Trust Accounts, Including the History, Preparation, Investigation and Audit Thereof

You are holding a reproduction of an original work that is in the public domain in the United States of America, and possibly other countries. You may freely copy and distribute this work as no entity (individual or corporate) has a copyright on the body of the work. This book may contain prior copyright references, and library stamps (as most of these works were scanned from library copies). These have been scanned and retained as part of the historical artifact.

This book may have occasional imperfections such as missing or blurred pages, poor pictures, errant marks, etc. that were either part of the original artifact, or were introduced by the scanning process. We believe this work is culturally important, and despite the imperfections, have elected to bring it back into print as part of our continuing commitment to the preservation of printed works worldwide. We appreciate your understanding of the imperfections in the preservation process, and hope you enjoy this valuable book.

*To The Master King,
Royal Courts of Justice

with the Author's Kind Regards*

TRUST ACCOUNTS

"Estate Books" and all appropriate forms of account for use in practice, in accordance with the system recommended in this work, are published by—

    Sir JOSEPH CAUSTON & SONS, Ltd.,

        8, Portugal Street,

            London, W.C. 2.

TRUST ACCOUNTS

INCLUDING THE HISTORY, PREPARATION, INVESTIGATION AND AUDIT THEREOF

BY

PRETOR W. CHANDLER
MASTER OF THE SUPREME COURT

THIRD EDITION

BY

THE AUTHOR

AND

JOHN HERBERT STAMP, M.A
OF LINCOLN'S INN, BARRISTER-AT-LAW
LATE FELLOW OF TRINITY COLLEGE, CAMBRIDGE

LONDON ·
BUTTERWORTH & CO., BELL YARD, TEMPLE BAR.

SYDNEY :	BUTTERWORTH & CO. (AUSTRALIA), LTD.
CALCUTTA :	BUTTERWORTH & CO (INDIA), LTD.
WINNIPEG :	BUTTERWORTH & CO. (CANADA), LTD.
WELLINGTON (N.Z.).	BUTTERWORTH & CO. (AUSTRALIA), LTD.

1919.

LONDON.
PRINTED BY C. F. ROWORTH, 88, FETTER LANE, E.C.

AUTHOR'S PREFACE.

THE present Volume is a New Edition as regards the Text, but the Accounts in the Appendices practically remain unaltered, as Solicitors are now not only familiar with those forms, but an increasing number have them in daily use.

Two additional Chapters have been added—the one on "Hotchpot," the other on "Releases."

I hope the law in this Edition may be found to be more accurately stated than in either of the other Editions, having regard to the assistance which has been rendered in that behalf by the joint Editor.

I am again much indebted to my former Clerk, Mr. Henderson, for his invaluable assistance in passing the work through the press.

P W. CHANDLER.

CO-EDITOR'S PREFACE.

I REGRET that I am unable to lay claim to any share of authorship in the system of accounts propounded and recommended in this work; *per contra* I am free to express my high appreciation of its merits without infringing any canon of modesty. I say, then, that it appears to me to be an admirably formulated system, ready to perform with ease all the services that the Author wishes it to perform, and adapted in all respects to take its place as a universally accepted common form framework for trust accounts

My part in this edition is to share responsibility with the Author for its statements of law; this responsibility is a heavy one in the case of a work prescribed for the use of students, and I should have welcomed much greater leisure for the task than has been at my disposal within the allotted time. Unfortunately the true scope and effect of the case law involved is not in all cases easy to gauge, and it is sometimes very difficult to deduce a working rule which can be relied upon.

J. H. STAMP.

TABLE OF CONTENTS

	PAGE
TABLE OF STATUTES	xi
TABLE OF CASES	xv
INTRODUCTION	1

CHAPTER I

The History of the Subject	5
As to Accounts	8
As to Information	11
Accounts for Probate Division	13
Accounts for Chancery Division	14
The Paymaster-General's Account	16
Accounts for the Inland Revenue	18
Accounts under Charitable Trusts Acts	19
Accounts of Trustees in Bankruptcy	20
Accounts in Lunacy	20
The Judicial Trustee Act, 1896	22
The Custodian Trustee	22

CHAPTER II

The System explained	24

CHAPTER III

The Memoranda	33

CHAPTER IV

The Schedule	35

CHAPTER V

	PAGE
The Capital Account	43
Cash Entries	45
Classification of Entries	47
Narrative of Entries	48
Mortgages by Trustees	49
Loans to Trustees	49
Investment Entries	51
Narrative	52
Deposits by Trustees	53
Secured Debt not paid in full	53
Valueless Securities	54
Advancements	54
Schedule references	55
Investments in Hand	58
Balancing the Accounts	60
Separate Trusts	64
Vouchers	64
Review of the Account	66

CHAPTER VI

The Income Account	69

CHAPTER VII

Apportionments	74
Apportionment Act, 1870	75
Accounts for the Apportionment of Dividends and Interest pursuant to the Statute	81
Calculation of Dividend and Interest Apportionments	85
Dividends on Government Securities, &c.	86
,, ,, other Stocks, &c.	86
Interim Dividends	88
Transfer Items	89
Accounts for the Apportionment of Rent pursuant to the Statute	89
Calculation of Rent Apportionments	92
Transfer Items	94

CHAPTER VII—*continued*

	PAGE
Advantages of Tabular Forms	95
Apportionments governed by Rules of Equity	96
The Rule in *Howe* v. *Earl of Dartmouth*	98
The Rule in the *Earl of Chesterfield's Case*	101
The Rule in *Allhusen* v. *Whittell*	103
Insufficient Mortgage Security	107
Covenant to pay an Annuity	109
Suspense Apportionment Account	110

CHAPTER VIII

Hotchpot 113

CHAPTER IX

The Bank Account 121

CHAPTER X

Final Statement for Beneficiaries 127

CHAPTER XI

A Marriage Settlement Trust 133

CHAPTER XII

Investigation and Audit of Trust Accounts	137
The Provisions of the Act and Rules considered	138
Proposed Form of Application	148
Proposed Form of Notice of Application	149
Proposed Form of Report and Certificate	150
The Audit	151
The Conduct of the Audit	155
The Investigation of the Condition of the Trust	168
The Auditors' Report, Certificate and Account	170

CHAPTER XIII

	PAGE
Releases	172
Auditors' Reminders	179
APPENDICES	195
INDEX	317

TABLE OF STATUTES.

	PAGE
21 Hen. 8, c. 5, s. 4 (1529) Administration of Estates	6
22 & 23 Car. 2, o. 10, s. 3 (1670) Statute of Distribution	6, 113, 114
14 Geo. 3, c. 78, s. 83 (1774) Fires Prevention Act	183, 185
39 & 40 Geo. 3, c. 98 (1800) Thellusson Act	179
1 Vict. c. 26, (1837) Wills Act,	
s. 15	191
ss. 25—33	186
12 & 13 Vict c. 51, s. 5 (1849) Mental Incapacity (Scotland) Act	126
15 & 16 Vict. c. 80, s. 38 (1852) New Practice on Abolition of Masters in Chancery	27
16 & 17 Vict. c. 51, (1853) Succession Duty Act	190
c. 137, s. 62 (1853) Charitable Trusts Act	19
17 & 18 Vict. c. 113 (1854) Locke King's Act	187
20 & 21 Vict. c. 77, ss. 89, 81 (1857) Court of Probate Act	6
22 & 23 Vict. c. 35, s. 29 (1859) For relief of Trustees	179
25 & 26 Vict. c. 116, s. 63 (1862) Charitable Trusts Act	19
30 & 31 Vict. o. 69 (1867) Locke King's Amendment Act	187
33 & 34 Vict. c 35 (1870) Apportionment Act,	
s. 1	75
s. 2	76, 188
s. 3	75
ss 4 & 5	76
s. 6	77, 188
s. 7	77
36 & 37 Vict c. 66, s. 25 (6) (1873) Judicature Act	176
38 & 39 Vict. c. 54 s. 257 (1875) Public Health Act	190
40 & 41 Vict. c. 34 (1877) Locke King's Amendment Act	187
44 & 45 Vict c 41, s. 43 (1881) Conveyancing Act	187
45 & 46 Vict. o. 38 (1882) Settled Land Act,	
s. 11	79
s. 31, sub-s 1 (11)	189
s. 34	80
s. 35	80
c. 75, s 3 (1882) Married Women's Property Act	187
46 & 47 Vict. c. 47, ss 3—5 (1883) Provident Nominations and Small Intestacies	183

TABLE OF STATUTES

	PAGE
51 & 52 Vict. c. 59, s 8 (1888) Trustee Act	174
53 Vict. c. 29 (1890) Intestates Act	182, 185
53 & 54 Vict. c 39 (1890) Partnership Act	160, 188
54 & 55 Vict. c 73, s. 5 (1891) Mortmain Act, Amendment of..	187
55 & 56 Vict. c. 58 (1892) Accumulations Act	176
56 & 57 Vict. c. 39, s. 25 (1893) Industrial and Provident Societies Act	183
c. 53 (1893) Trustee Act,	
s. 1	98
s. 9	155
s. 14	189
s. 18	185
s. 21	176, 177
s. 43	184
57 & 58 Vict. c. 30 (1894) Finance Act	7
59 & 60 Vict. c. 25, s. 35 (1896) Friendly Societies Act	182
c. 35, s. 3 (1896) Judicial Trustee Act	22, 169
c. 28 (1896) Finance Act,	
s. 13	183
s. 19 (1)	189
60 & 61 Vict. c. 65, s. 1 (1897) Land Transfer Act	7
2 Edw. 7, c. 41, s 9 (7) (1902) Metropolitan Water Board Act	36
6 Edw. 7, c. 55 (1906) Public Trustee Act,	
s. 13 (1)	138
s. 13 (2)	142, 143
s 13 (3)	143
s. 13 (4)	144
s. 13 (5)	144, 145
s. 13 (6)	146
s. 13 (7)	147
s. 13 (8)	148
8 Edw. 7, c 69, s. 113 (1908) Companies Act	151
10 Edw. 7, c 8, s 59 (1909-10) Finance Act	7, 184, 189, 191
1 & 2 Geo. 5, c. 37, s. 7 (1911) Conveyancing Act	188
4 & 5 Geo. 5, c. 10, s. 14 (1914) Finance Act	189
c. 59, s. 42 (1914) Bankruptcy Act	191
ss. 88 and 89 (1914) Bankruptcy Act	126
8 & 9 Geo. 5, c 40, Sched. A. No. 8, Rules 1 and 7 (1918) Income Tax Act	92
Rule 19 of all Scheds (1918) Income Tax	110
Order XXIX. of 1852	27
Rules of Supreme Court, Order XLIV	146
IV. r. 10 a	25
IV. r 64	185
IV. r 75	14, 15
Public Trustee Rules 19 and 20	126

TABLE OF STATUTES xiii

	PAGE
Public Trustee Rule 29	13
32 (1)	139
32 (2)	139
32 (3)	145
33	142
34	140
35	142, 145
36 (1)	143, 144
36 (2)	143, 145
37 (1)	145
37 (2)	145
37 (3)	145, 146
40 (1)	147
40 (2)	147
40 (3)	147
41	147
Public Trustee Fees	145
Audit	146
Bankruptcy Rules, 1915, Nos. 360—364	20

(xv)

TABLE OF CASES

	PAGE
Abrahams, Re, Abrahams v. Bendon, (1911) 1 Ch. 109	185
Akerman, Re, (1891) 3 Ch 212	189
Allen, Re, (1896) 2 Ch. 345	189
Allhusen v. Whittell (1867), L R 4 Eq 295	103, 104, 183
Alsbury, Re (1890), 45 C. D. 237	88
Ambler, Re, (1905) 1 Ch. 697	187
Atkinson, Re, (1904) 2 Ch. 160	108, 187
Attorney-General v. Gibbs (1847), 1 De G. & Sm. 156	9
Attorney-General v. Jefferys, (1908) A. C. 411	187
Bacon, Re (1893), 62 L. J Ch. 445	109
Bagot, Re, (1894) 1 Ch 177	190
Bain v. Brand (1876), 1 A. C. 767, 768	183
Baines v. Chadwick, (1903) 1 Ch. 250	190
Barker, Re, (1918) 1 Ch. 128	114
Beddington, Re, (1900) 1 Ch 771	120
Bell, Re, (1896) 1 Ch. 1	187
Betts, Re, (1907) 2 Ch. 149	182
Betty, Re, (1899) 1 Ch. at 829	188
Beverly, Re, (1901) 1 Ch. 681 and 688	181
Bird, Re, Evans, Re, Dodd v. Evans, (1901) 1 Ch. 920	108
Bladon, Re, Dando v. Porter, (1911) 2 Ch. 354; (1912) 1 Ch. 45	181, 183, 185
Blow, Re, (1914) 1 Ch. 233	169
Bolivia, Republic of, &c , Ltd., (1914) 1 Ch 139	153
Bostock v Blakeney (1789), 2 Bro. C. C. 653	80
Bosworth, Re, Martin v. Lambe (1889), 58 L J. Ch. 432	12
Bouch v. Sproule (1887), 12 A. C. at 397	86, 87, 88
Bowlby, Re, (1904) 2 Ch. 685 and 712	185
Bristol (Marquis of), Re, (1897) 1 Ch. 946	120
Brown, Re, (1895) W. N. 115	25
Bugden v. Tylee (1856), 21 Beav. 545	12
Bulkeley v. Stephens, (1896) 2 Ch. 241	81
Burrowes v. Lock (1805), 10 Ves jun. 470	11
Burrows v. Walls (1855), 5 De G. M. & G. 233	9
Cadell v. Palmer (1832-3), 1 Cl & Fin. 372.	184, 188
Cartwright, Re (1889), 41 C. D. 532	188
Cater's Trust, Re (No. 2) (1858), 25 Beav 366	176
Cavendish, Re, (1912) 1 Ch. 794	120
Chadwick v. Grange, (1907) 1 Ch. 313; 2 Ch. 20	36
Chadwick v. Heatley (1845), 2 Col. 130	173, 176

TABLE OF CASES.

	PAGE
Chesterfield's (Earl of) Trusts, Re (1883), 24 C. D 643	101, 189
Clarke, Re (1881), 18 C. D 160	80, 81
Clarke v. Ormonde (Earl of) (1821), Jac. 108	8, 9, 10, 11
Cole v Graham (1750), 1 Ves senr 507	172
Collyer v. Dudley (1823), T. & R 421	9, 172
Constable v. Constable (1879), 11 C. D 681	78
Cooke, Re, (1916) 1 Ch. 480	114, 117
Cordwell's Estate, Re (1873), 20 Eq 644	186
Cottrell, Re, Brickland v. Bedingfield, (1910) 1 Ch. 402	180
Courtier, Re (1887), 34 C. D 136	188
Courtney v. Williams (1844), 3 Hare, 539	186
Cowin, Re, Cowin v. Gravett (1886), 33 Ch. D at 185	10, 12
Cowley (Earl of) v. Wellesley (1866), 1 Eq 656	186, 190
Cox's Trusts, Re (1878), 9 C D 159	79
Craven, Re, Watson v. Craven, (1914) 1 Ch. 358	117, 180, 181
Crocker, Re, (1916) 1 Ch 25	120
Cuff v. London & County, &c Co , (1912) 1 Ch. 440	151
Dando v. Porter, (1911) 2 Ch 354	185
Dartnall, Re, Sawyer v. Goddard, (1895) 1 Ch at 478	11
Davy, Re, (1908) 1 Ch. 61	114, 179
Dawson, Re, (1906) 2 Ch. 211	109
Dealtry, Re, (1913) W. N 138	182
De Teissier's Settled Estates, (1893) 1 Ch. 153	188
Docker v. Somes (1834), 2 My. & K. 655	125
Dollond v. Johnson (1854), 2 Sm. & G. 301	186
Dowse v. Gorton, (1891) A C 190—203	181
Drybutter v. Bartholomew (1723), 2 P Wms 127	36
Edwards, Re, (1918) 1 Ch 142	78
Egmont (Earl of), Re, (1908) 1 Ch 821	166
Ellis v. Ellis, (1908) W. N 215	65, 191
Ellis v. Rowhotham, (1900) 1 Q. B. at 744	77, 79
Evans, Re, (1913) 1 Ch. 23	88
Evans' Contract, Re, (1910) 2 Ch. 438	180, 186
Field v. Field, (1894) 1 Ch. 425	191
Field v. Peckett (No 3) (1861), 29 Beav. 576	184
Fish, Re, Bennett v. Bennett, (1893) 2 Ch at 425	9
Foligno's Mortgage, Re (1863), 32 Beav. 131	176
Ford, Re, Myers v. Molesworth, (1911) 1 Ch 455	78
Forster Brown, Re, (1914) 2 Ch 584	117, 118
Fountaine v. Amherst (Lord), Times, (1909) 2 Ch. at 394	8
Fowler, Re (1881), 16 C D 723	188
Fraser, Re, (1913) 2 Ch. 232	120
Freeman, Re, (1898) 1 Ch 28	188
Freeman v. Fairlie (1812), 3 Mer at 39	8
Freman v. Whitbread (1865), L R. 1 Eq. 266	80

TABLE OF CASES. xvii

	PAGE
George, Re (1877), 5 C. D. 837 and 843	185
Gibbons, Re (1887), 36 C. D 486	182
Gibson v. Bott (1802), 7 Ves. 89	180
Gilbert, Re, (1908) W N. 63	117
Giles, Re (1886), 34 W. R. 712	182
Gjers, Re, (1899) 2 Ch. 54	188
Gough v. Offley (1852), 5 De G. & Sm. 653	10, 12
Gray v Haig (1855), 20 Beav 219	8, 11
Griffith, Re (1879), 12 C. D. 655	78
Grosvenor, Re, (1916) 2 Ch. 375	190
Hadley, Re, (1909) 1 Ch. 20	183
Hancock v. Podmore (1830), 1 B. & Ad. 264	184
Hardoon v. Belilios, (1901) A. C. at 123	10, 12
Hardwicke (Earl of) v. Vernon (1808), 14 Ves. jun. at 510	8
Hargreaves, Re (1903), 88 L. T. R. 100	117, 118
Harris, Re, (1914) 2 Ch. 395	189
Harvey v. Olliver (1887), W. N. 149	2
Hasluck v. Pedley (1874), 19 Eq 271	78
Hatfield v. Minet (1878), 8 C. D. 136	118
Henderson v. M'Iver (1818), 3 Madd 275	10
Henry Squire, Cash Chemist, Ltd. v Ball, Baker & Co., Times (1911), 17th February	153
Herbert v. Herbert, (1912) 2 Ch. 268	181
Hilton, Re, (1909) 2 Ch. 548	107, 181
Hockey v. Western, (1898) 1 Ch 350	128, 187
Hollebone, Re, (1919) W. N. 144	103
Horton v Brocklehurst (No. 2) (1858), 29 Beav. 504	8
Hoskin, Re (1876), 5 C. D 229	176
Howarth, Re, (1909) 2 Ch 19	179
Howe v. Dartmouth (Earl of) (1802), 7 Ves. jun 137	36, 83, 98, 106, 167, 180, 184
Howe (Earl of) v. Kingscote, (1903) 2 Ch at 83	182
Hume Nisbet's Settlement, Re (1911), 27 T. L R. 461	87
Hunt, Re (1913), 107 L T R. 757	117
Inman, Re, (1915) 1 Ch. 187	107
Irving v. Houstoun, 4 Pat. 521	87
Jeffreys v Marshall (1870), 23 L. T. 548	9
Jenkins v. Jenkins (1897), 76 L T. R. 164	7
Johnson v. Baker (1826), 2 Car & P. 207	187
Jones, Re (1886), 31 C. D. 440	189
Jones v. Ogle (1872), L R 8 Ch. 192	79, 188
Kelly's Settlement, Re, (1910) 1 Ch. 78	119
Kemp v. Burn (1863), 4 Giff 348	8, 9, 10
Kempson v. Ashbee (1874), 10 Ch. 15	173
Kenyon v. Walford, (1912) 1 Ch. 219	185

c.   b

TABLE OF CASES.

	PAGE
King v. Mullins (1852), 1 Dr. 308	173
Kingston Cotton Mill, Re (No 2), (1896) 2 Ch. 284	153
Lacon's Settlement, Re, (1911) 2 Ch 17	182
Lambert, Re, (1897) 2 Ch 169	118
Lambert v. Lambert (1874), 22 W. R 359	79
Leeds, &c. Co. v Shephord (1887), 36 C. D at 802	152
Legh's Settlement Estates, (1902) 2 Ch. 74	188
Leng, Re, (1895) 1 Ch 653	187
Lewis, Re, (1907) 2 Ch. at 299	78
Lloyd v. Attwood (1858), 3 De G. & J. at 649	172
Lockwood, Re (1892), 92 L. T. Jour. 237	25
London, &c Bank (No 2), (1895) 2 Ch 673	152
Lord v Lord (1867), 2 Ch at 789	185
Low v. Bouverie, (1891) 3 Ch. at 99	11
Lowis v. Rumney (1867), 4 Eq. 451	190
Lysaght v. Lysaght, (1898) 1 Ch. 115	78
Macdonald v Irvine (1878), 8 C. D. 101	181
McEwen, Re, McEwen v Phelps, (1913), 2 Ch 715, 716	103
Malam, Re, (1894) 3 Ch 578	88
Mansfield v. Ogle (1859), 4 De G. & J. 38	179
Mead v. Ball, Baker & Co, Times, 17th February, 1911	153
Middleton, Re (1881), 19 C. D. 552	190
Moore, Re, Strickland v. London, (1907) W. N. 181	182
Muirhead, Re, (1916) 2 Ch. 181	78
Myddleton v. Rushout (1797), 1 Phill 246	6
New, Re, (1901) 2 Ch. 584 at 547	181
Newton v. Askew (1848), 11 Beav. at 152	11, 12
North, Re (1897), 76 L. T. R 186	120
Oddy, Re, (1911) 1 Ch 532	140, 142, 146
O'Grady v. Wilmot, (1916) 2 A C 231	183
Oppenheimer, Re, (1907) 1 Ch 399	79
Ottley v. Gilby (1845), 8 Beav 602	9, 10, 11
Overton v. Banister (1844), 3 Ha 503	9, 172
Page, Jones and Morgan, Re, (1893) 1 Ch 309	9
Palmer, Re, Lancs., &c. Co v. Burke, (1907) 1 Ch. 486	191
Parker-Jervis, Re, (1898) 2 Ch. 643	179
Payne v. Evens (1874), 18 Eq. 356	8, 9
Pearce, Re, (1909) 1 Ch 819	189, 190
Pearse v. Green (1819), 1 Jac & W 135	8, 9
Peel's (Sir Robert) Estate, (1910) 1 Ch. 464	81, 186
Perkins, Re (1892), 67 L T R. 743	120
Perkins, Re, (1907) 2 Ch. 596	97, 109, 180
Phillips, Re, (1903) 1 Ch. 183	187
Phillips v. Bignell (1811), 1 Phill. 240	6
Piercy, Re, (1907) 1 Ch. 289	88

TABLE OF CASES. xix

	PAGE
Pimm, Re, Sharp v. Hodgson, (1904) 2 Ch. 345	182, 190
Pizzi, Re, (1907) 1 Ch 67	190
Pollock v. Pollock (1874), 18 Eq. 329	78
Popham, Re, (1914) W N 257	79, 110
Powell v. Hellicar (1858), 26 Beav 261	183
Powis v. Blagrave (1854), Kay, 496	188
Poyser, Re (1888), 1 Ch. 828	117
Poyser, Re, Landon v Poyser, (1910) 2 Ch 448	97, 109, 180
Pritt v Clay (1843), 6 Beav 503	178
Prockter, Re, (1916) 1 Ch. 25	119
Pullan v. Koe, (1913) 1 Ch. 9	179
Pullen, Re, 54 Sol Jour. 341, 354	191
Pyke, Re, (1912) 1 Ch 770	182
Raven v. Waite (1818), 1 Swans 553	185
Rees, Re (1881), 17 C. D 701	114, 184
Rhoades, Re, (1899) 2 Q. B 347, 354	188, 189
Rhodes v. Bate (1866), 1 Ch at 257	172
Rochester (Bishop of) v Le Fanu, (1906) 2 Ch. 513	77, 78
Roberts, Re, (1902) 2 Ch. 834	45
Ross, Re, (1900) 1 Ch. 162	180
Rowlls, Re, (1900) 2 Ch. 107	101, 107
Ryder v. Bickerton (1743), 3 Swans 90	9
St. Albans (Duke of), In re, (1900) 2 Ch. 873	179
Salaman, Re, (1907) 2 Ch 46; (1908) 1 Ch 4	184
Salmon, Re (1889), 42 Ch. D. 351	154
Salvin, Re, Worseley v. Marshall, (1912) 1 Ch. 332	180
Samson, Re, (1906) 2 Ch 584	189
Saunders (T. H.), Re, (1908) 1 Ch. 415	190
Scholefield v Redfern (1863), 2 D. & Sm. 173	80
Scott, Re, (1903) 1 Ch 1	179
Seagram v. Knight (1867), 2 Ch 630	128
Sharman, Re, (1901) 2 Ch. 280	183
Sharp v. Lush (1879), 10 C D 468	190, 191
Shuttleworth, Re (1911) 55 Sol. J. 366	184, 186
Simpson v. Bathurst (1869), L R 5 Ch. at 202	12
Sisson, Re, (1903) 1 Ch at 264	188, 191
Skeene v Cook, (1901) 2 K B at 12	36
Skinner, Re, Cooper v. Skinner, (1904) 1 Ch. at 292	8
Society of the Deaf and Whittle's Contract, (1907) 2 Ch. at 493	181
Spencer Cooper, Re, (1908) 1 Ch 130	45, 187, 191
Springett v Dashwood (1860), 2 Giff 521	8, 9, 11
Stokes, Re (1892), 67 L. T R 223	45
Strickland v. London, &c., (1907) W. N. 181	45
Talbot v. Marshfield (1868), L R 3 Ch. at 628	9
Thomas, Re, (1916) 1 Ch. 384, and 2 Ch. 331	86

TABLE OF CASES.

	PAGE
Thomas v. Crabtree (1912), 106 L. T. R. 49	181
Thomas v. Devonport Corporation, (1900) 1 Q. B. at 20, 21	153
Thompson v. Dunn (1870), 5 Ch. App. 573	9
Tillott, Re, Lee v. Wilson, (1892) 1 Ch. 86	10, 11, 12
Tod, Re, (1916) 1 Ch 567	117
Torre v. Browne (1855), 5 H. L C. 555	180
Trevalion v. Anderton (1897), 66 L. J. Q. B. 489	79
Trevor v. Hutchins, (1896) 1 Ch. 844	189
Trotter, Re, (1899) 1 Ch. 764	191
Turner v. Collins (1871), 7 Ch 329	172
Turner v. Turner, (1911) 1 Ch 716	186
Underwood v Trower (1867), W. N. 83	9, 12
Utley, Re, Russell v. Cubitt, (1912) W N. 147	146
Van Straubenzee, Re, (1901) 2 Ch 779	180, 184
Vincent, Re, (1909) 1 Ch. 810	184, 186
Vyse v. Foster (1872), 13 Eq. 602	8
Walker v. Symonds (1818), 3 Swans 58, 3 Swans at 59.	8, 9, 11, 172
Ward's Settled Estates, Re, (1919) W. N. 51	189
Wasdale, Re, Brittin v. Partridge, (1899) 1 Ch. 163	187
Watson v. Watson (1864), 33 Beav. 574	118, 119
Wearmouth, &c. Co., Re (1882), 19 C. D. 640	79, 188
Wedderburn v. Wedderburn (1838), 4 My. & Cr. at 50	172
Weeks v. Daniels, (1912) 2 Ch. 90	80
Wheatley v Davies (1876), 35 L. T. R. 306	180
White, Re, (1898) 2 Ch 217	184, 186
White v. Lincoln (Lady) (1803), 8 Ves. jun. 363	8
White v. Jackson (1852), 15 Beav. 191	9
White, Re, Theobald v. White, (1913) 1 Ch 231	78
Whitehead, Re, (1894) 1 Ch. 678	180
Whitehead v. Palmer, (1908) 1 K. B. 151	186
Williams, J., deceased, Times, 8th July, 1910	142, 143, 146
Willis, Re, (1902) 1 Ch 15	188
Willoughby, Re, (1911) 2 Ch. 597	121
Wills, Re, (1915) 1 Ch. 769	103, 183
Wood, Re, (1913) 2 Ch. 583	121
Wood v. Turner, (1907) 2 Ch. 134	10, 12
Wright, Re (1857), 3 K. & J. 419	176
Wright v. Carter, (1903) 1 Ch. 27	173
Wroe v. Seed (1863), 4 Giff. 425	8, 9, 10
Wynch v. Wynch (1788), 1 Cox, 433	185
Wynne v. Humberston (1858), 27 Beav at 424	9
Wythes, Re, (1893) 2 Ch 369	190, 196
Young, Re, (1914) 1 Ch 581	114, 179
—— v. —— (1819), 4 Madd. 273	9

TRUST ACCOUNTS

INTRODUCTION

MANY men of business at one time or another are called upon to act as executors or trustees, and perhaps even more, sooner or later in their lives, become entitled to participate in trust estates. On each of these occasions the solicitor is or may be consulted: the executor or trustee usually retains his solicitor to guide him in the proper administration of the trust estate and to take care that suitable accounts are kept; whilst the beneficiary frequently engages a solicitor to see that the administration of the trust has been properly conducted, and that the accounts are all in order.

No attempt will be made in this book to explain the general law of trusts; that has already been done by many learned text-writers, but the object of this Treatise is to deal with and explain one all-important incident of every trust, and that is the accounts which must be kept by the trustees.

The passing of the Public Trustee Act, 1906, has increased the importance to trustees, executors and administrators of having their accounts well arranged and entered up ready, as far as possible, for examination, because any beneficiary or trustee may, in pursuance of the powers contained in that Act, call for an official investigation of the condition of the trust and an audit of the accounts. If the accounts are imperfect, or the costs of the investigation and audit have been substantially increased in consequence of neglect, then it is not unnatural to imagine that the defaulting trustee may be ordered to pay the costs occasioned by such neglect.

If, at any time, the trust passes into the hands of new trustees, it would be their immediate duty to ascertain of what the trust fund consisted (*Harvey* v. *Olliver* (1887), W. N. 149), to acquaint themselves with the details and circumstances of the trust estate, and to take such steps as might be necessary for the due protection thereof. It is difficult to see how this duty can be safely discharged without some examination of the accounts, the extent of which examination will depend upon the circumstances of each case.

Further, it is necessary to bear in mind that every appointment of an auditor under the Act may involve an examination by him of the capital and income accounts from the commencement of the trust; so that a continuous account of all trusts should always be kept, and available for inspection at any time.

At present there is no uniform and well-recognised practice in England with regard to the form in which trust accounts are rendered to beneficiaries out of Court. When, however, a solicitor is called upon to examine a trust account prepared for the Chancery Division or the Inland Revenue Department, he approaches the work knowing full well that the account will be drawn in accordance with a prescribed form, just as he would expect to find a deed based upon some established precedent.

In Scotland, the reverse is the case, for speaking generally the accounts of private trusts are there kept by the solicitor who acts for the trustees, and he annually or periodically puts the account current into the form of an "Account Charge and

Discharge," and thus submits it with the vouchers for audit. This is the form in which a Judicial Factor, when appointed, is bound by law to render his accounts, and it is very generally adopted by solicitors acting for private trustees. Such accounts are easily understood by trustees who are non-professional men, they become familiar with the form, and are consequently left free to direct all their attention to the substance of the account.

It is intended in the following pages to examine the existing obligations imposed upon a trustee with regard to his accounts, and when that examination has been completed it is proposed to attempt the construction of the framework of a common form for keeping and rendering such accounts.

A satisfactory common form must be simple enough to be understood by persons who are neither lawyers nor accountants, and at the same time must be full enough to contain all the information which a trustee is by law required to furnish, and the arrangement should be such as to enable the information to be furnished in the shape required by the Court when taking trust accounts, and should therefore be based upon the practice of the Court in dealing with trusts

Great advantages would ensue from the general adoption of such a form: advantages not confined to the limits of a solicitor's office, but extending to the external intercourse of one solicitor with another, with his clients and with the Courts of Justice. If all trust accounts were kept upon the same simple and well-known principles, any competent solicitor's clerk could be trusted to carry on an account, and if every trust account coming to a solicitor for examination from the office of any other solicitor were rendered in the same common form, it would be at once intelligible and self-explaining. Further, every order of the Court for accounts could be complied with automatically from the books, and every application from trustees or beneficiaries, for inspection or information, could be promptly met. These advantages and others would quickly and inevitably follow the general adoption by solicitors of a properly constructed common form for keeping and rendering the accounts of private trusts.

CHAPTER I

THE HISTORY OF THE SUBJECT

BEFORE proceeding to lay down the outline of any system upon which trust accounts should be kept, it is proposed in the first place to mention certain obligations which are imposed upon trustees and the personal representatives of a deceased person, to preserve records of what the trust estate consisted in its inception, and in the next place the general rules to be extracted from the reported decisions of the Courts with regard to the accounts of executors, administrators and trustees, then to see what accounts are liable to be required by the practice of the Chancery and Probate Divisions of the High Court, and finally to notice the accounts which have to be rendered to the Estate Duty and other departments of the State.

The Trust Estate

All trustees are liable to be called upon by the Chancery Division to answer such inquiries concerning their trust estate, as may be deemed necessary. When an order is made for the administration of a trust estate, an inquiry will often be directed " of what particulars the property comprised in the settlement consisted at the date of the settlement and of what the same now consists."

Executors and administrators are under a similar obligation, and may be ordered either by the Chancery Division or the Probate Division to exhibit an inventory of the real and personal estate of their deceased.

The granting of Probates of Wills for many centuries in this country was a function of the Ecclesiastical Courts, and the Prerogative Court required the executor to exhibit his inventory of the personal estate of the deceased even before probate could issue. *Burn's Ecclesiastical Law*, 9t edit. Vol. IV. p 404.

6 TRUST ACCOUNTS

In the year 1529 executors and administrators were by statute (21 Hen. VIII. ch. 5, s. 4) required to deliver upon oath an inventory of the deceased's personal estate, and in 1670 an administrator was, again by statute (22 & 23 Car. II. ch. X.), required to give a bond that he would deliver his inventory before a named day.

Originally the inventory was furnished as a matter of course, but in the process of time (say by 1797), that practice was relaxed until it became customary only to render the inventory when it was called for by some beneficiary or creditor (*a*). Even now in some cases a schedule of the estate, which amounts to an inventory, must be lodged in the Probate Registry on application for a grant, *e g.*, when sureties have to justify (Rule 42, non-contentious business), or when power is reserved to another executor to prove.

The Probate Act of 1857 (20 & 21 Vict. ch. 77), s. 80, repealed so much of the above-mentioned Acts " as requires any surety bond or other security to be taken from a person to whom administration shall be committed " (*b*), and by sect. 81 of the same Act every administrator is required to give a bond in such form as the judge shall from time to time direct, conditioned for duly administering the personal estate of the deceased.

According to the present practice under this section, an executor and administrator in his oath to lead to probate or administration, gives a specific undertaking to render his inventory and account when called for, which undertaking is contained in the familiar words, "*I will administer according to law all the estate which by law devolves to and vests in the personal representative of the said deceased, and I will exhibit a true and perfect inventory of all the said estate, and render a just and true account thereof whenever required by law so to do.*" Now that the beneficial interest in such real estate as is covered by sect. 1 of

---

(*a*) *Myddelton* v. *Rushout* (1797), 1 Phill. 246. The Court refused a creditor an order in a case in which he had commenced Chancery proceedings. He could not proceed in both Courts. (*Phillips* v. *Bignell* (1811), 1 Phill. 240.)

(*b*) Some writers think that the above words are sufficient to repeal the obligation to furnish any inventory at all.

the Land Transfer Act, 1897, becomes vested in the personal representative of a deceased, the inventory must contain particulars of the real as well as of the personal estate (c).

This jurisdiction of the Probate Division to demand an inventory and account, is in addition to, and altogether distinct from that exercised by the Chancery Division over executors and administrators. Seldom is application now made to the Probate Division for an order upon an executor or administrator to bring his inventory and account into that Division, although in a comparatively recent case such an order was made (d). It is, however, a useful way of obtaining particulars of the estate when nothing more is required.

The Commissioners of Inland Revenue are another authority to which trustees, executors and administrators are obliged to render an inventory of the trust property.

In the case of executors or administrators the obligation is complied with by the affidavit for inland revenue, which is lodged in the Probate Registry with the other papers proving the right of the executor or intended administrator, as the case may be, to a grant of probate or letters of administration, and which is required to contain full particulars of the deceased's real and personal estate.

This last-mentioned obligation arises whenever death duties have to be assessed in respect of the trust estate (e).

The Trust Accounts

The requirements which the laws of England make of executors, administrators and trustees with regard to their trust accounts as laid down by the judges in various actions which they have tried, and in which the question under consideration has been raised, may be summarised as follows:—

It is the duty of trustees, executors and adminis-

(c) See Tristram and Coote's Probate Practice, 14th edit. p. 819

(d) *Jenkins* v. *J.* (1897), 76 L. T. R. 164.

(e) 57 & 58 Vict. c. 30 ; 10 Edw. 7, c. 8.

8 TRUST ACCOUNTS

trators (for in this respect they stand in the same situation) (*f*)—

I. To keep proper (*g*) accounts of the trust estate, which accounts must be regular (*h*), clear and distinct (*i*), faithful and accurate (*k*):—

    (a) The accounts must contain particulars of all receipts and of all payments (*l*), and care must be taken not to suppress, conceal, or overcharge (*m*).

    (b) The accounts must be kept separate and apart from others (*n*).

    (c) Vouchers must be preserved to justify all items on both sides of the account, that is, items of receipt as well as of payment (*o*), and the accounts and vouchers must be preserved even after release granted (*p*).

II. To produce to any beneficiary (*q*) at his request

(*f*) *Pearse* v. *Green* (1819), 1 Jac & W. 135.

(*g*) *Kemp* v. *Burn* (1863), 4 Giff 348, *Wroe* v *Seed* (1863), 4 Giff. 425. See also *Re Skinner, Cooper* v. *Skinner*, (1904) 1 Ch. 292.

(*h*) *White* v. *Lady Lincoln* (1803), 8 Ves. Jun. 363.

(*i*) *Freeman* v. *Fairlie* (1812), 3 Mer. 39, *Springett* v. *Dashwood* (1860), 2 Giff. 521.

(*k*) *Hardwicke (Earl of)* v *Vernon* (1808), 14 Ves. Jun. at p. 510, *Springett* v. *Dashwood, ante*.

(*l*) *White* v. *Lady Lincoln* (1803), 8 Ves. Jun. 363.

(*m*) *Hardwicke (Earl of)* v. *Vernon* (1808), 14 Ves. Jun. 510, *Walker* v. *Symonds* (1818), 3 Swans at p 59. If trustees stand by and sanction the rendering of improper accounts, they become liable themselves for the misrepresentations. (*Horton* v. *Brocklehurst* (No. 2) (1858), 29 Beav. 504.)

(*n*) *Freeman* v. *Fairlie* (1812), 3 Mer. 39, *Fountaine* v. *Lord Amherst*, (1909) 2 Ch. 394. See also *Vyse* v. *Foster* (1870), 10 Eq. 602.

(*o*) *White* v. *Lady Lincoln, ante*. See also *Payne* v. *Evens* (1874), 18 Eq. 356; *Gray* v. *Haig* (1855), 20 Beav. 219.

(*p*) *Clarke* v. *Ormonde (Earl of)* (1821), Jac. 108; *Payne* v. *Evens, ante*. A defendant in an administration action may, by his own oath, discharge himself of sums under 40*s*. Where an account was of twenty years' standing the Court ordered that the defendant should prove his account by his own oath for so much as he could not prove by books and cancelled bonds. (*The Practical Register*, 1714, p. 2.)

(*q*) A beneficiary is one who is now or may hereafter be entitled to participate in the income or capital of the trust estate. He must at least establish a

the accounts in which he is interested (r). The accounts must be constantly ready for production (s) even after they have been settled (t).

III. To render without requisition to all beneficiaries—

(a) In the case of income, at reasonable intervals,
(b) In the case of capital, when the same falls into possession (u),

a statement of what they are then entitled to receive (x). Releases will not discharge the trustees in respect of rights not disclosed (y). (See also Chapter XIII.)

IV. To allow beneficiaries—

(a) To inspect (z) and investigate (a) the accounts, vouchers (b), and other documents relating to

---

primâ facie case of the relation of trustee and *cestui que trust* (see *Wynne* v. *Humberston* (1858), 27 Beav. at p. 424), and his rights are dependent to some extent upon the nature of his interest, *e g* , a person only interested in reversion cannot in general call for accounts of income.

(r) —— v. —— (1819), 4 Madd 273 ; *Springett* v. *Dashwood* (1860), 2 Giff. 521 ; *Kemp* v. *Burn* (1863), 4 Giff. 348 , *Wroe* v. *Seed* (1863), 4 Giff. 425 , *Payne* v. *Evens, ante*. See also *Talbot* v. *Marshfield* (1868), L. R. 3 Ch. at 628, and *Jeffreys* v. *Marshall* (1870), 23 L T. 548.

(s) *Pearse* v *Green* (1819), 1 Jac. & W. 135 , *Kemp* v. *Burn, ante , Springett* v. *Dashwood, ante ; Thompson* v. *Dunn* (1870), 5 Ch. App. 573.

(t) *Talbot* v. *Marshfield, ante , Underwood* v *Trower*, W. N (1867) 63.

(u) *Collyer* v. *Dudley* (1823), T. & R. 421 A trustee is in a sense bound to inform the beneficiaries what their interests are in the trust funds ; and therefore what their rights are as against the trustees. Per Wigram, V.C., in *Overton* v. *Banister* (1844), 3 Ha. 503. See also *White* v *Jackson* (1852), 15 Beav. 191, where the trustees did not persistently refuse his accounts. See also *Re Page, Jones & Morgan*, (1893) 1 Ch at p. 309.

(x) *Att.-Gen.* v *Gibbs* (1847), 1 De G & Sm. 156. And this is especially so on a beneficiary attaining twenty-one. See *Burrows* v. *Walls* (1855), 5 De G. M. & G. 233

(y) *Walker* v *Symonds* (1818), 3 Swans. at p. 59 ; *Clarke* v. *Ormonde (Earl of)* (1821), Jac. 108. See also *Ryder* v. *Bickerton* (1743), 3 Swans. 90.

(z) *Ottley* v. *Gilby* (1845), 8 Beav. 602 ; *Kemp* v. *Burn* (1863), 4 Giff 348.

(a) *In re Fish, Bennett* v. *Bennett,* (1893) 2 Ch. 425.

(b) *Ottley* v. *Gilby, ante.*

the trust (*c*). This they may do either personally or by their solicitor (*d*); but see *post*, as to Trust and Title Deeds.

(b) To take copies of the accounts and vouchers (*e*); but when trustees supply copies on request (*f*) then the applicant must pay for them.

(c) To examine the mortgages and deeds appertaining thereto, the scrips, the securities, and other like documents appertaining to the trust (*g*).

If, for any reason, trustees cannot keep their accounts themselves, it is their duty to employ a competent person to do the work for them (*h*), and it is presumed that in all cases in which it is reasonable for the trustees to employ an agent, *e.g*, where the accounts are long or intricate, or the trustee is ignorant of such matters or burdened with other business, the cost would be allowed out of the trust estate. Trustees "have an indemnity against every penny incurred by them in discharge of their duty" (*i*), and since to keep accounts is one of their first and most important duties, the cases must be few indeed in which trustees would be disallowed the reasonable charges for the skill and time occupied by an agent employed in preparing the accounts which the law requires them to keep. The length and complexity of the account would both be elements involved in fixing the reasonable charge.

(*c*) *Clarke* v. *Ormonde (Earl of)*, ante; *Re Cowin, Cowin* v. *Garett* (1886), 33 Ch. D 185.

(*d*) *Kemp* v. *Burn*, ante.

(*e*) *Clarke* v *Ormonde (Earl of)*, ante.

(*f*) *Ottley* v. *Gilby*, ante. But as to rendering accounts, see *ante*, Accounts, III.

(*g*) *In re Tillott, Lee* v. *Wilson*, (1892) 1 Ch 86. See also *Gough* v. *Offley* (1852), 5 De G. & Sm. 653.

(*h*) *Wroe* v. *Seed* (1863), 4 Giff. 425 See also *Henderson* v. *M'Iver* (1818), 3 Madd. 275.

(*i*) *Hardoon* v *Belilios*, (1901) A C 123, *Wood* v. *Turner*, (1907) 2 Ch. 134.

As to Information.

Every beneficiary is entitled to demand of the trustees—

I. Full and accurate information as to the amount and state of the trust property (*k*).

II. All reasonable information with reference to all matters relating to the trust generally (*l*) as are or ought to be within the trustee's knowledge (*m*), and the mode in which the trust property has been dealt with by the trustee and where it is (*n*).

But a trustee is under no obligation to answer questions as to what incumbrances the *cestui que trust* has himself created, nor as to which of his incumbrancers have given notice of their respective charges (*o*). Trustees are often asked to answer such questions to satisfy a proposed mortgagee or purchaser from the *cestui que trust*.

III. Proper authorities enabling him to make application to the Bank of England or any other corporation or company for the purpose of verifying the trustees' statement with regard to any investment, and at the same time to ascertain that no one has a paramount title to the investment (*p*).

If any beneficiary requires information which the trustees

(*k*) *Clarke* v *Ormonde (Earl of)* (1821), Jac. 108; *Ottley* v *Gilby* (1845), 8 Beav. 602; *Re Dartnall, Sawyer* v. *Goddard*, (1895) 1 Ch. 478, *Walker* v. *Symonds* (1818), 3 Swans. at p. 59. But see trustees' liability for misrepresentation as to *cestui que trust's* interest and value thereof, *Burrows* v. *Lock* (1805), 10 Ves. Jun. 470; *Gray* v. *Haigh* (1854), 20 Beav. 219; and for giving half information, *Walker* v. *Symonds, ante*.

(*l*) *Springett* v. *Dashwood* (1860), 4 Madd. 273 See also *Newton* v. *Askew* (1848), 11 Beav. at p. 152.

(*m*) *Walker* v. *Symonds, ante*

(*n*) *Low* v. *Bouverie*, (1891) 3 Ch. 99, *Re Tillott, Lee* v. *Wilson*, (1892) 1 Ch. 86.

(*o*) *Low* v. *Bouverie*, (1891) 3 Ch. 99

(*p*) *In re Tillott, Lee* v. *Wilson, ante*

cannot furnish without incurring expense, whether by the necessity of obtaining assistance or otherwise, then if and so far as such expense is not chargeable against the trust estate the beneficiary demanding the information must defray the expenses of obtaining it, and if required so to do must in proper cases undertake to pay them before the trustee is under any obligation to incur them; and where the trustee is a solicitor with power to charge for his services, the rule extends to the trustee's proper remuneration for his own work in supplying the desired information (*q*). When a demand for security is made by the trustees they must be careful not to ask that it should cover a wider class of costs than those to which they will be entitled from the *cestui que trust* on that occasion in connection with the information asked for (*r*). Where the beneficiary is solvent and offers a personal undertaking to defray any expenses, it is thought that the trustee ought to be satisfied with this.

IV. And every beneficiary has a *primâ facie* right, in the absence of any special circumstances—

> To examine the trust deeds and title deeds relating to the trust estate, unless the production of the latter might possibly disclose some flaw in the title (*s*). But this exception does not extend to the deeds of estates which have been mortgaged to the trustees (*t*).

V. The information which the Public Trustee is bound to render when acting as an ordinary, a judicial, or custodian trustee is regulated by Rule 29

(*q*) *In re Bosworth, Martin* v. *Lambe* (1889), 58 L. J. Ch. 432, *Hardoon* v. *Belilios*, (1901) A. C. 123; *Wood* v *Turner*, (1907) 2 Ch 134

(*r*) *Underwood* v *Trouer*, W. N. (1867) 83.

(*s*) *Re Cowin, Cowin* v. *Gravett* (1886), 33 Ch. D 185, *Re Tillott, Lee* v. *Wilson*, (1892) 1 Ch. 86. See also *Newton* v *Askew* (1848), 11 Beav 145; *Bugden* v. *Tylee* (1856), 21 Beav. 545, *Simpson* v. *Bathurst* (1869), L R. 5 Ch at p. 202.

(*t*) *Gough* v. *Offley* (1852), 5 De G. & Sm. 653, 655.

of the Public Trustee Rules, 1912, which is as follows :—

(1) Upon an application in writing by or with the authority of any person interested in the trust property the Public Trustee—

- (a) shall permit the applicant, or his solicitor, or other authorized agent, to inspect and take copies of any entry in any register or book relating to the trust or estate, and (so far as the interest of the applicant in the trust property is or may be affected thereby) of any account, notice, or other document in the custody of the Public Trustee ;
- (b) shall, at the expense of the applicant, supply him, or his solicitor, or other authorized agent, with a copy of any such entry, account, notice, or document as aforesaid, or with any extract therefrom ;
- (c) shall give to the applicant, or his solicitor, or other authorized agent, such information respecting the trust or estate and the trust property as shall be reasonably requested in the application, and shall be within the power of the Public Trustee.

(2) Subject as aforesaid, the Public Trustee shall observe strict secrecy in respect of every trust or estate in course of administration by him.

Such is a concise summary of the case and statute law declaring the obligations imposed by law upon trustees, executors, and administrators with reference to their accounts.

Probate Division

The inventory and accounts which the Probate Division will, on the application of a legatee or creditor, order the personal representative of a deceased to render consist of—

- (a) An inventory of the real and personal estate of the deceased ;
- (b) A cash account shewing the receipts and payments of the personal representative.

From very early times executors and administrators have been required to keep and furnish an inventory of the personal estate of their testator or intestate, and from times almost as remote to keep and render proper accounts of their dealings with the deceased's estate. (See *ante*, pp. 5 *et seq*.)

This jurisdiction of the Probate Division is practically disused, except where it is desired to make an administrator's sureties liable for his default.

Chancery Division

The accounts to be rendered to the Chancery Division in administration proceedings have been the subject of very careful deliberation at the hands of at least two separate bodies of Royal Commissioners (*u*). The use of the forms of accounts settled in pursuance of the recommendations of those Commissioners was in the origin optional, but those forms have long since been prescribed by the Rules of Court, and to-day must be used in all administration proceedings in the Chancery Division. (R. S C Ord. LV. r 75.)

Whenever this Division of the Court is called upon to administer a trust estate the first order made in the proceedings is that which is called the "administration order." That order imposes upon the executor or other accounting party the obligation of bringing into Court all such accounts and answering all such inquiries as the Court may direct in each case As soon as the accounts and answers to the inquiries have been delivered, they are all carefully examined by the proper officer of the Court, who, upon completion of the examination, certifies the result. Until that certificate has become binding upon the parties the Court will not, except under very special circumstances, make any distribution of the estate.

The accounts and inquiries usually directed by such administration orders are the following:—

(1) An account of the personal estate of the deceased come

(*u*) See Report of Chancery Commission, 1826, and First Report of Chancery Commission, 1852, pp. 34—5.

THE HISTORY OF THE SUBJECT 15

to the hands of the personal representative, or to the hands of any person by his order, or for his use.

(2) An account of the debts of the deceased.

(3) An account of the funeral expenses.

(4) An account of the legacies given by the testator's will.

(5) An inquiry what parts (if any) of the personal estate are outstanding or undisposed of.

(6) An inquiry what real estate the deceased was seised of or entitled to at the time of his death.

(7) An inquiry what incumbrances (if any) affect such real estate, or any and what parts thereof.

(8) An account of the rents and profits of such real estate received by the personal representative.

All these accounts, and the answers to all these inquiries, must be prepared in accordance with the forms in Appendix L to the Rules of the Supreme Court, which forms are prescribed by Ord. LV. r. 75. These forms include four schedules and a capital account (x).

The first schedule contains a complete inventory of all the personal estate of which the deceased died possessed.

The second contains particulars of the personal estate outstanding or undisposed of.

The third contains particulars of the real estate (if any)

The fourth contains short particulars of the incumbrances affecting the real estate, shewing what part is subject to each.

The capital account must shew all moneys received, and all payments or allowances made on account of the personal estate.

An account of proceeds of sale of real estate, rents of real estate and other accounts, would be directed in suitable cases, but the personal estate account is always necessary.

Through these accounts and schedules the executor or administrator places the Court in possession of the following *data*.—

(1) Particulars of the gross estate of the deceased at the time of his death, real as well as personal.

(2) Particulars of all moneys received, when, from whom

(x) See Daniell's Chancery Forms, 6th edit. p. 609 *et seq.*

and on what account received, and similar information with regard to all payments.

(3) Particulars of the real and personal estate outstanding or undisposed of, including (1) such of the items of real and personal estate set forth in the first and third schedules as still remain, (2) any new investments.

From these *data* can be ascertained—(a) What has become of each asset of which the deceased died possessed, and (b) What property remains to be dealt with, that is to say, what original assets are left, what new investments have been made and are still in hand, and what is the cash balance.

Such is the information which every executor or administrator must furnish to the Court in an administration action and which every beneficiary having a sufficient interest is entitled to demand, and such accordingly is the information which every executor's or administrator's account ought to furnish.

The Paymaster-General's Account.

To the Paymaster-General of the High Court is entrusted the custody of all cash and securities paid and transferred into Court, and the duty of keeping proper accounts of all dealings with that cash and those securities.

The Treasury requires the Paymaster to keep a separate account for every trust. On each side of this account (besides a column for money on deposit), there are two money columns, one for cash and the other for investments. Thus whenever money is received by the Paymaster-General an entry is made in the money column, and whenever investments are received by him an entry is made in the investment column on the same side of the account, and this is so whether the moneys and investments have been paid or transferred into Court under an order of the Court, or whether they have arisen from dealings with funds already in Court or from income of funds in Court. On the other side of the account similar entries are made of cash and investments paid away, sold, or transferred out of Court by the Paymaster-General, thus the one and the same account shews continuously in order of date all dealings whether with cash or with investments appertaining to that account; these cash and investment columns may at any moment be separately balanced shewing the cash balance and investment balance at that moment, and in this way there is no difficulty in issuing a certificate of both balances as at any desired date.

Attention is directed to the fact that *for the purpose of the trustee's accounts* there is no occasion to ascertain the value of the various properties of which a man died possessed and of the securities from time to time representing the trust. It will have been noticed that in the accounts required by the Chancery Division and in the Paymaster's accounts the value of an asset is never mentioned, and in taking the executors' accounts in an administration suit the common form order does not direct any inquiry with regard to the value of assets. Of course in the administration of every trust estate it is necessary to satisfy the Inland Revenue authorities as to the value of the trust property when duty has to be paid upon it, but values ascertained on one day may be different on the next day, and the values thus ascertained are good only as between the accounting party and the Revenue authorities, and are in no way binding upon a residuary legatee. It is therefore a surplusage for trustees to attempt to adjust the value of their trust estate from time to time. Parties interested in the capital of the estate may be desirous at times of ascertaining approximately the value of their shares, and in every such case the beneficiary should be left to make his own valuation. He will find in every properly drawn account all the information necessary for the purpose. When preparing the accounts of an estate for the beneficiaries the one duty of the executor is to disclose the whole of the testator's estate, to set forth particulars of all assets which he has got in, to shew the payments and allowances he has made in a due course of administration, and what assets remain outstanding, but the executor is not concerned with shewing by his accounts the value of those outstanding assets.

In conclusion, reference may be made to the Inland Revenue accounts, and the accounts which various special classes of trustees are required to render to particular departments of the State, and to the statutes relating thereto.

Accounts for the Inland Revenue

The principal accounts required by the Inland Revenue are two: the one is contained in the schedules to the affidavit upon which estate duty is paid and which in the case of executors and administrators has to be lodged before probate or administration is granted, and the other is contained in the residuary account, upon which legacy duty is paid.

In the executor's affidavit for estate duty particulars of the testator's free real and personal estate are set out, and the value given as at the death. From the total value of the estate the amount of the testator's liabilities at his death (with statutory exceptions) and the funeral expenses which have since been incurred are deducted, duty being paid on the balance. The residuary account is rendered when the debts and funeral and testamentary expenses and pecuniary legacies have been paid or provided for and the residue is ready for distribution. The items in the residuary account are numbered and arranged in the same order to correspond with the estate duty affidavit, and the interim income to date is brought in. The object of this account is to ascertain the value of the residuary estate at the time when the account is rendered. It is necessary to bring into account all the personal estate not specifically bequeathed and so much of the residuary real estate as was devised upon trust for sale, and any sales by executors of real estate under the statute to shew what each item realised or produced on sale, and what the remaining items are worth on the day on which the account is rendered, and what income has then accrued in respect of the estate from the date of the death of the testator down to the delivery of the account. Then on the other side of the account there are the discharges: these consist of the debts due by the deceased, the expenses of his funeral, the expenses of administration, the legacies, the duties payable to the Revenue and charged upon the gross estate, future and contingent debts, and any other like payments In the result the total of the moneys received and the value of the unrealised assets are ascertained, from which is deducted the total of the discharges, and the balance is the amount upon which duty is payable.

Accounts under the Charitable Trusts Act

These Acts require that the trustees acting in the administration of every charity within the scope of the Acts (for exemptions see sect. 62 of the Charitable Trusts Act, 1853) shall, in books to be kept by them for that purpose, regularly enter full and true accounts of all money received and paid respectively on account of such charity, and shall on or before the 25th day of March in every year, or such other day as may be fixed for that purpose, prepare and make out the following accounts in relation thereto (that is to say):—

(1) An account of the gross income arising from the endowment, or which ought to have arisen therefrom, during the year ending on the 31st day of December then last, or on such other day as may have been appointed for this purpose;

(2) An account of all balances in hand at the commencement of the year, and of all moneys received during the same year and on account of the charity;

(3) An account for the same period of all payments;

(4) An account of all moneys owing to or from the charity, so far as conveniently may be.

The Charity Commissioners (except in the case of endowments held solely for educational purposes, and charities excepted by sect. 63 of the Charitable Trusts Act, 1862) are empowered to make such orders as they may think fit in relation to the delivery or transmission of the said accounts, and the forms of such accounts, and it is provided that such orders shall be executed by all trustees and persons from whom the accounts to which they may relate are required.

The forms of account prescribed by the Charity Commissioners involve a schedule of assets resembling that used in Chancery, in that investments are carried in at face value. Receipts and payments on account of Capital and Income are classified under separate headings.

Accounts of Trustees in Bankruptcy

The trustee in bankruptcy is under the supervision of the Board of Trade. He is required to render his accounts every six months, to pay all moneys into an approved bank to a separate account, and any interest receivable in respect of the account forms part of the assets of the bankrupt's estate. He must never without the authority of the Board of Trade retain in his hands for more than ten days a sum exceeding 50*l*., and in default is liable to pay interest at 20 per cent. on the money retained with no claim for remuneration, and to be removed from his office.

The trustee is required to keep a record book in which he shall record all minutes, all proceedings had and resolutions passed at any meeting of creditors or of the committee of inspection, and of all such matters as may be necessary to give a correct view of his administration of the estate. Such a book would correspond with the Memorandum in this system. He also has to keep a cash book in which must be entered from day to day receipts and payments made by him.

The trustee is required to forward at the first audit a summary of the bankrupt's statement of affairs; in other words, a schedule shewing the particulars of the bankrupt's estate as stated by the bankrupt. The amount realised for each asset must be shewn on the face of the schedule in red ink. (See Bankruptcy Rules, 1915, Nos. 360—364.)

Accounts in Lunacy.

The affidavit which leads to a first order in lunacy contains a schedule of the patient's estate. In cases where the committee or receiver collects rents in person the account is divided into three parts:—

(1) The rent account, which so far as the receipts are concerned is in tabular form (very much the same as Appendix G., p. 285). The payments are included in (3) below.

(2) The general receipts are classified so that all the income received in respect of each investment during the period covered by the account is clearly shewn.

(3) The payments are also classified under separate headings.

With the schedule at hand it thus becomes easy to ascertain that all the income in respect of each asset has been duly received and accounted for. Where, however, rents are collected for the committee or receiver by an agent, only the net amounts received from such agent during the period covered by the account are brought into the committee's or receiver's account, and these amounts are included in the general receipts. The agent's accounts are produced to check these rents.

In the majority of cases accounts are rendered yearly.

In submitting an account in lunacy the main objects to be borne in mind are—

(a) To shew whether the estate is being well managed.

(b) To shew that the patient is being properly maintained, and that he is getting the greatest possible benefit from his income.

(c) To consider the investments, with the view of selling out where advisable, and re-investing the proceeds to greater advantage.

(d) To find the income for the purpose of assessing the lunacy percentage payable.

As regards (b). The word "maintenance" as applied to a patient is not always understood. Generally speaking, under the heading of "maintenance" should be included all payments made in respect of the patient's personal wants, such as board, lodging, clothing, medical and other attendance, pocket money, &c. And, where the patient is living in his own or a rented house, all the ordinary outgoings of the establishment are "maintenance."

(c) If the official taking the account in consultation with the committee or receiver or his solicitor considers any investment should be altered, it is usual to obtain the expert advice of a broker. A separate statement of the patient's fortune should be lodged with the first account, and this is revised on passing each subsequent account.

(d) The income for this purpose is the actual income, including arrears of income, received during the period covered by the account, less the proper deductions.

Accounts in lunacy are not sworn to and no certificate of the result is issued, but an office copy of the account can be obtained on request by the committee or receiver or the solicitor acting in the matter.

An unpaid receiver should keep an accurate account of receipts and payments, but when the time comes for him to present his account to the Master in a different form he is entitled to a reasonable allowance for the purpose of having the accounts so prepared. (Per Lord Cozens-Hardy, M.R., Law Society's Gazette (1917), Vol. XIV., p. 104.)

It must be borne in mind that this is not a case involving a trustee's account, but rather the account of a manager of a gentleman's private estate.

The Judicial Trustee Act, 1896

When a judicial trustee is appointed a separate banking account must be kept in his name, and he must pay all money coming into his hands on account of the trust without delay to the trust account at the bank.

The Court gives directions to the judicial trustee as to the date to which the accounts of the trust are to be made up in each year, and such accounts are to be audited by an officer of the Court, but no form of account has been prescribed, a departure from the Scotch practice as seen in the orders directing the judicial factor as to the form in which he must render his account.

The Custodian Trustee

By virtue of the Public Trustee Act, a "custodian trustee" may be appointed: it will be his duty to take possession of the trust property, including all securities and documents of title relating thereto, when powers of management alone will be left in the hands of the ordinary trustees. In such cases the management of the trust does not include the receipt of income or capital, which will be paid to the custodian trustee unless he directs otherwise. He may direct the dividends and other income of the trust property to be paid to the managing trustees, or to such person as they direct, or into such bank to the credit of such person as they may direct, thereby facilitating the payment of the income to the bankers of the tenant for life.

No form of account has been prescribed for the use of a custodian trustee.

CHAPTER II

THE SYSTEM EXPLAINED

BEFORE proceeding to explain any general system upon which trust accounts may be kept, a few additional considerations which will help to shew the desirability of some such system as is about to be recommended may here be mentioned.

It has already been seen that beneficiaries are entitled to certain information at the hands of their trustees (using the term "trustees" here and throughout this chapter so as to include executors and administrators), which information necessarily involves in substance a list or schedule of investments or property and an account. If default is made in complying with the legitimate demands of a beneficiary in this behalf, the Court compels obedience by ordering the trustees to bring the schedule and account in question into Court; but the information which the beneficiary is entitled to receive is the same whether he gets it without the assistance of the Court or through the instrumentality of the Court; therefore, in either event, there should be no difference in the substance of the information furnished, although the form in which it is rendered may vary widely.

The Chancery Division of the High Court is concerned in the administration and investigation of a vast number of trusts, some of which are of the largest, whilst others are but small, and again some are of the most complicated whilst others are of the simplest; therefore, the system of accounting which has been prescribed for use in the Courts, and which has in fact stood the test of fifty years' experience, may reasonably be expected to comply with most of the requirements of the case.

The present Rules of Court provide that applications for administration may be ordered to stand over for a certain time so that the executors, administrators or trustees in the meantime may render to the applicant a proper statement of their accounts. (Ord. LV. r. 10a.) This order was made after Lord Esher's Committee sat, and the practice of directing accounts to be furnished and vouched out of Court has been adopted by some judges (*Re Lockwood* (1892), 92 L. T. Jour. 237), but not by others. (*Re Brown*, W. N. (1895) 115.) In such circumstances the question arises, what is a "proper statement of their accounts"? Certainly that account which the Court itself would order the accounting party to bring into the judge's chambers must of necessity be a proper statement.

It has been pointed out that trust accounts should contain the same information whether prepared for the Court or not, and that the form in which they are rendered in the Chancery Division has stood the test of time. When, therefore, the problem is proposed of formulating a general system upon which trust accounts may be kept, it is natural to turn to the existing practice in the Chancery Division and in the Paymaster's office, behind which there is so much weight of authority and experience, to see what there is in that system which can be utilised, and no one who considers the matter will be surprised to know that this Chancery practice in conjunction with the practice of the Paymaster-General's office provides the basis of a system which may with confidence be recommended for general adoption.

An endeavour will now be made to describe a general system upon which the accounts of trustees may be kept. Such a system should not only satisfy all the requirements which have already been referred to, but should at the same time be quite simple and capable of being readily understood by a beneficiary who may not have had any special training in accounts.

The objects to be attained by such a system are as follows:—

(1) To shew what original assets were brought into trust.

(2) To shew the dealings with those assets.

(3) To shew of what the estate consists at the present date, and of what it consisted at any other given date.

(4) To shew (in cases where income has to be accounted for) what income has arisen from the trust estate and how it has been applied.

These objects are attained in the system proposed by means of three essential features, viz.:—

(1) A schedule of all original assets;
(2) A "Cash and Investment Account" on the model of the account kept by the Paymaster-General.
(3) An income account.

The Schedule

To begin with, there must be a *Scheaule*, or that which the Probate Division terms an Inventory. In this schedule will be set forth particulars of all original assets, both real and personal, which have been brought into the trust, and of all incumbrances affecting the trust.

The schedule will (if and so far as necessary) be divided into three parts.

Part I. will contain full particulars of the real estate of which the deceased died possessed, or (as the case may be) which was brought into trust

Part II. full particulars of the personal estate of which the deceased died possessed, or (as the case may be) which was brought into trust, each item being separately described; by this arrangement no asset can be lost sight of.

Part III. will contain short particulars of the incumbrances affecting the estate, whether created by the deceased, by the settlor, or by the trustee, shewing what part of the estate is subject to each incumbrance. It will serve as a perpetual reminder of the liabilities to which the estate is subject.

The Cash and Investment Account

In the next place there must be a capital account. This will follow the form of a receiver's cash account, as recommended by the Royal Commissioners in 1826 and again in 1854, in which the items of cash coming into and going out of the estate

THE SYSTEM EXPLAINED 27

are set forth in chronological order and numbered consecutively on the two sides of the account, in accordance with Ord. XXIX. of 1852 (a).

In the early stages of the administration many of the original assets will have to be realised, and later on investments will have to be made, and again later still the then existing securities may have to be sold and the proceeds reinvested, and the question arises, how are these dealings with securities to be recorded, and at the same time the accounts of the trust estate kept in regular chronological order? The answer is that the receiver's cash account above referred to will be supplemented by adding a second set of money columns, so as to assimilate its form to that of the Paymaster-General's "Cash and Investment Account," in which he records all his dealings with investments having a pecuniary denomination, as well as his dealings with cash, carrying the figures representing the nominal amounts of the investments into the one set of money columns, and the cash figures into the other. In this account the Paymaster enters the nominal amounts of the Consols and other stocks, &c., coming in and going out of the account, in just the same way as he debits and credits himself with his dealings in cash, so that at any moment he can ascertain from his account what amount of cash and what nominal amount of investments he holds, and if necessary, by referring back, he can trace the history of an investment, that is to say, he can ascertain who transferred any investment into Court, or, if he purchased it, he can see when, and what was the price paid; similar particulars *mutatis mutandis* can be ascertained concerning every sale. By this means no sum of cash and no investment can be lost sight of, as any omission on either side of the account would affect the balance. Any person examining the account can easily ascertain from the cash columns what cash was in hand on any

---

(a) Order dated 16th October, 1852, made under 15 & 16 Vict. c. 80.—

XXIX Where any account is directed to be taken the accounting party is, unless the judge shall otherwise direct, to make out his account and verify the same by affidavit. The items on each side of the account are to be numbered consecutively, and the account is to be referred to by the affidavit as an exhibit, and to be left in the judge's chambers.

particular day and how long it remained uninvested; and from the investment columns the securities held in trust on any day can also be ascertained.

Where the estate consists of real and personal property, the account will consist of two parts, so that the entries appertaining to realty may be all included in Part I., and those appertaining to personalty in Part II. of the account.

Many of the entries may have to be distinguished from others at a later stage; thus, money paid to creditors must be distinguished from funeral expenses; both must be distinguished from death duties and other testamentary expenses, and from payments to legatees or other beneficiaries, and, in order to facilitate this process, it is a good plan to commence the entries on alternate lines of the account book, and to write on the spare line over each entry the name of the separate set of payments to which the entry belongs—*e.g.*, "Executorship expenses," "Pecuniary legacies," "Debts due at the death." The headings must of necessity vary with the circumstances of each case, but they can soon be determined in each particular estate and a list of them prefixed to the account. When selecting these headings it is well to have regard to the way in which the items in the estate duty affidavit are classified, but when a residuary account has to be rendered to the Inland Revenue the classification in such residuary account should be followed.

If a business forms part of the trust estate the accounts of such business will be kept separately in the usual commercial way, the resultant figures alone being entered in the trust account.

As and when each asset in the schedule is dealt with so as to require it to be entered in the cash and investment account, a note will be made in the reference column of the shedule shewing the nature of such dealing. Thus, as every original investment having, or capable of being reduced to an English pecuniary denomination (*b*) is taken by the trustee into his own name or

---

(*b*) French investments in francs may be reduced to £ sterling at the rate of twenty-five to the £, or dollars at the rate of five to the £.

control, it will be entered in the investment column of the "Cash and Investment Account," and the serial number of that item in the account will be entered in the reference column of the schedule. If a sum of cash is received—*e.g.*, a bank balance—that will be entered in the cash column of the same account, whilst the original item in the schedule recording such bank balance will be "discharged" by entering in the reference column the number of the item in the account representing the cash received.

If there are settled legacies these would naturally be carried over to separate capital accounts, and would constitute separate trusts. These separate accounts will in their turn follow the form of the "Cash and Investment Account."

The Income Account

A second or income account must be kept, in which will be entered particulars of all receipts and payments appertaining to income. This, again, will be in the form of a receiver's account, as above described, unless for any reason the income has to be accumulated and invested, in which case a "Cash and Investment Account" will be used.

If rents have to be collected they should be carried to a separate rent account, and where there are rents of real estate as well as of leaseholds, the account will be divided, one part for each class of property.

Where the rents of freehold or leasehold properties, or the dividends and interest upon investments, have to be apportioned, it will be useful to shew the apportionment of the income derived from each class of property upon separate accounts reserved exclusively for the purpose.

In large and complicated estates the cash and investment account book may be used as an ordinary cash or "day" book which receives all entries in the first instance and from which the items will be posted to appropriate accounts, in a ledger in order to classify the receipts and payments under appropriate heads. Where this plan is adopted, the heading in the "Cash and Investment Account" would be dispensed with, because a separate account would be opened in the ledger for the items which would otherwise have been entered under each separate heading.

Results of the System

Such in brief is the system recommended. It has been found simple to use and at the same time adequate, and the principles involved, together with the forms used, have the sanction of the highest authority; indeed, it is an adaptation, with but few additions and alterations, of the simple forms prescribed by the Rules of Court for use in the Chancery Division. It is capable of expansion to meet the special requirements of large estates.

If this framework of common form is adopted, the following results are obtained, viz. :—

In the first place the schedule defines the trust property : that is to say, it gives full particulars of the original assets and incumbrances, and so provides the materials for the accounts required by the Inland Revenue and for the answer to the first, sixth and seventh inquiries in an administration action.

In the second place the Cash and Investment Account will give a complete and continuous history of all dealings with capital money from the commencement of the trust, and will also give particulars of, practically speaking, all investments, so that it can readily be ascertained what was the cash balance and what were the stocks, shares, mortgages, debentures, &c., representing the trust estate on any day which might be named during the currency of the trust. Any other property, such as land, which remained subject to the trust, would be ascertained by reference to the items remaining undisposed of in Parts I. or II., as the case may be, of the schedule.

In the third place.—When an executor is ordered by the Probate Division to render an Inventory and Account, it could be prepared with the least possible adjustment from the schedules and account above referred to.

In the fourth place.—Should an executor be ordered by the Chancery Division to render all or any of the accounts and answer the inquiries usually directed in an administration action, he would have the principal schedules and account

THE SYSTEM EXPLAINED 31

actually ready by omitting the investments from the "Cash and Investment Account" and re-numbering the items; the only schedule to be prepared would be that containing particulars of the outstanding personal estate, the material for which would be ready at hand in the same account and in the schedule.

The Estate Book

The system has now been explained. In practice the accounts must be put together in a convenient form, and this as soon as possible; for instance, in the case of a will or intestacy, as soon as probate or letters of administration have been granted; and in the case of a settlement contemporaneously with the preparation thereof. To meet these requirements an "Estate Book" may be compiled, which will consist of the following documents :—

(1) The copy of the Will (made when taking Probate), or an Epitome of the Settlement.
(2) An Epitome of the grant of representation.
(3) The Memoranda (for the present a blank sheet of foolscap thus headed).
(4) The Schedule (c).
(5) The forms for the Cash and Investment Account (c).
(6) The forms for the Income Account (c).
(7) Apportionment Accounts, when necessary (c).

All these documents (which will be on foolscap) will now be put together and in the order above mentioned, and after suitable covers have been procured the whole may be laced up and will constitute "The Estate Book." When this has been done the pages of the book should be numbered throughout and indexed, and whenever additional pages are wanted for the memoranda or for any account the book will be unfastened, the additional pages inserted in the appropriate place, and the previous page number will be continued, with the addition of a, b, c, or any other letter of the alphabet.

If proper entries are made in the estate book throughout the

(c) All these accounts will be in accordance with the forms set forth in the Appendices

administration it would be difficult to imagine any ordinary inquiry which a trustee or beneficiary could make concerning the accounts which would not immediately be answered by reference to the estate book. From the practitioner's point of view such an estate book results in a great economy of time, because at any moment he can see how the course of the administration is progressing, what securities have been realised, what have yet to be realised, what cash there is in hand, and indeed he can review the whole situation at a glance.

The estate book above described, when compiled for a particular trust, will have no place in it for transactions appertaining to any other trust or any other matter of business, but even where there is no such estate book it is irregular to enter the accounts of two trusts in the same book, or to enter the account of any one trust in the same book with any other account whatever. Solicitors or agents having trust moneys passing through their hands will, of course, keep their own accounts and record their dealings with those moneys, but that is the solicitor's account with his client, and not the trustees' account with their beneficiaries. (*Fountaine* v. *Amherst, Ltd.*, (1909) 2 Ch. at 394.)

Moreover, the ledger of the solicitor or other agent of the trustee is his property, and the account in that ledger can only be of moneys actually passing through the agent's hands, which will not be much where a separate banking account for the trust is kept. But on the other hand, the trustees' account must be exhaustive of all dealings with the trust estate, including those moneys passing through the hands of their agents. It therefore follows that the ledger of the solicitor or other agent of the trustee is in no way whatever a substitute for that complete account which it is incumbent upon every trustee to keep and have always ready for production.

In order to elucidate the situation by examples, the estate book appertaining to the trust of an imaginary testator—W. Roberts—has been set forth in Appendix A., pp. 195 to 260, which book includes a full schedule, cash and investment account, apportionment accounts and income account.

The items involved in the estate of this imaginary testator have been used throughout this book wherever possible.

CHAPTER III

THE MEMORANDA

EVERY one who is accustomed to deal with trust estates will recall occasions when events occur in the course of administration of considerable importance to the trust, for which there is no acknowledged place of record in the trust accounts. In order to meet this need, the estate book is made to include a blank sheet headed "The Memoranda," where it is proposed to record all these events.

It is generally convenient to make entries of the marriage of a settlor, also of the births, marriages and deaths of his children, and sometimes of his grandchildren; and in the case of a testator and more particularly of an intestate to collect and enter all those details which would enable the executor or administrator at any time to procure the necessary certificates to prove who was the heir and who were the next of kin of the deceased.

The date when notice of any dealing by a beneficiary with his interest is given to each trustee is of very considerable importance. Particulars of any such notice, whether by way of settlement, sale, or mortgage, which may have been served upon all or any of the trustees should be recorded, including the name, address, and description of the assignee or incumbrancer, as well as that of the solicitor (if any), who gives the notice and the date when the notice was received.

If any beneficiary becomes bankrupt, the event should be recorded as soon as it comes to the knowledge of any trustee, with particulars of the Court in which the proceedings took place, the record number and the dates.

If a beneficiary dies, or a lady entitled to a share of the estate marries, the event should be recorded, and the date when and the place where the death or marriage took place should, if possible, be included in the entry.

If any appointment of new trustees is made, the death or retirement of any previous trustee, or other event which gave rise to the power, will be recorded, and the deed or order of Court appointing the new trustee referred to.

The notice of an appointment made in pursuance of a power in favour of any beneficiary will be entered.

Advancements made to or on behalf of beneficiaries must be entered in the accounts, and an entry may with advantage be made in the Memoranda as well.

Any order of Court made in any action or on any originating summons in the matter of the trust should be entered, together with short particulars of the effect of the order and the title of the record, so as to enable office copies, if necessary, to be procured. Opinions of counsel taken upon questions arising in the administration should be noted as well.

If meetings of the trustees are held, the minutes of the proceedings at such meetings, and a note of any audit and of every periodical examination of the accounts by the trustees, or a beneficiary, whether on a balancing, or at any other time, should be entered.

A record of every event of sufficient importance which may affect the residuary legatees, and which has no place elsewhere in the books, should be preserved by being entered in the Memoranda.

(For Specimen Memoranda, see pp. 205, 206 *and* 293—295.)

CHAPTER IV

THE SCHEDULE

IMMEDIATELY after the inception of a trust, whether created by deed, will, or otherwise, the trustee (a term which in this chapter includes executors and administrators) would do well to start or open an Estate Book, and enter therein a copy or an epitome of the trust instrument, if any. The provisions of the document creating the trust and the nature of the assets representing the estate should then carefully be considered with the view of deciding what are the most appropriate accounts to keep of the trust estate, because every trustee is bound to keep accounts (see Chapter I), it not being sufficient merely to preserve the materials from which to prepare them. It therefore becomes necessary at the outset to decide upon the system of account keeping to be adopted.

A general outline has already been given in Chapter II of a common form system upon which all trust accounts may be kept, and it will have been noticed that the schedule, the cash and investment and income accounts are the essential features thereof. In this chapter it is proposed to deal with the schedule (a specimen of which will be found at pp. 207—210) and subsequently with the accounts.

Whoever has studied the history of the subject under consideration will have realised the supreme importance of commencing the administration of every trust by preparing a schedule of the original assets which constitute the trust estate. It is essential that this schedule should be drawn with great care and distinctness, pains being taken to include in it a full statement of every item of real or personal property brought into trust.

A special word of warning is necessary with regard to the estate of a deceased lunatic, because, as a rule, the character of the beneficial interest in his property is not changed by any dealings with it by the committee or receiver, so that securities representing proceeds of real estate sold during the lunacy will still retain their character of real estate and be scheduled accordingly with notes explaining the reasons. If, however, the lunatic had mortgaged his real estate, which was subsequently sold, in the lunatic's lifetime, by his mortgagee, then the balance of the sale moneys was converted into and became personalty. (*Chadwick* v. *Grange*, (1907) 1 Ch. 313, and 2 Ch. 20.)

There are some properties which constitute real estate which might well have been thought to form part of the personal estate and *vice versâ*, as, for instance, shares in the New River Company and a few of the older companies are real estate. (*Drybutter* v. *Bartholomew*, 2 P. Wms. 127.) These New River shares have now been converted to a large extent under the Metropolis Water Act, 1902, s. 9 (7) (2 Edw. VII. c. 41), but the Water Stock issued in respect of any Adventurer's or King's share is for all purposes of devolution and transmission to be considered as land until the 24th June, 1904, but thereafter only until some person being *sui juris* becomes absolutely beneficially entitled in possession. Redeemed Land Tax, which has not been merged, is personal estate. (*Skeene* v. *Cook*, (1901) 2 K. B. 12.) Tithes in lay hands are real estate. Real estate given upon trust for sale, the testator being entitled to a share in the proceeds of sale, is personal estate.

In the case of a deceased's estate, particulars of the assets will be extracted from the estate duty affidavit made when proving the will or taking administration. In the case of a settlement by deed, the particulars will be taken from the deed itself.

Each separate asset will be shortly but accurately described, and any important fact connected therewith will be mentioned; *e.g.*, an estate has been mortgaged, or leased, or that an investment is subject to the rule in *Howe* v. *Lord Dartmouth*. (See pp 98—101.) The subject of every specific devise or bequest will constitute a separate entry in the schedule, and "specifically devised" or "specifically bequeathed," as the case may be, should be added at the end of the description. (Item 2, p. 207, and Item 7, p. 208.)

The schedule will be divided into three parts, in order to keep real and personal property always separate and to have a list of the incumbrances affecting the trust estate.

Part I (Real Estate)

Here will be entered particulars of all the real estate which has been brought into trust. The particulars of real estate contained in the estate duty affidavit will be examined, and after making necessary alterations, may well be re-copied, so that Part I. of the new schedule will, in most cases, be ready, and thus the same order will be preserved, thereby facilitating reference.

A distinctive number will be given to each property the title to which is contained in a separate bundle of deeds. Then the particulars of the tenancies and leases may be set forth as in App. A., pp. 207, 208. If this plan is adopted, a label should be attached to each bundle of deeds, bearing the schedule number, and all the leases may, if sufficiently numerous, be numbered consecutively both in the schedule and (in pencil) on the counterparts; but the other documents of title should on no account be marked in any way whatever. In this way country estates or building estates can be scheduled with great facility, especially if an extract from the Ordnance map, which includes the property, is included in the estate book fronting that part of the schedule containing the particulars of the property in question.

Part II (Personal Estate)

Here will be entered particulars of all the personal estate which has been brought into trust.

The arrangement of the items should, so far as possible, follow the same order as that which is adopted in the Estate Duty Affidavit. This will facilitate reference, and now that the items in the Inland Revenue Residuary Account have been arranged in the same order as those in the Estate Duty Affidavit, the desirability of adopting this plan is obvious. An exception, however, must be made when scheduling leaseholds. They will be entered either before or after all other items of personalty, preferably before.

In the money column between the number of the item and the particulars thereof will be inserted *the nominal or face value* in sterling of any item which has a pecuniary denomination, and in the very few cases of foreign investments having no English currency denomination then the foreign money may be reduced to English currency at a rate to be mentioned in the entry; as, for instance, an American security of 500 dollars would be carried in at 100*l.*, and in the description of the security it would be mentioned that the dollar had been taken as of the value of 4*s.* (See Item 11, p. 208.)

The exact description of stock exchange securities must be given, and in the case of bonds the number appearing on the face. Whatever classification is adopted care should be taken to arrange the items strictly in alphabetical order. When a number of investments is involved, and particularly when a residuary account has to be rendered to the Revenue, this classification and alphabetical arrangement will be found in practice to be of great assistance.

The due proportion to death of all rents and dividends then current may be included in Part II. by inserting a common form item " Proportion of Income on ditto to Death " (see Item No. 8, p. 208) immediately after each investment. Rents of leaseholds may be treated in a similar manner. At the end of Part II. may be entered " Proportion of Rents of Freeholds to Death " (see Item No. 29, p. 209), because, although the property producing the rent is real estate, yet this proportion of accruing rent is personalty.

The number of the apportionment items in the schedule may be materially reduced by inserting one only for the proportion of all dividends accruing due at the death, and referring to a separate apportionment account for particulars. In such cases a separate entry will be made in the schedule—" Proportion of dividends accruing due at the Death as per separate Apportionment Account."

In similar circumstances a separate entry may also be made

with regard to the rents of real and leasehold property accruing due at the death referring to the separate account for details.

All rent, whether of real or leashold property, due prior to the death, but not received by the deceased, must be separately entered in this part of the schedule, and if the rents are numerous, the total may be entered in one sum, "Rents in arrear and unpaid at death as per List A.," reference being made to the list for details. There is no apportionment involved in these cases, and the Revenue will require a separate list of all such rent in arrear.

When this part of the schedule is first prepared the amounts of several of the items will not have been ascertained, and so will be left blank, as in the case of dividends accruing at the death the due proportion of which cannot be supplied until the next dividend is declared; but the advantage of making these entries is that the items cannot be lost sight of, and when the counterfoil of the next dividend warrant is returned by the bankers, the information necessary to make the calculation will be available, and the figure ascertained and entered in the space in the schedule left for the purpose.

When an item in the schedule consists of a reversionary interest, the particular sum of cash and the securities which will be received in respect thereof cannot yet be ascertained, so the figures must be left blank, but none the less it is most important that the reversionary interest should be entered; and if the rule in *Chesterfield's case* can apply (as to which, see p. 101, *post*), a note of the fact should be added, so that the application thereof may not be overlooked. Upon falling into possession the particulars of the assets, as soon as ascertained, will be entered in the appropriate money column of the schedule in the same way as the proportion of dividend accruing due at the death is entered. (Item 26, p. 209.)

The same practice will be adopted in the case of a settlement in which a lady covenants to settle after-acquired property. The covenant will be a separate item in the schedule, and each time it attaches, particulars of the assets received will be entered as described in the case of the reversionary interest, but with this addition, that the original item of the covenant must again be repeated under the last item in the schedule, and if it again attaches the same process as that already explained will be repeated. (Appendix I., p. 296, Item 8, and p 297, Item 8.)

Parts I. and II.

As soon as all the items in Parts I. and II. of the schedule have been entered they will be numbered consecutively throughout, those in Part II. being continued from the last number in Part I., and a line drawn under the last entry in each part.

The object of the entries in the reference column of the schedule is to enable the disposition of every item therein readily to be traced, a convenience which will materially facilitate an examination or audit of the accounts. The full effect of these references can hardly be realised until after the next chapter has been studied, but it will be sufficient here to state that every investment having a pecuniary denomination, and every sum of cash mentioned in the schedule will, as soon as received by the trustee, be entered in the cash and investment account and "discharged" from the schedule. In this way the schedule will contain particulars of every original trust asset, from which it follows (and this will be made clearer in the chapter dealing with the cash accounts) that every sum of money, every property, and every investment received by the trustee, must have been one of the items mentioned in the schedule, or must have had its root of origin in the schedule, *i.e.*, derived either directly or indirectly from one or another of those original items. For instance, if after proof of the will a new asset is discovered, say a fund in Court which is now ready for distribution, the money when received should not be entered in the account until after an entry of the new asset has first been made in the schedule. On the other hand, if a testator died possessed of 1,000*l*. Consols, which was duly entered in the schedule, then when that investment is sold and the proceeds re-invested, neither the cash proceeds nor the new investment can have any place in the schedule, because the source of origin of the cash and of the new investment is to be found in the Consols already entered.

The advantage of the schedule is that the trustee always has ready at hand a complete record of all original trust assets, and can readily comply with the common form inquiries in an administration suit with reference to such assets. Further, with the aid of the account he will at once be able to say what has become of every original asset, and finally no asset can possibly be lost sight of in the course of the administration.

If any book-keeper rejects the plan of keeping in one account records of his dealings with securities side by side with his dealings with cash, then he will keep a cash account shewing on the one side cash received and the other cash paid. In such a case the original items in the schedule will be discharged when delivered to a beneficiary or when sold, and appropriate references entered in the reference column. The rest of the estate would remain in schedule, and if at any time a new investment is made, the schedule would be extended by adding another part in which the new investments would be recorded. The numbering of the items in the new part will be continued from Part II., so that all the items in schedule will be consecutively numbered throughout, and it will be easy to distinguish the original items from the new investments.

This alternative form of account is not to be recommended, as it is much more satisfactory to keep a Cash and Investment Account, and so doing involves but little extra work.

Part III (Incumbrances)

There yet remains the third part of the schedule to be explained. Here will be entered in order of date every incumbrance affecting the estate. The entry should specify—

(1) The date of the mortgage deed.
(2) The names of the parties.
(3) The sum of money borrowed.
(4) The property mortgaged.
(5) The names of the parties (if any) covenanting to pay the debt.

This schedule of incumbrances will act as a continual reminder of the liabilities to which the estate is subject.

A note may be made in Part I. or Part II. of the schedule, as the case may be, against the entry there of any item which has been mortgaged, and there should be included in that entry the number of the item in this part recording the incumbrance.

This Part III. will be sub-divided into two other parts, to be called A. and B. respectively (see p. 210).

Division A. of Part III.—In this division will be set forth particulars, as above, of all mortgages affecting the trust estate—
- (a) created by the deceased or the settlor;
- (b) created by the trustees pursuant to power in that behalf, but without any covenant by them to pay the debt;
- (c) charges arising by operation of law, *e.g.*, compensation under Agricultural Holdings Acts, charges for paving under Local Government Acts, payments of estate duty by tenant for life, &c.

Division B. of Part III.—In this division will be set forth particulars of all mortgages created by the trustees pursuant to powers in that behalf, under which they render themselves personally liable to pay the money borrowed.

(*For specimen Schedules, see pp.* 207—210 *and* 296, 297.)

CHAPTER V

THE CAPITAL ACCOUNT

The General Capital Account is the most important of the accounts in the estate book, and will now be explained in detail.

It is imperative that every entry necessary for preserving the records of the assets of which the estate originally consisted, and of every dealing with those assets or the money and securities representing the same, should be made in the books, because the trustee or his successors will in the more or less distant future have to divide the trust estate amongst beneficiaries who will become entitled to participate in the capital, and who at the outset are generally not in existence or not *sui juris*. For these reasons the capital account will be one continuous and uninterrupted record from the inception of the trust down to and including the distribution of the estate.

With the exception of real estate, leaseholds, chattels, and some few other assets, the capital of any ordinary trust consists at all times either of cash or of stocks, shares, mortgages, or other investments having a nominal cash value capable of being entered in an account, added up and balanced in like manner as cash. Accordingly, when all dealings with capital money and trust investments have been entered in the same account, such an account will contain particulars of all cash and other assets (except property having no pecuniary denomination) which at any time represented the trust estate, and of all dealings with those assets and of all payments made by the trustee on account of the trust. Such an account is the "Cash and Investment Account," and is the form in which the capital account involved in this system will be kept.

It is of primary importance to understand the exact nature of this account, the objects to be attained by keeping it, the construction of it, and the details involved in working it.

The nature of the account is that of a capital account as between the trustee (a term which in this chapter includes executors and administrators) and the beneficiaries.

The object of the account is to preserve records of all dealings by the trustee with cash received by him forming part of the capital of the trust estate, and of all payments made by him, or on his behalf, on account of the trust. But it is more than a mere cash account, as it is to include receipts of and dealings with investments having a pecuniary denomination in the same way as cash. This account will contain in figures and words a continuous history of the trust, so far as cash and investments are concerned, and it will shew how far payments have been made in a due course of administration. From it particulars can be taken out of the cash and investments which represented the trust on any named day.

The account, as set forth in Appendix A., p. 211, is in the form of a receiver's cash account, enlarged into the Paymaster's "Cash and Investment Account," in which investments are dealt with in the same way as cash. All the entries, whether of cash or investments, will follow one another in order of date, and will be numbered consecutively throughout on both sides of the account, in order to facilitate reference, the cash figures being carried out into the first of the two sets of money columns, which are ruled on either side of the account, the investment figures being carried out into the second set.

Every cash entry on the debit side of the account will commence with the words "To Cash," and on the credit side with the words "By Cash," and every investment entry on the debit side with "To Amount," and on the credit side with "By Amount." The adoption of this plan at once distinguishes the cash and investment entries.

When a trustee has to deal with a mixed fund representing personalty as well as proceeds of sale of realty, he must divide this account into two parts, carrying the entries appertaining to real estate into one part and those belonging to personal estate into the other part of the account. (See Appendix A., pp. 212

and 228.) By this means the separate dealings with each class of property will be shewn. It is necessary thus to separate real and personal assets, because the devisee or heir-at-law of any real estate which has been resorted to for payment of debts or legacies is entitled to call for a schedule of the real and personal estate of the deceased, and an account of all moneys received and paid in respect of each estate for the purpose of ascertaining that no undue burden has been cast upon the real estate. (See *Re Stokes* (1892), 67 L. T. R. 223, and *Re Roberts*, (1902) 2 Ch. 834.) Again, debts and legacies may have been charged upon real and personal estates in such a way as to be payable proportionately out of each estate (*Strickland* v. *London, &c.*, (1907) W. N. 181), and so far as legacies are under these circumstances found to issue out of real estate there is this further complication that there has to be deducted from those legacies (in the absence of any indication in the will to the contrary) their share of the estate duty paid in respect of such realty. (*Re Spencer Cooper*, (1908) 1 Ch. 130.)

The detailed working of this account has yet to be explained. It will have been noticed that there are two essential elements in the account, viz. :—

(1) Entries of cash transactions; and
(2) Entries concerning investments having a nominal pecuniary denomination.

Each of these will now be explained in further detail.

The Cash Entries

Some confusion often exists in the minds of the public as to the use of the terms "debit" and "credit." It will be well, therefore, to make the application of those words quite clear at the outset.

The left-hand side of the account is always the "debit" or "debtor" side, and is marked with the letters "Dr." The right-hand side is always the "credit" or "creditor" side, and marked with the letters "Cr." The principle is that an accounting party is "debtor" for that which he receives, and "creditor" for that which he pays away, but what appear to be receipts are sometimes found on the Dr. side and sometimes on the Cr. side of an account. The answer to the difficulty entirely depends upon the heading of the account. If the account is headed "The Executors in Account with the Beneficiaries," here the executors are the accounting parties, and will debit or charge themselves with all receipts, and accordingly make those entries on the Dr. or left-hand side, because they do or did owe those moneys to the beneficiaries; in like manner they will credit or discharge themselves with all cash paid, and those entries will be made on the right-hand or credit side. It is only necessary to reverse the title of the account and make it "The Beneficiaries in Account with the Executors," and the arrangement of the entries will immediately be transposed. The beneficiaries then become the accounting parties, so they in their turn will debit themselves with all moneys received by them from the executors and credit themselves with all moneys paid to the executors. Seldom, however, in the title of a trust account does the name of the beneficiary come first, so that the receipts almost invariably appear on the left-hand side.

In his Cash and Investment Account on the left-hand side and in the cash column thereof the trustee will enter, and by so doing will charge himself with all cash capital belonging to the trust received by him or on his behalf, that is, all capital sums of money which the Court would charge him with when taking an account of the trust. He should be careful not to charge himself with other moneys for which he is not accountable to the beneficiaries, in fact, he should not include in this account any sum of capital which was not mentioned or had not its root of origin in the schedule.

A trustee is not responsible in the beginning for every item mentioned in the schedule, but his duty is to obtain possession of all such assets as soon as possible, and he is liable to account for them as and when received. He is *primâ facie* responsible for all cash entered in the account as having been received by him, because by making the entry he admits the receipt of the money, and is therefore liable to be charged with it in account, consequently he should not make that acknowledgment until the liability is complete. The appropriate time, therefore, to enter cash is as soon as it has been actually received.

There will be entered on the opposite side of the same account, and in the cash column thereof, every capital sum of money paid by or on behalf of the trustee in a due course of administration—in other words, every sum of capital money which the trustee would be entitled to take credit for as against the trust estate; by this means he will discharge himself of his receipts so far as such payments will extend, but the account may shew payments representing sums in excess of receipts, which means that, so far as the excess is concerned, the trustee may have advanced money out of his own pocket, or may have overdrawn some other trust account (*e.g.*, the income account); still the entries are correctly made, and the capital account will shew the true position of the capital of the trust estate as between the trustee and the beneficiaries If there is not at the time enough cash in hand to balance the capital account, then some part of the estate sooner or later must be sold in order to recoup the trustee, as he has a lien on the whole estate for any balance owing to him in a due course of administration.

Classification of Entries.—Each item (or several items when the succeeding one is of a similar character to the previous one) should be preceded by words indicative of the class to which the item belongs (*e.g.*, " Legacies "); such words might form the title of a separate ledger account if there was occasion to further classify the capital. These headings are in accordance with the form of account issued by the accountant of Court for the guidance of the Judicial Factors under the Judicial Factors (Scotland) Acts. When deciding upon the headings to be used in any particular account, the book-keeper should at least have a separate heading for each class of items appearing in the Estate Duty Affidavit, and he should also have regard to the additional classes of items which may have to appear in the Inland Revenue Residuary Account in order to avoid the possibility of any further subdivision being necessary when the time comes for preparing that account: for instance, dividends due and dividends accruing due at the death should never be entered under the same heading, because particulars of the dividends due at the death are included in the Estate Duty Affidavit, but not those accruing due, whilst both may have to be included in the Inland Revenue Residuary Account.

If a payment is made which must be charged exclusively to any beneficiary, then the name of such beneficiary should be incorporated in the heading preceding the entry, and a note may well be made in the Memoranda, *e.g.*, Residue settled in equal moieties on a daughter and step-daughter, involving different rates of legacy duty.

The duties on each share will, in the absence of any direction to the contrary, be a charge upon the share, and must be distinguished, so that when the time for distribution comes it may be charged against such share. In addition to this the account may be debited with the duty as an investment in the same way as an advance as explained at p. 54 *et seq.*

On the other hand the estate may be divided into shares, and a separate capital account opened for each beneficiary. When this plan is adopted, the payments made exclusively on behalf of any beneficiary would be charged to his or her section of the capital account.

Narrative of Entries.—Care must be taken in composing the narrative of each entry; it must express the transaction in simple accordance with fact, narrating distinctly the data necessary to check its accuracy, such as dates, periods, rates of interest, dividends, and stock amounts. The name of the person from whom money is received or to whom money is paid should always be stated, and it must appear on what account the money is received or paid. For instance, when entering the receipt of the cash proceeds of a sale of stock, the date of the receipt, the amount of stock sold, the price obtained, the name of the broker, the amount paid or allowed for brokerage, and the net amount realised should all be stated. (See Item 11, p. 214.) If, on the other hand, the entry had been merely "Proceeds of sale of L. & N. W. Ry. Stock, £358 : 2*s*. 6*d*.," there would be no material with which to verify the accuracy of the entry made. In a word, when making an entry, it should be borne in mind that the account is to contain a continuous history of all dealings with trust assets, and all that information which is necessary to attain this end should be recorded. When entering any balance of money received from the broker upon a sale and re-investment, or indeed when the whole has been re-invested, so that there is no balance to account for, care should be taken to enter full particulars of the sales and purchases.

Mortgages by the Trustee.—If a trustee mortgages a part of the trust estate the deed will in the ordinary way negative any personal liability on the part of the trustee to pay the money lent. In such circumstances the trustee is not personally liable, and the transaction is in effect a conditional realisation of a trust asset; the trustee will charge himself in the capital account with the money received and make a note in the schedule against the items included in the mortgage to the effect that they have been mortgaged, which will explain the absence of the deeds when an investigation and audit is made. He will also enter the mortgage in Division A. of Part III. of the schedule, and this will justify the payment of interest on the mortgage in the future to be charged in the income account. (See p. 210, Division A.)

Loans to the Trustee.—Where a trustee borrows money for the benefit of the estate, making himself personally liable, this is a borrowing by the trustee personally, therefore no entry of such a transaction is made in the capital account, which is an account as between himself and the beneficiaries. The trustee should be very careful to give an acknowledgment in writing, stating the amount, the date, the rate of interest and the terms, and place a copy with his trust papers, and enter full particulars in the Memorandum. Should the trustee at the same time or subsequently give security to such a creditor by creating a charge upon any of the trust assets the position so far as this capital account is concerned is unaltered, but the trustee, of course, makes an entry in Division B. of Part III. of the schedule which will explain the absence of the deeds and justify the payment of interest on the loan to be charged in the income account. (See p. 210, Division B.)

> *Example.*—The trustees borrow 200*l.* from the bank, and use the money so borrowed in paying estate duty. No entry will be made in this capital account of the money so obtained, but an entry will be made of the estate duty paid. Subsequently the trustees take the deeds of "West View" (one of the trust assets) to the bank, and deposit them to secure that loan. No entry can be made in the cash account of this deposit, but one will be made in Division B of Part III. of the schedule. Here the trustees, by not debiting the capital account with the money borrowed, but by crediting that account with the payments made, preserve a true record of the receipts and payments as between themselves and the beneficiaries, and the account will shew a balance due to them of 200*l.* at least. It is true that they are personally liable to the bank, but the estate is liable to them, and the account shews that liability. When "West View" is sold, whether by the mortgagor or mortgagee, or when the trustees realise other sufficient assets, the whole proceeds will be brought into the capital account as moneys received by the trustees, though part will of course be applied by the trustees (or retained by the bank) in discharge of the debt. There may also have to be an entry on the credit side shewing interest on the loan or the costs in relation to it. The entry would be, *e.g.*, "By Trustees' (or 'Bank's') costs of loan of 200*l.*"

Such are the entries as between the trustees and the beneficiaries, but there is yet another view of the situation to be considered, as some account must be debited with the receipt of the money borrowed. It has been shewn that it cannot be debited in the capital account, therefore a new or loan account must be opened, which will be one as between the borrowers and the lender (the bank), in which the 200*l.* will be debited and in which every capital payment to the bank by the trustees in discharge or on account of the loan will be credited.

When under these circumstances the capital account shews a balance in hand, inasmuch as any balance in hand will be at the bank, it follows that there must be money at the bank belonging to the trustees. They are then free to draw a cheque in repayment of the loan, which payment will be entered in the loan account as above explained (see Item 1, p. 233), and the money afterwards remaining in the bank should be sufficient to discharge the net balance due on all open trust accounts.

The Investment Entries

Attention must now be directed to that part of this account which relates to investments. The trustee will enter on the receipt side of this account and in the investment column thereof—and by so doing will charge himself with—every trust investment mentioned in the schedule having an English pecuniary denomination, or capable of being reduced to such, which has been received by him or has come under his control. In the very few cases of foreign investments having no English currency denomination, then the foreign money may be reduced to English currency at a rate to be mentioned in the entry, as for instance, an American security of 500 dollars would be carried in at 100$l.$ and in the description of the investment it would be mentioned that the dollar had been taken as of the value of 4$s.$ (See Item 5, p. 212.)

All original stocks and shares mentioned in the schedule will be entered in the account as soon as the probate has been registered with the company, secured debts or mortgages as soon as notice of the probate has been given to the debtor or mortgagor, and bearer bonds as soon as actual possession is obtained, in fact in each and every case the investment should be entered as soon as the trustee could be held accountable therefor. He will also enter and so charge himself in like manner with every investment which he makes or takes in exchange. (See Item 24, p. 218.)

If the trustee transfers an investment, whether to a purchaser or a beneficiary, or if he surrenders an investment on conversion of the investment or reconstruction of the company, or if an investment is extinguished by dissolution of the company, in each of these cases the amount of stock with which he stands charged is thereby reduced, and he is accordingly entitled to take credit for the nominal amount of the stock dealt with. This is done by entering on the payment side of the account and in the investment column the amount of stock sold, transferred, or surrendered, the consequence of which is that the investments in his hands are to that extent discharged; and in the case of a conversion or reconstruction the trustee will debit himself with the new stock.

The **Classification** of investment entries, where any is required, will follow the principle already explained in the case of cash entries.

The **Narrative** of an investment entry will always be short, as all that is necessary is to include such a description of the investment as will be sufficient to identify the asset, and record the manner in which it is acquired or disposed of. The nominal or face value alone will be entered, but in the case of bonds, and more particularly when they are payable to bearer, the serial number appearing on the face of each must be specified. The face values in these cases are merely a matter of account, and not of valuation. This will be apparent on reference to Item 5, p. 308, where there is an entry of 11l. East Indian Railway "B" Annuity. Here is an annuity, and not a nominal amount of stock, which may have been worth in the market about 240l cash. The 11l. is, however, inserted in the investment column, as, for the purpose of identification, that is sufficient.

If an investment is sold, it will be entirely unnecessary to enter here all the information which will have to be recorded when entering the receipt of the cash. On this occasion the date of the contract and particulars of the investment, as appearing on the broker's note, will alone be recorded. (See Item 6, p. 215.) The reason for this is that when the items constituting each class of assets, identified by appropriate headings, have to be taken out the particulars of the amounts produced by the sales must appear in the cash classification (see Item 11, p. 214), and the investment sold and the date of sale will appear in the investment classification. (See Item 6,

p. 215.) Upon referring to these examples it will be obvious how unsuitable it would be to have the cash details of a sale in the investment and not in the cash classification, and, of course, it would be a surplusage to record the details more than once. Exactly similar entries, *mutatis mutandis*, will be involved when an investment is purchased.

Deposits by the Trustee.—Whenever a trustee has in his hands an appreciable sum of cash which is not required in the immediate future, it is his duty to place it on deposit, in order that it may be earning interest pending a permanent investment. In such a case an entry must be made on the payment side of the account in the cash column, and at the same time a cross entry must be made on the receipt side of the account in the investment column, the transaction thus recorded being in fact a temporary investment which forms part of the trust estate. When the money is withdrawn from deposit the investment entry will be discharged, and the cash will be entered in the usual way. Any interest on the deposit will be carried to the income account.

> *Example.*—The payment of the cash for deposit is shewn in Item 12, p. 217. The entry which records the deposit as one of the investments for the time being is Item 16, p. 216; then when the money is withdrawn, the cash received (Item 19, p. 216) and the investment discharged (Item 14, p. 217), are entered in the usual way.

A secured Debt not paid in full.—This will be dealt with in the following manner, for instance:—When the trustee originally assumes control of a mortgage it is entered on the debit side in the investment column at the full amount. When the mortgage is realised the full amount of the mortgage is entered on the credit side of the account in the investment column. The actual amount of cash received is then entered on the debit side of the account in the cash column.

> *Example.*—If the mortgage was for 500*l.*, and the mortgagee had to realise his security, which produced on sale, say, 300*l.*, the sum of 500*l.* would appear in the investment columns on either side of the account, and the sum of 300*l.* on the debit side in the cash

column. The two entries in the investment columns will balance each other, and shew that the security was originally brought into account, and has since been realised, and no part of it remains in the estate, while the entry in the cash column will shew that the sum of 300*l.* cash is in the trustees' hands in place of the 500*l.* mortgage security previously held. (See Item 8, p. 212; Item 34, p. 225; and Item 35, p. 224.)

Valueless Securities.—Any investment which proves to be valueless, as, for instance, if a company goes into liquidation and pays no dividend, then the item should be discharged in the account by an entry on the credit side in the investment column, *e.g.*, "By amount of 50 shares of £1 each in the English Investment Trust, Ltd. (valueless), liquidated in 1900," and some document preserved with the vouchers giving a reference to the liquidation proceedings, or it may be a broker's certificate. (See Appendix, Item 2, p. 215.) If there is no market for the shares, that in itself is not sufficient to justify their being discharged on the account, and again, what is worthless to-day may become valuable years hence. Therefore, except where the asset has been properly disposed of, as in the case of liquidation or bankruptcy, the book-keeper should be slow to discharge an item on these grounds.

Advancements.—Most settlements and many wills authorise advancements to be made out of the capital of the trust estate for the benefit of an infant beneficiary, or money may be advanced for payment of estate duty. Where such a power is exercised, or such a payment made, the proper entries recording the transaction must appear in the accounts. It is manifest that such an advancement or payment, although made *out of* the general estate, must not ultimately be charged against that general estate, but against the share of the beneficiary for whose benefit the same was made. The amount advanced is taken out of the trust altogether and paid over to the object of the power, but, nevertheless, when winding up the trust and distributing the estate this sum will have to be brought into account by the beneficiary advanced in the investment column of the capital account; the trustee will therefore debit himself with the amount of the cash so advanced as if it were an investment in order to preserve a permanent record of the advance, and he may at the same time open a separate account in the name of that particular beneficiary for the purpose of shewing all dealings with that beneficiary's share. In this account the amount of the advance will at once appear on both sides: "To cash transferred from capital account" and "By cash advanced for . . ."

> *Example.*—A sum of India 3 per cent. Stock has been sold and the usual entries made. Out of the capital then in hand 380*l.* is paid by way of an advance for the benefit of one of the beneficiaries. This is a cash transaction, and entered as such in the ordinary way. Another entry is made of this advance, as although the cash no longer forms part of the trust estate, yet it will have to be brought into account when the time comes to distribute the estate, so the sum in question is entered on the debit side of the account and in the investment column. When the trust estate has to be divided this advance will be disposed of by being charged in account against the beneficiary on whose behalf the payment was originally made. (Item 7, p. 303; Item 8, p. 302; Item 8, p. 303; Item 9, p. 302; and Item 15, p. 307.)

It now remains to divide the residue of cash. To this end there must, for the purpose of computation, be added to the cash balance in hand the total of any advances made. The result will be divided by the number of the beneficiaries, and from each share thus ascertained will be deducted the advance made to each beneficiary.

Schedule References

Some means must be adopted of connecting any item of cash in the account with the *same* item in the schedule, and any item of cash in the account which represents the proceeds of sale of any or any part of a specific asset mentioned in the schedule, and of connecting any investment entered in the account with the *same* investment mentioned in the schedule, because one of the chief features of this system is that at the commencement of the trust every original asset is entered in the schedule, and all assets which are cash, or have a pecuniary denomination, are *also* entered in the account as and when received, so that the one and the other must be easily connected. At an early stage in the administration all cash and every investment gets entered in the account, and nothing remains on the schedule except assets having no pecuniary denomination: and excepting the last mentioned assets every capital asset and the entire history of every dealing with every part of the capital of the trust estate is to be found in this account. It follows that means should be adopted whereby the original investments and items of cash mentioned in the schedule may be traced into the account with the greatest possible facility.

This connection between the items in the schedule and the corresponding items in the account will be accomplished by inserting in the reference column of the schedule opposite every item entered there the number of the corresponding item in the account and the page in the account on which such item is to be found.

Examples of Cash References.—The testator's balance at his bank at the time of his death amounted to 47l. 4s. 2d. (see Item 20, p. 209), which was received in due course on the 16th day of November, 1902, and will be found entered on the debit side of the capital account. (Item 2, p. 212.) The reference therefore to be inserted opposite the original entry of this bank balance in the schedule will be "Item 2, p. 212."

Again, if a man owing a simple contract debt, which has not been entered in the investment column of the account, becomes bankrupt, and a dividend or dividends is or are received in respect of the debt, then similar references to those cash receipts will be entered in the schedule, and when the final dividend has thus been entered, the original item in the schedule will have been completely discharged. (Item 25, p. 209.)

If at any time a mortgage is paid off, the number of the item in the account and the page of that account recording the payment will be entered in the reference column of Part III. of the schedule opposite the incumbrance in question, and if the incumbrance has been noted in Part I. or II. of the schedule, the entry of the mortgage will be struck out and the above

THE CAPITAL ACCOUNT

references to the payment off inserted. (Part IIIB., Item 1, p. 210.)

In a similar manner, as each original investment is received by the trustee or becomes subject to his control, it will be entered in the account and the appropriate reference will be entered in the schedule.

> *Example of Investment Reference.*—The executors obtained control of 600*l*. Consols by registering the probate at the Bank of England, accordingly they entered this investment in the account. This being one of the original assets of which the deceased died possessed, the number of this entry and the page will be inserted in the reference column in the schedule. (See Item 4, p. 208.)

Specifically devised or bequeathed property which has no pecuniary denomination will be discharged on the schedule, as it is incapable of being transferred to the account. This discharge will be effected, when the executor consents to the devise or bequest, by entering in the reference column of the schedule some such words as " consent granted," and the number of the legatee's receipt or the item in the memoranda (if any) referring to the matter may be added. (Item No. 2, p. 207.)

Any other property having no pecuniary denomination which is not ultimately transferred to the beneficiaries *in specie* will remain on the schedule until sold, and when sold the proceeds will be entered in the cash and investment account, and the usual references entered in the schedule. (Item 3, p. 208.) If a part only of an original item having no pecuniary denomination is sold, then the proceeds will be entered in the cash and investment account, and similar reference numbers entered in the schedule as in the previous case, but with this addition, that the figures in the reference column will be preceded by the words " Part sold."

By means of these references the history of every original item can readily be traced. Suppose long after the death of William Roberts (the imaginary testator) the residuary legatee inquired as to what had become of the 800*l*. London & North Western Railway Stock of which the testator died possessed. On searching the schedule the stock is at once identified in items numbered 7 and 9 (p. 208), and from the reference column there the two items, together making 800*l*., are traced to the cash and investment account, Item No. 4, p. 212. The next question is, What has become of it? This is ascertained by examining the entries in the investment column on the other side of the account, when Item No. 6 on p. 215 is discovered, from which it appears that 300*l*. part of the stock was sold. Then reference is immediately made to the other side of the account, and there it will be found that the stock realised 358*l*. 2*s*. 6*d*. (Item No. 11, p. 214), at that date a balance of 500*l*. of the same stock was still in hand, and by examining the entries on the payment side of the account it will be seen that on the 1st February, 1903 (Item No 13, p. 217), that sum of stock was transferred to the specific legatee.

If the item in question formed the subject-matter of a property having no pecuniary denomination which had not been sold (*e.g.*, a specific devise of real estate), there would be no necessity to go beyond the schedule itself to ascertain its history, because the property would have remained there until discharged by "Consent granted," but if such an item had been sold, then again, from the information in the reference column, the proceeds of sale could at once be traced into the cash and investment account.

In a similar manner the history of every other asset in the schedule can be traced.

Investments in Hand

The entries on the debit side of the capital account and in the investment column thereof represent the *face value* of the various investments brought into account, and the entries on the credit side represent the *face value* of those which have been parted with, therefore the balance should represent the total *face value* of the investments in hand at the date of the balance.

Where the investments are few it will be seen from a glance at the account what they are, but when there are more than three it is useful to keep a slip in the account book in the following form:—(See slip opposite p. 224).

INVESTMENTS IN HAND

	Face Value.	Description of Investments.	How Disposed of.
1.	£ s. d.		
2.			
3.			
4.			

and to fill up the form with the shortest possible description of the various items of investment in hand. If between one balancing and another any investment or part of an investment mentioned on the slip is sold, a note will be made on the slip against that investment, stating how it has been disposed of. In the event of only a part of any item mentioned having been sold, in that case the original entry will be struck out, but will be repeated as a new item so far as the number and description of the security is concerned immediately following the last on the list, and the *reduced amount* will be substituted for the original sum held. Again, any new investment made will be added to the existing list, but will have no number, so that the items still remaining on the list, which were included in the last balance, can always be identified by their numbers. When next the accounts are balanced and a balance of investments is brought down all the assets which go to make up that balance will be enumerated in the account in an inner column by the side of the balance, and to each item a distinctive number will be given and the list copied on to a fresh slip for use as before explained. In this way the book-keeper will be able to produce the balance of the investments and the items constituting that balance as readily as he will be able to furnish any inquirer with the balance of cash in hand. In practice it is found convenient to record on the back of the slip the place where the scrips for the various investments have been deposited.

Having regard to the fact that all the entries in the cash and investment account are made in chronological order, it will be easy to ascertain what was the state of the account at any date, both as to cash and investments. This is important, as there are occasions when it becomes necessary to discover what the balance of investments consisted of years previously: as for instance, four children of a testator are residuary legatees, and each is entitled to his share on attaining majority, and that the eldest was paid his share years ago, since when the assets have very materially depreciated in value; this subsequent wasting of assets will not entitle the remaining three children to call upon the eldest brother to refund any part of that which he received if that truly represented his share at the date when he settled with the trustees, but it is obvious that those three younger children would require an account of the state of the trust as of the day on which the eldest child received his share in order to satisfy themselves that he was entitled to all that he then received.

Balancing the Accounts

As soon as substantial progress has been made in the administration of a trust, the accounts should be balanced, so as to ascertain that all is in order; the first balancing should take place at the expiration of six, or at the latest, twelve months from the testator's death. To do this,

(1) The balances due to capital and income respectively on any apportionment accounts must be transferred and the accounts closed.
(2) The balance on the income account, which will be dealt with in the next chapter, must be paid over to the tenant for life, so that that account may also be closed.
(3) Any appreciable sum of capital in hand should be invested.
(4) The balance on every account remaining open must be brought down.

When these preliminaries have been dealt with, then, in the majority of cases, the capital account will alone shew a balance, which will agree with the balance at the bank; but if there are other open accounts, and still more if any one of them shews a contra balance, the following plan must be adopted to prove the accuracy of the account. All the debit balances on the trust accounts must be taken out and added together. The same with the credit balances on the trust accounts; then the total of the credit balances will be deducted from the total of the debit balances, and the result will ordinarily be a sum equal to the balance at the bank. But if a loan account is open (which is not a trust account), then the balance due on that loan account must be subtracted from the above-mentioned result.

The net figure thus arrived at must now be agreed with the balance at the bank. To this end the bank pass-book must be examined, and all the items checked with the entries in the capital and income accounts, a tick being placed against the items in the pass-book and also in the accounts as they are found to be correct, and, assuming that no cheques are outstanding, the balance at the bank should equal the figure already found to be the net balance on the trustees' accounts.

Attention must now be directed to the investments to ascertain that all are in hand and in order.

In the first place the schedule should be carefully gone through and all the references against investment items verified by tracing each item into the account; where the reference is found correct and the investment has been duly entered in the account the original entry will be marked off the schedule as discharged therefrom. The remaining items in the schedule which have not been thus discharged must now be brought down and re-entered consecutively on the schedule itself after the last entry under a fresh heading, entitled "Balance of assets remaining in schedule," as of the date of the closing of the accounts, so as to form, as it were, a second edition of the schedule revised to date. The original numbering of the items thus brought down will be preserved and so facilitate the identification of every original item. Each of these entries should be in the fewest words possible, because the original entry can readily be referred to for full particulars. (See p. 209.)

In the second place the investment slip in the account book will be brought down to date, the balance on the investment columns taken out, and it must be seen that that balance equals the total of the face value of the investments on the slip.

Finally all these three balances thus ascertained, viz. :—

    (1) the cash balance;
    (2) the balance of assets remaining in schedule;
    (3) the investment balance,

must be proved to be correct in the following manner:—

In the case of No 1.—If there are no loans in Part IIIB. of the schedule unsatisfied, the cash balance on the capital account will be the cash balance at the bank after deducting the balance on the income account (if any), but if there are any outstanding loans in Part IIIB. of the schedule then the total of such loans will have to be set off against the balance due to the trustee on the capital account before the bank balance can be agreed.

In the case of No. 2.—By inspecting the deeds themselves appertaining to each separate property or otherwise ascertaining that they are in proper custody, and in the case of furniture that it is in the possession of the person lawfully entitled thereto.

If the trustee has borrowed money upon the security of any of the trust assets, then the documents of title relating to the security will be missing, and rightly so. Particulars of the mortgages undischarged will be found in Part III. of the schedule.

In the case of No. 3.—All the investments must be produced and examined in order to see that the list is true and exhaustive, and at the same time it should be ascertained that all these investments stand in the names of the trustees for the time being, and that the documents are in proper custody.

When these balances have thus been proved to be correct, the aggregate balance of investments will be brought down on the account, and the details making up such balance entered in

THE CAPITAL ACCOUNT

an inner column. If any conversion of an original investment has taken place, care must be taken to see the new stock is within the powers of the investment clause, otherwise it would be unauthorised, and if so must be sold. Again, the list must be examined to see that all the other investments are duly authorised, but if any are not, then they must be sold and the proceeds reinvested; or it may be that there is a power to retain or postpone conversion, and in either of such cases the trustees should consider and decide whether they will continue to hold such unauthorised investments: if they do, care must be taken to see whether the tenant for life (if any) is entitled to the income accruing in respect of such investments the sale of which is thus postponed. After the investments have thus been entered and considered, they will be re-numbered consecutively.

At the same time a second edition of Part III. of the schedule should be prepared, by repeating in the fewest words possible with the original numbering any mortgages still remaining undischarged.

It is most desirable that the trust accounts should be periodically examined and the balances which have been brought down ascertained to be correct, particularly on all important occasions, as for instance, when new trustees are appointed, when a tenant for life dies, or when a share is paid out of residue. This is so in consequence of the fact that in years to come it may, and in the last case certainly will, be necessary to ascertain what were the investments subject to the trust as well as the cash balances on the dates named.

The verification of the balances as above described wherever possible should be conducted in the presence of the trustees, or some or one of them, with or without a tenant for life or remainderman, for which purpose a meeting would be called. The accounts would then and there be examined, and the investments checked as explained above. When the parties have satisfied themselves that all is in order, the deeds and other documents of title would be restored to their original custody and the vouchers put away ready for production to anyone else who has a right to call for them, and a minute made in the memoranda recording the examination, which might well be signed by all the persons—especially the trustees or beneficiary—who took part in the work.

As soon as the executorship comes to an end, that is, when all the debts and legacies have been paid, investments made in accordance with the trusts, and nothing further remains to be done during the lifetime of the tenant for life except to pay her the income, a convenient opportunity arises to close the accounts. If these have been kept by an agent, it may be well to have them independently examined; after this has been done, it is a good plan to forward to every trustee a copy of the account, following the practice prescribed by the Public Trustee Act in the case of an audit, and at the same time notice may be given in such quarters as the trustees may think suitable, that the executorship has been closed, and that a copy of the schedule and capital account can be obtained upon the usual terms.

Separate Trusts

Whenever an estate is entailed, whether by a family settlement or by a will, it constitutes a separate trust.

Whenever trustees are appointed under the Settled Land Act, they will, of course, keep a separate account.

Where a legacy has been given upon separate trusts, and the executors either pay, or appropriate certain investments to satisfy the legacy, that cash or those investments will be transferred to a separate capital account, and, if necessary, a separate income account will be opened for the legacy trust.

A separate estate book should be opened for each separate trust as soon as the payment or appropriation is made. An example of such is given on pp 235 to 237.

Vouchers

A voucher must be obtained whenever possible for every item appearing on either side of every account. The book-keeper, when drawing a cheque in payment of a bill, should make the appropriate entries in his account before despatching the bill and cheque to cover same. If this entry is made at the time, he will be able to pick out from the bill before him all necessary information for the narrative of the entry in his account. The entry will have its appropriate number, and he should affix that same number to the bill and also to the cheque before parting with them, which will reduce the task another day of arranging the vouchers to that of merely putting them in numerical order. A separate bundle of vouchers must be made up for each separate account

There must be some regular place for denoting the number on the voucher. Sometimes the debit vouchers are numbered in the left-hand top corner, when the credit vouchers would be numbered in the right-hand top corner, whilst in other cases they are all numbered in the right-hand top corner, the number being preceded by "Dr." or "Cr.," according as it may be a debit or credit voucher.

Where one voucher is common to two accounts it should be numbered for the first account and included in that parcel of vouchers. In making up the second account the voucher will not be removed from its original place, but a slip will be prepared embodying so much of the information contained in the original voucher as may be necessary for the present occasion, which slip will be numbered and filed as if it were itself the voucher for the payment in the second account, and a note put at the foot of the slip giving the number of the original voucher contained in the other bundle for reference

The same rules will apply to the vouchers appertaining to the investments. The broker's notes for sales or purchases of investments will constitute the vouchers; the appropriate number will therefore be written on the face of these notes at the time when the credit entry on sale is made or the cheque is drawn, and they will be filed consecutively with the cash vouchers.

Every payment of 2*l*. and upwards must be evidenced by a stamped receipt. (See also p. 161.) Vouchers representing payments made by an agent on behalf of a trustee with his money are the trustee's property, and must be handed over to him. (*Re Ellis & Ellis*, (1908) W. N. 215.)

The following are examples of vouchers which should be available. In the case of freehold or leasehold property sold,

C.   F

the contract, the completed draft conveyance, and the statement of account for completion agreed between the parties.

In the case of the sale or purchase of securities, the broker's "sold" or "bought" note; for the cash at the bank at the testator's death and for any sums withdrawn from deposit and interest, the banker's pass-book or letter; amount of life assurance policy, the letter from the insurance office admitting the claim; for the moneys produced at any auction, the auctioneer's account and marked catalogue; rents and mortgage interest, the account of the agents who collected same; for amount due under partnership articles, the articles themselves and a balance sheet or statement signed by the surviving partners.

Review of the Account

The advantage of keeping such an account following immediately the schedule as above described is that the latter will shew the state of the assets at the testator's death, and the account will shew all capital receipts and payments in respect of the assets as well as all dealings with the investments having a nominal pecuniary denomination from the commencement to the end of the trust. Further, the account will shew how every sum of cash was disposed of, and from the schedule and account it can readily be ascertained what was the state of the trust at any particular time.

Thus, where a testator leaves a sum of bank stock which the executors afterwards sell, and invest the proceeds in Consols, the bank stock will appear in the schedule, and from there can be traced to the debit side of the account, the nominal value being entered in the investment column. The stock when sold will be discharged by an entry on the credit side of the account, and the amount will be carried into the investment column; the proceeds of the sale will be entered on the debit side, the amount being carried into the cash column. The Consols will be entered on the debit side of the account, the amount being carried into the investment column, and the money paid for the Consols will be entered on the credit side, the amount being carried into the cash column.

It will be observed that at the commencement of this imaginary transaction there was a sum of bank stock with which the executors stood charged; immediately that stock was sold they discharged themselves of the liability to account for that original sum of bank stock, and therefore entered the same to their credit on the credit side of the capital account; then on settling day they received the purchase-money for the stock, and on the same day debited themselves with the cash so received. Then, again, as soon as they have entered into a contract to buy the Consols, and have paid the purchase-money, they discharged themselves of the liability to account for the cash received on sale of the bank stock by crediting themselves with the payment of the cost of the new investment, and at the same time that they pay their purchase-money they will receive the Consols in exchange, which will involve the last entry whereby they will debit themselves with the new investment—namely, the Consols, which if not sold in the interval, will ultimately be divided amongst the residuary legatees.

The history of all dealings with the trust will be apparent on the face of the account; and with this and the schedule it can readily be ascertained—

(1) How far the assets have been realised and debts and legacies paid in a due course of administration.

(2) When every scheduled asset was got in, what it produced, and how the proceeds were dealt with.

(3) When any investment was made, what it cost and from what source the purchase-money was derived.

(4) When the sale of any investment subsequently acquired took place, what each sale produced, and how the proceeds were applied.

(5) What investments were in the hands of the trustee at any given date during the administration

(6) What was the cash balance in the hands of the trustee at any particular time, and how long it remained uninvested.

(7) What was the cash balance due to the trustee at any particular time, and how long it remained unpaid.

At the expiration of about six months from a testator's death, it will usually be found that every sum of cash and every investment having a cash denomination has been entered in the account and discharged from the schedule, leaving nothing there but real and leasehold estates and chattels; with those few exceptions the whole of the records of the estate will then and in the future be found in the Cash and Investment Account.

Having thus explained the principles involved and the working of the system, it may be useful to refer the reader to the accounts of the estate of William Roberts set forth in the Appendices, where the system will be found worked out in detail and its practical application demonstrated.

(*For Specimen Capital Account, see pp.* 211—229.)

CHAPTER VI

THE INCOME ACCOUNT

In addition to the capital account which has been previously dealt with, it is the duty of a trustee to keep an account of all income received, and of all payments made by him or on his behalf on account of income.

This will be purely a cash account, recording such receipts and payments, except when income has to be accumulated and invested (*e.g.*, during an infant's minority), in which case the account will be enlarged into a Cash and Investment Account.

If the estate consists of stocks and shares, as well as of lands and houses, this account will be divided into two parts, the one for rents and the other for the rest of the income. The rent account will again be divided in order to separate the rents of real estate from those of leaseholds.

The narrative of the entries will in principle be similar to that already described in the case of entries in the capital account. Where there is an appreciable amount of property in hand, and the payments are more or less numerous, then the entries may usefully be prefaced by headings as in the case of the capital account. By this means the gross receipts and payments appertaining to each property can readily be ascertained, and the net income of each farm or estate fixed.

When an agent is employed to collect the rents and manage the property, careful instructions should be given to him as to the form of the account which he is to keep and render periodically. In the first place, he should be supplied at the cost of the estate with a separate book, and instructed to enter therein all his receipts and payments appertaining to the estate. The book will be the property of the trustee. In large estates a separate account should be opened for the property included in each separate tenancy, but generally it will be sufficient for the agent to keep his account in the form set forth in Appendix G. (see p. 285), taking care in suitable cases to preface his payment entries by headings. Then at the end of the period of account he should add a summary shewing the total receipts and payments and net revenue derived from the property included in each tenancy during the period covered by the account, which may be quarterly, half-yearly, or otherwise. Yet there may be many exceptions to this rule of having a separate item for each tenancy, as, for instance, when dealing with a block of (say) fifty cottages all let upon weekly tenancies. Here it would be more suitable to have one entry in the agent's summary (*e.g.*, " fifty cottages ") than to make fifty separate entries, but these are details which must be left to the discretion of the book-keeper.

The agent when submitting his account will forward to the trustee a cheque for the balance due The amount of that cheque will be entered by the trustee in his Income Account, and reference made to the agent's first or other account, as the case may be, for details, and the agent's account will be filed together with his vouchers, which are the property of the trustee, because they are payments for the trustee out of his money.

As in the case of capital, so with income, the question will periodically arise as to the form in which the Income Account should be rendered to the beneficiary. The trustee cannot part with his account, and his agent's account is part thereof; therefore a fresh account must be prepared for the occasion, and the material will be found in one or both of the accounts already described, but by a little arrangement and classification the situation can be nicely focussed In deciding upon the arrangement to be adopted, it must be borne in mind that there will be a periodical account of the same estate, and for this reason it is desirable that the items in each succeeding account should be set out in the same order as they appear in the preceding account, subject, of course, to necessary variations consequent upon sales and re-investments. The various properties constituting the real estate will come first, any leaseholds second, and both will be set forth in an account the form of which is given at p 286, and

THE INCOME ACCOUNT

in which will be entered the gross receipts and payments and net result in respect of each property which has been separately entered in the agent's summary. If details are called for they are ready at hand in the agent's rent book or other account kept by the trustee. In the first account particulars of all tenancies will be given; these details will not be repeated in the subsequent accounts, but when a new tenancy is created, the terms thereof will be mentioned.

The investments representing the rest of the estate will be set forth in an account the form of which is given in Appendix H. (p. 287).

All the items mentioned in the investment balance on the capital account will be included, and against each will be entered the gross and net income produced during the period of account, with particulars of any deductions such as income tax; a memorandum may be added at the foot of the account specifying any arrears.

Each investment will be repeated in every subsequent account until discharged by sale, or transfer, or becoming valueless, and the reason for the discharge will be stated.

In the first of both these accounts the balance of each rent or dividend received after deducting the proportion due to capital at the death will be entered, the particulars being extracted from the appropriate apportionment account.

The order in which assets are brought on to an account is important, and particularly is this so when there is a series of accounts involving the same assets, *e.g.*, an Income Account. The assets in the schedule were entered in the same order as they appeared in the Estate Duty Affidavit, and it would be convenient now, when preparing the first Income Account, to adhere to the same classification, so that English Government Securities would come first, Colonial Securities next, and so on.

Every asset should be entered in the Income Account notwithstanding that a particular item produced no income during the period covered by the account, and in such cases a note will be added opposite the item in question explaining the loss of income.

This plan avoids the possibility of any item of income being forgotten, it facilitates the examination of the account by the beneficiary, and enables him in the most convenient way to detect any fluctuations of his income. He can see in what part of the estate the rents are on the increase or decrease, what arrears exist, and what part of the estate is unlet. He can readily detect the quarter in which there is any increase or decrease on dividends, and what mortgagors are in arrear with their interest, and he will see at once the nature and amount of each class of investment held by the trustees.

It is a common practice for a trustee to allow the dividends to be paid direct to the tenant for life. In such a case a list of the investments in respect of which such dividends are paid will be included in a separate classification, and a note added to the effect that the dividends on all these investments have been paid direct to the tenant for life pursuant to an authority in that behalf lodged with the company at the request of the beneficiary.

Perhaps a safer practice still is for the trustees to have all dividends, rents and income paid direct to their own trust income account, leaving with the bank an authority to transfer the same, or the due proportion thereof, to the private accounts of the tenant for life or other beneficiaries. The advantage of this plan is that the pass book of the account belongs to the trustees, and will contain full records of receipts and payments. They will also have the counterfoils of the dividend warrants.

A memorandum should be added at the foot of the account which is rendered to the beneficiary to be signed by him acknowledging that the account is correct, and particularly that the moneys therein appearing to have been paid to him have been so paid, and that he has received the dividends stated to have been paid to him through his bankers

If for any reason these forms are not thought suitable, and the trustee prefers to send to the beneficiary merely a copy of the cash account appertaining to income, then on the first occasion a schedule of all properties held in trust should accompany it, and on subsequent occasions a statement should appear on the face of the account that the trust assets are the same as those held, mentioned or referred to in the last account, subject to any exception which should be mentioned, *e.g.*, a sale and re-investment, and it should be made clear upon the account which of the investments now included represents the proceeds of sale of that omitted.

(*For Specimen Income Accounts, see pp.* 286, 287.)

CHAPTER VII

APPORTIONMENTS

THE administration of trusts often involves questions of apportionment, as, for instance, on the death of a testator, of an intestate, and of a tenant for life. In all these cases rents, dividends and interest which were not actually due, but which were accruing due at the death, have to be apportioned in order that the proportions which accrued before and after the event may be allocated and paid to capital, to income, to the estate of a deceased tenant for life, or to parties entitled in remainder, as the case may be. On some few other occasions income derived from certain investments has also to be apportioned.

All these apportionments are necessary in consequence either of the provisions of the Apportionment Act of 1870 or of rules of equity which require, under certain conditions, income to be apportioned as between a tenant for life and those entitled in remainder, in order to give effect to a testator's intention, express or implied, and in other cases to do justice between the parties. An inaccurate apportionment may on occasions affect the rate at which estate duty is to be calculated, and therefore great care must be taken in working out these apportionments.

Before dealing with the statute of 1870, it must be made quite clear that all rents and interest actually paid or accrued due, and all dividends declared, although not necessarily paid or even yet payable, before the death of a testator or intestate, are capital, and therefore in respect of any such rent, interest or dividend, no question of apportionment can arise. All these arrears in a deceased's estate will have been included in the schedule, and must, as and when received, be entered in the capital account. (Item 10, p. 214.)

The Inland Revenue, in the case of a deceased's estate, will require particulars of all arrears of rent, interest and dividends, and also of the due proportion of rents to death, but there will not be required for the purposes of estate duty particulars of the due proportion of dividends on stocks or shares accruing due at the death, as those proportions were all included in the capital value of the stocks or shares when the prices were fixed as of the day of the death and upon which duty was paid, unless, indeed, the stocks or shares were valued ex dividend, in which cases such dividends are taken as being in arrear, and must be accounted for accordingly. It is important, therefore, in the accounts to be able to distinguish moneys due at the death, even if not then payable, from those then accruing due.

The Apportionment Act, 1870 (a)

This Act was passed, as the preamble recites, for the better apportionment of rents and other periodical payments, and of some payments not periodical.

The sections of the Act are as follows:—

SECT. 1.—This Act may be cited for all purposes as "The Apportionment Act, 1870."

SECT. 2.—From and after the passing of this Act all rents, annuities, dividends, and other periodical payments in the nature of income (whether reserved or made payable under an instrument in writing or otherwise) shall, like interest on money lent, be considered as accruing from day to day, and shall be apportionable in respect of time accordingly.

SECT. 3.—The apportioned part of any such rent, annuity, dividend, or other payment shall be payable or recoverable in the case of a continuing rent, annuity, or other such payment when the entire portion of which such apportioned part shall form part shall become due and payable, and not before, and in the case of a rent, annuity, or other such payment de-

(a) 33 & 34 Vict. c. 35.

termined by re-entry, death, or otherwise when the next entire portion of the same would have been payable if the same had not so determined, and not before.

SECT. 4.—All persons and their respective heirs, executors, administrators, and assigns, and also the executors, administrators, and assigns respectively of persons whose interests determine with their own deaths, shall have such or the same remedies at law and in equity for recovering such apportioned parts as aforesaid when payable (allowing proportionate parts of all just allowances) as they respectively would have had for recovering such entire portions as aforesaid if entitled thereto respectively; provided that persons liable to pay rents reserved out of or charged on lands or other hereditaments of any tenure, and the same lands or other hereditaments, shall not be resorted to for any such apportioned part forming part of an entire or continuing rent as aforesaid specifically, but the entire or continuing rent, including such apportioned part, shall be recovered and received by the heir or other person who, if the rent had not been apportionable under this Act, or otherwise, would have been entitled to such entire or continuing rent, and such apportioned part shall be recoverable from such heir or other person by the executors or other parties entitled under this Act to the same by action at law or suit in equity.

SECT. 5.—In the construction of this Act—

The word "rents" includes rent service, rent-charge, and rent seck, and also tithes and all periodical payments or renderings in lieu of or in the nature of rent or tithe.

The word "annuities" includes salaries and pensions.

The word "dividends" includes (besides dividends strictly so called) all payments made by the name of dividend, bonus, or otherwise out of the revenue of trading or other public companies, divisible between all or any of the members of such respective companies, whether such payments shall be usually made or declared at any fixed times or otherwise; and all such divisible revenue shall, for the purposes of this Act, be deemed to have accrued by equal daily increment during and within the period for or in respect of which the payment of the same revenue shall be declared or expressed to be made, but the said word "dividend" does not include payments in the nature of a return or reimbursement of capital.

SECT. 6.—Nothing in this Act contained shall render apportionable any annual sums made payable in policies of assurance of any description.

SECT. 7.—The provisions of this Act shall not extend to any case in which it is or shall be expressly stipulated that no apportionment shall take place.

A few decisions on the Act may with advantage be referred to before passing on :—

The Act only applies to sums which are accruing, but have not accrued due at the time when the apportionment was said to be required (*b*).

The Act apportions liabilities as well as rights (*c*).

(*b*) *Ellis* v. *Rowbotham*, (1900) 1 Q. B. 744
(*c*) *Bishop of Rochester* v. *Le Fanu*, (1906) 2 Ch. 513, and cases there cited.

Interest on money lent is considered as accruing from day to day, although payable at intervals (*d*).

Rents of specifically devised property are apportionable (*e*).

Rents include tithe rent charge (*f*).

Annual sums payable by a bishop in commutation of first fruits and tenths are " periodical payments," and so apportionable (*g*).

Income of specific bequests, also dividends on stocks, are apportionable (*h*).

Every "company" registered under the Limited Liability Act is a public company within the meaning of the word as used in the Act (*i*), and for the purposes of the Apportionment Act a private company under the Companies (Consolidation) Act of 1908 is included (*k*).

Dividends declared after the death for a period commencing prior to the death and terminating after the death are apportionable (*l*).

Sect. 7 is not excluded by a power to postpone a Trust for Sale coupled with a direction that pending sale "the whole income of property actually producing income" shall be applied as from testator's death as income (*m*).

The word "dividends" may include payments by way of bonus or surplus profits to the shareholders of a public company, even though such payments be only occasional (*n*)

The Act does *not* apply in the following cases:—

Profits arising from a private partnership: for instance, where a testator died in October, 1870, and the account was made up and profits distributed in January, 1871, such profits

---

(*d*) *Re Lewis*, (1907) 2 Ch. 299

(*e*) *Hasluck* v. *Pedley* (1874), 19 Eq. 271, *Constable* v. *Constable* (1879), 11 C D 681

(*f*) *Re Ford*, (1911) 1 Ch 455

(*g*) *Bishop of Rochester* v. *Le Fanu*, *ante*.

(*h*) *Pollock* v. *Pollock* (1874), 18 Eq. 329; *Lysaght* v *Lysaght*, (1898) 1 Ch. 115.

(*i*) *Re Lysaght*, *ante*.

(*k*) *Re White*, *Theobald* v *White*, (1913) 1 Ch. 231.

(*l*) *Re Muirhead*, (1916) 2 Ch. 181.

(*m*) *In re Edwards*, (1918) 1 Ch. 142.

(*n*) *Re Griffith* (1879), 12 C D. 655.

are not apportionable, but the whole belongs to the tenant for life (o).

Rents, annuities, dividends and other payments in the nature of income which have accrued due before the happening of the event by reason of which it is proposed to apply the Act, e.g., rent payable in advance (p).

Dividends declared after a testator's death for the financial year of a company ending prior to his death (q).

Poor rates and local district rates payable on the day they are made (r).

Jointure, rentcharges under a settlement without any covenant to pay (s).

The result is that on the death of every intestate, and also of every testator unless a contrary intention is expressed or implied by his will, and on the death of every tenant for life, the due proportion of all income then accruing due forms part of the capital of the deceased's estate. In order, therefore, to ascertain this proportion the next instalment of every rent, whether of freehold, copyhold or leasehold property, the next dividend on all stocks and shares, and the next instalment of interest on money lent must be apportioned. But such an apportionment, which is in pursuance of the statute, must not be confused with that which ensues in a testator's estate under the rule in *Howe* v. *Lord Dartmouth*, a rule which is fully dealt with later on (pp. 98—101). Here it is merely necessary to observe that the rule last referred to can only apply, if at all, to income accruing due from and after the death.

The Settled Land Act, 1882, is another statute which it may be well to mention. Section 11 provides that under a mining lease granted under the Act where the tenant for life is

---

(o) *Jones* v. *Ogle* (1872), L. R. 8 Ch. 192. See also *Lambert* v. *Lambert* (1874), 22 W. R 359 , *Re Cox's Trusts* (1878), 9 C D. 159

(p) *Ellis* v *Rowbotham*, (1900) 1 Q. B. 740 ; and *Trevalion* v. *Anderton* (1897), 66 L J. Q. B 489.

(q) *Re Oppenheimer*, (1907) 1 Ch 399.

(r) *Re Wearmouth, &c. Co.* (1882), 19 C, D 640.

(s) *Re Popham*, (1914) W. N 257.

impeachable for waste in respect of minerals, three-fourth parts of the rent and otherwise one-fourth part thereof shall be set aside as capital money arising under the Act, and in every such case the residue of the rent shall go as rents and profits. The above obligation may be avoided by the terms of the settlement. (*Weeks* v. *Daniels*, (1912) 2 Ch 90.) Section 34 provides for the apportionment of purchase-money arising from land for an estate less than the fee simple. Section 35 provides that where timber is cut under the provisions of the Act three-fourths of the net proceeds of sale shall be set aside as capital, and one-fourth shall go as rents and profits.

No Apportionment is generally made on Sale or Purchase of Stocks —The question is often asked as to the apportionment which should be made of the purchase-money derived from the sale of stock upon a change of investment which is made on an intermediate day between two dividends, as the price, of necessity, includes the capital value of the stock as well as the value of the accruing dividend thereon. Although the price of the stock has been increased owing to the near approach of the dividend, yet it is not the practice to make any apportionment, but the whole of the purchase-money is treated as capital, and no sum whatever is paid to the tenant for life in respect of the current dividend. (*Bostock* v. *Blakeney* (1789), 2 B. C. C. 654; *Scholefield* v. *Redfern* (1863), 2 D. & Sm. 173; *Freman* v. *Whitbread* (1865), L. R. 1 Eq. 266.) In the same way, when stock is purchased on an intermediate day, the price paid includes something for the *accruing* dividend, yet when the next dividend is paid no apportionment is made, and the tenant for life is entitled to the whole. (*Re Clarke* (1881), 18 C. D. 160.)

There are a few cases to be found in the books where apportionments were directed, but the circumstances in each case were special, and the cases are only exceptions to the general rule. In Scotland the practice is, upon every sale and purchase, to apportion the price received and paid.

Of course, any trustee who deliberately arranged changes of investment so as to benefit or injure the tenant for life by the application of these rules would be guilty of a gross breach of trust.

Upon the death of the last tenant for life it is very common to sell certain securities for the purpose of facilitating the division of the estate; in such circumstances the amount realised by the sale is compounded partly of the value of the stock itself, and partly of the value of that proportionate part of the current half-year's dividend, which may be considered to have accrued since the last dividend day. Even in such cases the executors of the tenant for life are not entitled to have any part of that purchase-money carried to income, neither is it the practice of the Court to recognise any such claim in the ordinary course of dealing with funds directed to be sold on the death of a tenant for life. (*Bulkeley* v. *Stephens*, (1896) 2 Ch. 241.) Sometimes the executors of a deceased tenant for life may succeed in obtaining payment of the due proportion of dividends to death where the will authorises a transfer of the investments to the beneficiaries. This was done in the case of *Bulkeley* v. *Stephens*, but the Court was careful to point out that the claim was allowed under the special circumstances of the case

If stock is purchased together with the right to receive a dividend, which has been earned and declared though not paid, then such a dividend is capital. (*Re Sir Robert Peel's Estate*, (1910) 1 Ch. 389.)

Where trustees appropriate investments to meet a legacy, there is no apportionment of the dividends of the appropriated property (*Re Clarke* (1881), 18 C. D. 160)

Accounts for the Apportionment of Dividends and Interest pursuant to the Statute

The necessity of apportioning income under certain circumstances has now been made clear; the question remains, What is the most convenient form of account in which to enter the particulars and shew the result of the calculations involved in these apportionments?

If a separate entry is made in the capital account for every dividend which has to be apportioned under the Act the narrative must of necessity be somewhat lengthy, and when we come to understand the entry which will be involved in an apportionment under the rules of equity, the entry will be found to be still longer and more complicated, but by means of a tabular form of account the same information can be recorded in comparatively few words and in much simpler form. Three of such accounts are given in Appendices B., C and D. (pp. 239 to 247): Form B. for dividends and interest; Form C. for rents; and Form D. for apportionments under the rules of equity of dividends, interest and rents. All these must be studied separately.

The primary object of the account in Appendix B. is to ascertain what proportion of all dividends and of all interest current at the death is due to capital, but if the investment is authorised by the terms of the trust, the balance of each such dividend, after deducting the proportion due to capital, will be the proportion due to income, and consequently ascertained at the same time and entered in this account. On the other hand, if the dividend or interest arose from an unauthorised investment, and was not given to the tenant for life, the amount due to income cannot be ascertained on this account at all; in such cases the balance of the dividend will be entered in column 10 and carried to the suspense apportionment account, there to be further adjusted in manner presently to be explained.

When the dividend apportionment account is kept in the form given in Appendix B., it will be well to enter in that account (and repeat each entry in the suspense apportionment account, Appendix D., when it is involved) at the same time as the schedule is prepared a list of all investments included in the schedule, so that when any dividend or interest current at the death is received in respect of any such investment the details may at once be entered against the appropriate item.

At the same time as these particulars are entered in Appendix B. a line may be drawn through the column "Proportion due to Income" opposite every investment to which the rule in *Howe* v *Lord Dartmouth* will have to be applied. This practice will serve as a reminder whenever the first instalment of income is received in respect of any such investment that the balance of the income, after deducting the proportion due to capital, is not pure income, but has again to be apportioned on the suspense apportionment account, to which these items will be carried for that purpose.

Whenever a dividend or interest is entered in the suspense apportionment account, the investment in question will at once be re-entered under the last entry, ready for the next dividend or instalment of interest. This procedure will continue until the investment is sold, when the entry will be marked "Sold ——— day of ———," and the investment will not again appear. (See Appendix D., p. 249.)

All these items thus carried down will have to be further adjusted under the rule in *Howe* v. *Lord Dartmouth*, which is explained later in this chapter at p. 98 *et seq.*

By making these entries at such an early stage of the administration there will be perpetually available a complete list of investments, the next dividend on each of which will have to be apportioned, and as the administration proceeds it can be seen in a moment by the blank spaces remaining on the account what dividends have yet to come in before the account can be closed, and no item can by any possibility be lost sight of.

If the plan above suggested is adopted, then, after particulars of all investments have been entered in Appendix B. as each dividend is received, the amount of such dividend, and of any deductions made from it, *e.g.*, income tax, and the inclusive dates covered by the dividend, will all be entered in the appropriate columns, the net amount available for apportionment being carried out into the seventh column.

The working out of these apportionments will be dealt with shortly. At this point it is only necessary to explain that those apportionments have been calculated for the number of days between that on which the last payment accrued due and that on which the then current payment became due, and for practical purposes this plan can be adopted. Much time can be saved and the possibility of mistakes avoided by working out these calculations with the aid of an interest table.

Take the first item in Appendix B., p. 240 : the net amount apportionable is carried out into the seventh column. Now it is necessary to ascertain what would be the interest on 600*l.* at $2\frac{1}{2}$ per cent. for 27 days, being the number of days which the testator survived in the current quarter. This figure is ascertained in the shortest space of time with the assistance of an ordinary interest table, and in the instance being dealt with, amounts, after deducting income tax, to 1*l.* 1*s.* 1*d* , which is the proportion due to capital, the balance of the 3*l.* 11*s.* 3*d.*, a sum of 2*l* 10*s.* 2*d.*, being due to income.

A perfect legal apportionment, however, would proceed upon somewhat different lines, with but slight difference in the result, the reason being that the number of days in the several quarters of the year is not equal. This will be found fully explained, with reference to rents, at page 92, and would be equally applicable to interest on a mortgage, or a fixed rate of annual interest on stocks or shares, although, in fact, paid quarterly.

Appendix B. (see p. 239) is the commonest form of apportionment account, and will be used for the apportionment pursuant to the statute of all interest and dividends current at a death which may have to be apportioned. The entries must include all those particulars which are necessary for the verification of every item, so that anyone examining the account hereafter may be able to work out the calculations involved. For instance, in the case of mortgage interest, there should be entered the shortest possible description of the security, the capital sum, the rate at which interest is payable, the date from and to which it is calculated, and the date when it is paid. Again, in the case of a dividend, the amount and the exact description of the stock should be stated at least on the first occasion ; the rate at which the dividend is payable, the dates from and to which such dividend is calculated, and the date when it is paid must also be given. In every case the amount apportionable will be entered

There is yet one other column in Appendix B., headed, "Proportion carried to Suspense Apportionment Account." In this column will be entered the balance of the income on any investment unauthorised as to income after deducting the amount due to capital; consequently in such cases there will be no entry in Appendix B. of any "proportion due to income," because that cannot be ascertained on this account, involving, as it does, other considerations, which will be explained later and worked out in Appendix D. (See p. 247.)

Income Tax must always be borne in mind when dealing with dividend or interest. A company when paying a dividend and a mortgagor when paying interest generally exercise the statutory right to deduct income tax at the current rate on each occasion Sometimes, however, a company will pay their dividends free of tax. The actual sum of money received, after allowing for tax (if any), is the amount which will have to be apportioned.

Having thus explained the first dividend apportionment account, it will now be convenient to explain in further detail the principles upon which those apportionments have to be calculated.

Calculation of Dividend and Interest Apportionments.

Interest.—This is the simplest instance of an apportionment, as interest must be taken to accrue from day to day; therefore, in the case of mortgages and such-like obligations, it is necessary to ascertain the capital sum involved, the rate at which interest is to be calculated, and the date to which interest was last paid, then to calculate the number of days from that date to the death or other determining event. Interest at the appropriate rate on this capital sum for the number of days thus ascertained can then be fixed.

An instance of this apportionment will be found in Item 7 in Appendix B., p. 241.

A more perfect adjustment of this apportionment would be arrived at by following the principle explained for the apportionment of rent at p. 92, but except in cases where large sums are involved the difference is so small that the above calculations are generally accepted.

Dividends on Government Securities and Stocks or Shares carrying a fixed Rate of Interest.—The apportionment of all these dividends proceeds upon the same basis as that already explained in the case of interest. It is to be observed that these dividends are generally paid at due date, which, as will be seen directly, is not the case with dividends upon ordinary stocks and shares. An instance of each of these apportionments will be found in the first and second items in Appendix B., p. 240.

Dividends on other Stocks and Shares.—This apportionment is not quite so simple a matter as those already dealt with. Holders of ordinary stock or shares in a company are not often entitled to insist upon having the whole of the profit made in any year of trading divided amongst them in the shape of dividends. On the contrary, the directors are almost invariably empowered to retain profits arising in any year either by carrying them to reserve or by bringing them forward in the profit and loss account, and such profits may be distributed among the shareholders in respect of some subsequent period either under the name of dividend or in the form of a cash bonus. Dividends and cash bonuses so distributed by a company registered under the Companies Acts, 1908 and 1917 (which includes companies previously registered under the repealed Act of 1862), will be income of the period in respect of which they are actually distributed irrespective of the period in which the profits were earned, and they will be apportionable accordingly. The general principle on the point is thus explained in the leading case of *Bouch* v. *Sproule* (1887), 12 A. C. at p. 397:—
" When a testator or settlor directs or permits the subject of his disposition to remain as shares or stock in a company which

has the power either of distributing its profits as dividends or of converting them into capital, and the company validly exercises this power, such exercise of its power is binding on all persons interested under him in the shares, and consequently what is paid by the company as dividend goes to the tenant for life, and what is paid by the company to the shareholder as capital or appropriated as an increase of the capital stock in the concern enures to the benefit of all who are interested in the capital "

Once such a company has decided to treat any part of its profits as a permanent addition to capital instead of retaining it as available for distribution in the shape of dividend, from that moment the money has become and remains capital (*x*). Where companies, however, which have by law no power to increase their capital have accumulated profits and use them in fact for capital purposes and afterwards distribute those profits amongst the proprietors, there, although not strictly capital, such moneys are treated as an accretion to capital (*y*).

Instead of distributing profits by way of dividend or cash bonus companies frequently retain them as a permanent addition to capital, issuing fully-paid shares of equivalent amount to the shareholders. In such a case the shares are capital as between tenant for life and remaindermen. In other cases a company declares a cash bonus and at the same time offers shares to the shareholders on the terms that the bonus is to be applied in paying up the shares, the shareholders having the right if they so desire to take the cash and refuse the shares. In such cases nice questions may arise between capital and income which would be beyond the scope of this treatise to discuss at length, but the general result appears to be that if (a) the company intends in fact that the whole amount of the bonus should be added to its capital, and (b) the value of the shares offered is

---

(*x*) *Re Hume Nisbet's Settlement* (1911), 27 T. L R. 461.

(*y*) *Irving* v. *Houstoun*, 4 Pat 521, as explained by Lord Herschell in *Bouch* v. *Sproule* (1887), 12 A. C at p 397.

such that the shareholders are certain to take them instead of cash, the shares are capital; but if the shareholder really has an effective option whether to take cash or shares the amount of the bonus is income, while the extra value (if any) of the shares in excess of the amount of the bonus is capital (a).

Two facts must therefore be ascertained before the apportionment of any such sums or bonuses can be made. The capital involved is of course a fixed quantity, but the rate at which the dividend or bonus is calculated, and the period of time for which it is paid, both must be ascertained.

Attention should also be directed to the fact that these dividends are generally calculated to a date anterior to that of payment; therefore, care must be taken in those cases to ascertain the earlier date, which is the material one for the purposes of apportionment The dates from and to which the dividend is calculated, as well as that of payment, are generally stated on the counterfoil of the dividend warrant.

An instance of such an apportionment will be found in the second item in Appendix B., p. 240.

Interim Dividends.—Some companies pay what is called an interim dividend, that is, a sum of money on account of the dividend for the whole year, and subsequently pay a final dividend, that is, a further sum of money which, added to that already paid, makes up the total dividend for the year; consequently, when such is the case, the final apportionment cannot be made until the whole of the dividend for the year has been ascertained.

If an interim dividend had been received by the testator, that is merged in his estate; but the amount will be treated as part of the year's dividend for the purpose of calculating the apportionment, and if the due proportion of the entire dividend for the year is less than the amount received by way of interim

---

(a) *Bouch* v *Sproule* (1887), 12 A C 385, *Re Alsbury* (1890), 45 C. D. 237, *Re Malam*, (1894) 3 Ch 578, *Re Evans*, (1913) 1 Ch. 23, *Re Thomas*, (1916) 1 Ch. 384; (1916) 2 Ch 331. See also *Re Piercy*, (1907) 1 Ch 289.

APPORTIONMENTS 89

dividend, nothing more is due to capital; but if the due proportion is greater than the amount received by way of interim dividend, then that due proportion so ascertained, less the interim dividend already received, is the net amount due to capital Instances of these apportionments will be found in the fourth and fifth items in Appendix B , p. 240.

Transfer Items

When the last dividend or instalment of interest requiring apportionment in Appendix B. has been received, all the calculations can be worked out and entered in the appropriate columns and the account closed. (See p. 241.)

The total of column 8 being the " proportion due to capital " will then be transferred to the general capital account in one sum, and that total will also be entered in the schedule in one sum, *e.g.*, "proportion of dividends and interest current at the death as per separate apportionment account," or the amount due to capital in each case may be entered in the schedule as has been done in Appendix A., p. 209. The practitioner can adopt whichever of these two courses may prove to be most convenient. Then the total of column 9, being the proportion due to income, will in like manner be transferred to the general income account, and the figures in the 10th column (if any) will be entered in the suspense apportionment account (see p. 248), opposite the appropriate investments already entered there, as explained at pp. 110 *et seq*.

Accounts for the Apportionment of Rent pursuant to the Statute

The primary object of the account in Appendix C. is to ascertain what proportion of any rent current at the death is due to capital. The proportion of rents of realty and of leaseholds, when the rent is given to the tenant for life, as from the death will also be ascertained on and entered in this account, but nothing more than the proportion due to capital of other leaseholds can be ascertained now, as the balance of such rents will have to be carried to the suspense apportionment account, there to be further adjusted in a manner presently to be explained, before the exact amount applicable as income can be ascertained

The plan already described of entering investments in the apportionment accounts at the same time as the schedule is prepared, and of drawing a line through the income column and carrying down to the suspense apportionment account the dividends on unauthorised investments the income of which is not given to the tenant for life, is equally applicable to the entry of property and of rents, and may therefore be adopted with similar advantages to those above described in the case of investments and the dividends thereon.

It will be observed that there are separate forms for the apportionment of dividends and rents current at the death, but there is one form only for the apportionment of income which is not given to the tenant for life, and which is derived from unauthorised investments, including leaseholds. All these will have to be apportioned under the rule in *Howe* v. *Lord Dartmouth*, because the same principle governs the apportionment of the income of all such unauthorised investments. Again, the items in the apportionment accounts of dividends and rents are limited to those current at the death, so that each of these accounts will be finally closed within a year from the death, whilst the suspense apportionment account will continue until the last unauthorised investment or other asset has been sold.

If the plan above suggested is adopted, and particulars of all properties have been entered in Appendix C., then, as each rent is received, the amount of such rent, any deductions made and the inclusive dates covered by the rent will all be entered, the net amount available for apportionment being carried out into the seventh column. (See p. 245.)

Appendix C. (see p. 243).—This is the form of a rent apportionment account and will be used for the apportionment, pursuant to the statute, of all rents of every kind current at the death of a testator or intestate or a tenant for life when he enjoys the rent. The entries must include all those particulars which are necessary for the verification of every item which is divided, so that any one examining the account may be able to work out the calculations involved. For instance, mention must be made of each property and the annual rent received, the amount of the quarterly or other instalment now paid, the date from and to which it is calculated, and the date on which it is paid.

Property Tax.—Reference has already been made to the income tax in respect of interest and dividends which is generally deducted at the appropriate rate on each payment, but when property tax has to be dealt with a material difference is involved. Property tax is, in fact, the landlord's income tax, which the tenant pays for the landlord once a year, by two instalments, in January and July, for the whole financial year, which runs from the previous 6th April to the subsequent 5th April. After the tenant has thus paid the tax, he is entitled to deduct the tax at the appropriate rate upon his rent for the year from the *next* instalment of rent which he pays. This does not necessarily entitle him to deduct the whole amount of the tax which he paid, because near the end of a long lease the rent paid by the lessee often is far short of the then full annual value. In such cases the balance of the tax falls upon the tenant himself, as being in respect of his temporary beneficial interest in the property.

There is often an allowance to be made by the executor in respect of the property tax. If he is still in possession of the property, he will allow to the tenant the full tax out of his Lady-day rent, and transfer from capital to income the proportion due from capital. (Item 11, p. 217.)

In cases in which an executor does not enter into possession of the property but only claims the due proportion of the rent current at the death, then the person liable to the executor in that behalf may deduct the due proportion of the tax at the appropriate rate from the sum actually paid to the executor. A similar deduction can be made by the person liable to pay to the personal representatives of a deceased tenant for life the due proportion of rent current at his death. (8 & 7 Geo. V. c 40, Sch. A. No. VIII., r 7.)

The situation can only be adjusted by way of deduction, and no action will lie for the recovery of any sum which might have, but has not, been deducted.

If, however, the owner was in occupation and died before the tax was paid, then the heirs, executors, administrators or assigns, or other person who may become entitled, must pay all arrears of duty according to their respective interests. (8 & 9 Geo. V. c. 40, Sch. A. No. VIII., r. 1.)

Deductions must be entered in the fewest words possible, e.g., "Property Tax, £——," or "Repairs, £——," and, if necessary, reference given to the agent's account for details. Then this total of the deductions will be subtracted from the last instalment of rent received, and the result carried out into the seventh column.

Calculation of Rent Apportionments.

Each item of rent, whether derived from freehold, leasehold, or copyhold property, will, in most cases, have to be separately apportioned. It is obvious that it would not often be possible merely to apportion the balance of all rents received from an agent as shewn by his first account after the death, because all the rents are not likely to have accrued in respect of the same period of time.

As soon as all these rents have been received and entered in the apportionment account, the amounts appearing in the seventh column must be duly apportioned between capital and income, and the results entered, the capital in the eighth and the amount due to income in the ninth, except in the case of properties mentioned in Part II. (Leaseholds), when the balance, after deducting the proportion due to capital, will be entered in the tenth column, to be carried to the suspense apportionment account, unless such rents have been given to the tenant for

APPORTIONMENTS

life. To arrive at a perfect apportionment of rent it is necessary to ascertain the following facts:—

(1) Whether the rent is payable for a year, or for any less period of time, taking care to fix the true dates of the commencement and expiration of the actual period, and to disregard the dates (if any) upon which payments have been made on account of the whole period—e.g., an annual tenancy is granted at 100l. per annum, payable quarterly; the fixed period in such a case is a year, and the quarterly payments are made on account of the whole period of one year.

(2) The number of days from the commencement of the fixed period down to and including the happening of the incident which gave rise to the apportionment.

(3) The amount of rent payable for the number of days thus ascertained, hereinafter referred to as "the gross amount apportionable"

(4) Any quarterly or other payment received since the commencement of the fixed period must be deducted from "the gross amount apportionable," and the balance is the exact amount due to capital out of the next periodical payment after adjusting any income tax deductions

Anything else is inconsistent with the agreement to pay at the rate of 100l. per annum, for no quarterly payment is at that rate. Precisely the same is the case of interest payable at the rate of 5 per cent. per annum by four equal quarterly instalments. This never is paid at the rate of 5 per cent. for the quarter, because the quarters of the year are not equally divided. In very large estates a perfect apportionment should be made of rents and interest.

In smaller estates it is not unusual to calculate the apportionment of the current instalment of rent upon the same principle as the current instalment of interest was calculated, as explained at page 85, and this course has been adopted in the entries contained in Appendix C.

Take the first item in Appendix C., p. 244: the net amount apportionable is carried out into the 7th column. If 15*l.* is a quarter's rent, then the annual rent will amount to 60*l.*, which is a sum equivalent to interest at 5 per cent. per annum on a capital sum of 1,200*l.* Now it is necessary to ascertain what would be the interest on 1,200*l.* at 5 per cent. for 33 days, being the number of days which the testator survived in the Christmas quarter. This figure is ascertained in the shortest space of time with the assistance of an ordinary interest table, and in the instance being dealt with amounts to 5*l.* 8*s.* 6*d.*, which is the proportion due to capital, the balance of the 15*l.*, a sum of 9*l.* 11*s.* 6*d.*, being due to income, each amount being subject to a possible deduction for tax.

Upon the death of a tenant for life all the forms (B, C, and D) will be adapted to the circumstances of the case, the object being to ascertain the due proportion of current income payable to her representatives, which will be calculated upon the same principles as before explained.

Transfer Items

When the last rent requiring apportionment in Appendix C. has been received the account can be closed, and the proportion due to capital will then be transferred to the general capital account and entered in the schedule, and the proportion due to income in like manner transferred to the general income account, as already explained with regard to dividends on investments   (See p. 89, *ante.*)

The balance of any freehold or copyhold rent, after deducting the amount due to capital, will belong to the tenant for life; but the proportion due to the tenant for life of any balance of leasehold rents which have not been given to the tenant for life cannot be ascertained on this account for the reasons given on p. 90, as to dividends on investments held under similar circumstances, consequently every balance of such leasehold rents will be carried to the suspense apportionment account, there to be further adjusted.

Advantages of Tabular Forms

Some of the advantages to be obtained by the adoption of these tabular forms are :—

(1) The capital account is relieved of a number of entries, the narrative of which must of necessity be somewhat lengthy. For instance, the general capital account in this estate has in consequence of the adoption of this apportionment account been relieved of eight items, the details appertaining to all of which appear in Appendix B., p. 240. This is all the more forcible with regard to the income account when dealing with an unauthorised investment.

(2) The duplication of the information in the capital and income accounts is thereby avoided.

(3) This part of the estate is nicely classified.

(4) It will be sufficient to have one entry in the schedule for each class of apportionments, *e.g.*, " Apportionment of Dividends and Interest as per separate Account."

(5) This classification will be found convenient when preparing an Inland Revenue residuary account, as the department requires particulars of :—

(a) All rents received (including those current at the death) in respect of real and leasehold property directed to be sold, if sold up to the time of sale; if unsold, to the date of the account, including apportionment of those current rents.

(b) All dividends declared, received and accrued due on stocks and shares up to the date of the account, or if sold, to the time of sale, including the whole of the dividend accruing at the death.

All these rents and dividends will be found in the income accounts except the capital fractions, which will be found in the Appendix B., C. or D.

(6) It greatly facilitates the work of an audit when all apportioned dividends, interest and rents are to be found collected together in separate accounts.

If, however, the book-keeper prefers to enter the proportion due to capital and income in the respective accounts, then the entries should be arranged so that each item in the capital account and the corresponding item in the income account may readily be connected.

An example of the entry in the capital account in such a case, shewing the apportionment of a quarter's dividend on 600*l*. Consols, will be as follows:—

1903. *Apportionments.*

Jan. 5. To cash, being proportion of quarter's dividend on 600*l*. Consols, at 2½ per cent., due 5th January, 1903, from 5th October to 1st November, 1902 = 27 days - - - - £1 2 2
   Less tax - - - 0 1 1
            1 1 1

(See also Item — in the income account.)

The entry in the income account will be as follows:—

1903. *Apportionments.*

Jan. 5. To cash, being quarter's dividend on 600*l*. Consols, at 2½ per cent., due 5th January, 1903, 3*l*. 15*s*. — less 3*s*. 9*d*. tax - £3 11 3
 Deduct proportion thereof for 27 days from 5th October to 1st November, 1902, due to capital - - £1 2 2
   Less tax - 0 1 1
         1 1 1
            2 10 2

(See also Item — in the capital account.)

Apportionments governed by Rules of Equity

At the commencement of this chapter it was stated that apportionments were rendered necessary in consequence either of an Act of Parliament or of certain rules of equity. The former class of apportionments has been explained; the rules of equity governing the latter class remain to be dealt with.

In all these cases when it is determined that there must be some apportionment as between tenant for life and remaindermen, the method of carrying it out is in the discretion of the Court (b).

Where the residuary personal estate (c) of a testator is given to or for the benefit of persons in succession, certain rules of administration have been established which must be observed in every case except so far as a different intention is manifested by the will.

These rules are not rules of law overriding the intentions expressed by the will, but merely *primâ facie* rules of administration established by the Court for the purpose of carrying the presumed intentions into effect; if and so far, therefore, as the rules are inconsistent with the intentions expressed by the will, they are excluded, and the express provisions of the will carried into effect.

The will must, therefore, in every case, be examined to ascertain whether it contains anything to modify the effect of the rules. There are certain well-defined classes of cases of frequent occurrence which are referred to below where the exclusion of the rules, either in whole or in part, is well established. In cases, however, not included in these classes, it must not be lightly assumed that the rules are excluded by expressions which might, at the first blush, appear inconsistent with them, and unless the will unmistakably excludes the rules and substitutes some other procedure, the question of their application or non-application must be treated as a mixed question of law and construction lying outside the scope of this work.

In the paragraphs which follow—(a) the case of a simple gift of residuary personal estate to or for the benefit of persons in succession without any further indication of the testator's intention, is referred to as "the simple case"; and (b) the expression "net income" is used to denote the income which remains after

(b) *In re Perkins*, (1907) 2 Ch. 596; *In re Poyser, Landon v Poyser*, (1910) 2 Ch. at p 448.

(c) The rules do not apply to specifically given property, or to property under a settlement by deed, but they are not excluded by the fact that part of the property constituting the residue may be specifically enumerated

paying all outgoings properly chargeable to income, and after making such contributions (if any) out of income as (having regard to the rules below stated) are proper to be made towards the payment of the testator's debts and funeral and testamentary expenses and legacies.

The Rule in Howe v. Earl of Dartmouth

RULE (1).—In "the simple case" it is the duty of the executors or trustees to convert into money the whole of the residuary personal estate, except so far as it consists of authorised securities, and (after payment of debts, and funeral and testamentary expenses and legacies) to invest the proceeds of such conversion in authorised securities, *i.e.*, securities authorised either by the terms of the will or by the general law. At the present time the general law for this purpose is, in effect, the Trustee Act, 1893, s. 1. This rule is known as "the rule in *Howe* v *Lord Dartmouth*." (See (1802), 7 Vesey, jun. 137.)

RULE (2).—Such conversion must be effected at the earliest moment at which the several assets can be realised at a reasonable price, and *primá facie* must be completed within a year after the testator's death, or (in other words) the onus of justifying the retention of unauthorised securities or property after the year rests upon the executors or trustees; such retention may, however, be justified by special circumstances, as (for example) if the property is such as cannot for any reason be sold, or if the markets during the year are exceptionally adverse, or if the property is of such a kind that it cannot be advantageously realised except in parcels at intervals of time.

RULE (3).—The tenant for life is entitled to the whole net income, as from the testator's death, from all authorised securities comprised in the residuary estate at his death, and to the whole net income of all authorised securities acquired by the executors or trustees after the testator's death as from the acquisition thereof.

RULE (4).—Where unauthorised investments or property forming part of the testator's residuary personal estate produce a net income during the period between the testator's death and the conversion of the unauthorised asset into money, the tenant for life is entitled to receive out of such net income an allowance to be calculated as follows, viz. (*d*):—

(a) If the unauthorised asset is realised within the year, the

---

(*d*) The decisions upon which the statement of this rule is based are neither very clear nor very easily reconciled with one another in their details, but the general principle is quite clear—viz., that where unauthorised investments

allowance should be equal to interest at the rate of 4 (formerly 3) per cent. (e) per annum on the net proceeds of such realisation, from the death of the testator until such realisation is effected.

Example.—A leasehold house, "The Elms," an unauthorised investment, is sold seven months after the death for 620*l*., consequently the tenant for life is entitled to interest at 4 (formerly 3) per cent. (e) on that sum from the death out of the net rents, if sufficient. All these sums of interest are worked out in the suspense apportionment account, and it will be sufficient to refer to one of these calculations. Take Item 6 on p 248. Here the property is mentioned, the amount for which it was sold, the quarter's rent 10*l*., the rate at which interest is to be calculated on the purchase-money (3 per cent.) (e) and the deductions, which amount to 5*l*., leaving 5*l* apportionable. The interest, less tax, amounts to 4*l* 8*s*. 5*d*., so on this occasion 11*s*. 7*d*. only is carried to capital.

(b) If the asset is an unauthorised investment or property which owing to its nature cannot without exceptional sacrifice be turned into money within the year in the ordinary course of administration, *e.g.*, partnership capital which by the terms of the partnership must be left in the business for a term of years, the allowance is to be a sum equal to interest at the rate of 4 (formerly 3) per cent. (e) per annum as from the testator's death on the value of the asset estimated as at the testator's death.

Example.—See Item 28 on p. 222. Here is a sum of 650*l*. paid nearly two years after the testator's death by the surviving partners in pursuance of the provisions contained in the articles of partnership. The executors could not earlier have compelled payment of the capital sum, which, however, was producing income all the time. Therefore that income is carried to the suspense apportionment account and there divided according to the rule.

produce income before realisation they ought to be treated as producing for the benefit of the tenant for life so much of that income as might reasonably have been expected to arise during the same period from a corpus of equal value invested in sound trustee investments.

(e) In the former edition of this work this rate was given as 3*l*. per cent. per annum, but since that time, in sympathy with the universally higher return now obtained from trust investments, the rate has been raised and interest is now calculated at the rate of 4*l*. per cent. per annum in all equitable apportionments. In the illustrative examples the rate of 3*l*. per cent per annum has been retained in order to avoid the reconstruction of the arithmetic and bookkeeping figures.

In this case the value of the asset at the date of the testator's death was par value, namely, 650*l*., therefore interest at 3 per cent. (*f*) for the period in question on 650*l*. will be paid out of the interest received, the balance being due to capital. (See Item 5, p. 248, and Item 14, p. 250.) All necessary particulars are set forth in the tabular form, with the result that Item 5 shews 7*l*. 19*s*. 4*d*. due to income and 18*l*. 11*s*. 11*d*. belongs to capital.

(c) If the asset is an unauthorised investment or property such as might under ordinarily favourable circumstances be realised in a due course of administration within the year, which, but for extraneous reasons, is retained beyond the year with a view to more favourable realisation, the allowance is to be at a rate commonly known as "Consol interest," that is to say, a price is put upon the asset as at the expiration of the year from the testator's death, and it is ascertained what sum of Consols might have been purchased for that price on the same day, and the tenant for life receives out of the income derived from the asset between the death of the testator and the realisation thereof an allowance equal to the dividends for the same period upon the imaginary sum of Consols so ascertained (*g*).

Example.—The Standard Bank shares were sold in May, 1904, therefore at the end of one year from the death it became necessary to ascertain their value. This was fixed at 400*l*., which sum of money on that day would have purchased 443*l*. 15*s*. Consols, which were standing at 90. The next dividend received in respect of the shares amounted to 19*l*. There were no deductions, the dividend being paid free of tax. The dividend, less tax, on this imaginary sum of Consols amounts to 5*l*. 5*s*. 5*d*., consequently that is the sum payable to income. The balance of the dividend on the bank shares, amounting to 13*l*. 14*s*. 7*d*., belongs to capital. See Item 8 on p. 248 and Item 13 on p. 250.

It will be noted that in each case the tenant for life's allowance is to be paid out of the income actually received by the executors or trustees in respect of the assets, and if and so

---

(*f*) See footnote (*e*) on p. 99, *ante*.

(*g*) This method of dealing with the matter is now very rarely applied, and the method stated in 4 (b) is almost universally adopted. The allowance of "Consol interest" has, however, the advantage of enabling the rate of interest allowed to vary automatically with the standard return from trustee investments.

APPORTIONMENTS

far as such income fails or is insufficient, the tenant for life's allowance fails also.

The surplus net income (if any) of the unauthorised assets, after paying the tenant for life's allowance, is added to the capital of the estate, but the tenant for life receives the income arising from the investments thereof.

The balance of income in all these cases is carried out into the 12th column in the suspense apportionment account, Appendix D., p. 251, the total of which at the end of the year (amounting to 69*l*. 18*s*. 5*d*. in this case) is transferred to the general capital account (Item 25, p. 218) and in due course invested (Item 28, p. 221), the dividends on which investments are paid to the tenant for life (Item 13, p. 256) together with the rest of the income derived from the trust estate.

The Rule in Earl of Chesterfield's Case

RULE (5).—Where a reversionary interest forming part of the residuary personal estate is not at once realised or is allowed to remain until it falls into possession, the sum actually realised by the executors or trustees in respect thereof must be apportioned as between capital and income by ascertaining the sum which, put out at interest at 4 per cent. per annum—at one time 3 per cent. (*Re Rowlls*, (1900) 2 Ch. 107)—on the day of the testator's death and accumulating at compound interest calculated at that rate with yearly rests and deducting income tax, would, with the accumulations of interest, amount on the day when the reversion falls in or is realised to the sum actually received, and the sum so ascertained should be treated as capital and the residue as income. (See *Re Earl of Chesterfield's Trusts* (1883), 24 C. D. 643.)

Example.—On the 1st November, 1904, being two years after the testator's death, a reversionary interest falls in, which produces 977*l*. 5*s*. 1*d*. Consols, then of the value of 879*l*. 10*s*. 7*d*., and 120*l*. 9*s*. 5*d*. cash, making together a total of 1,000*l*., or its equivalent. This sum of 1,000*l*. represents mixed capital and income, and must be apportioned in order to give effect to the rule in *Chesterfield's case*.

It will be noticed that the reversion fell in two years after the death of the testator; therefore that is the period in respect of which it is necessary to ascertain the amount attributable to income.

This appears at first sight to be a somewhat intricate calculation, but when each year is dealt with separately, no difficulty will be experienced. If a sum of 100*l.* be invested for one year at 3 per cent., then at the end of the year the capital with the interest, less tax, will amount to 102*l.* 17*s.* Having ascertained this much, it is only necessary to work out the following fraction in order to see what capital sum, with interest at 3 per cent. (*h*) (less tax) for *one* year, would produce 1,000*l.*, viz.—

$$\frac{1,000l. \times 100l.}{102l.\ 17s.\ 0d.} = 972l.\ 5s.\ 10d.,$$

thus shewing that for one year we have 972*l.* 5*s.* 10*d.* capital and 29*l.* 3*s.* 4*d.* (less 1*l.* 9*s.* 2*d.* tax), or 27*l.* 14*s.* 2*d.* income, these two sums making together 1,000*l.*

This calculation has to be repeated for every year that elapsed between the testator's death and the falling in of the reversion, taking the capital figure produced by the calculation for the last year as the basis upon which to proceed with the previous year. Thus, in this case, the capital figure already ascertained for the last year is 972*l.* 5*s.* 10*d.*, so that the fraction for the previous year will be—

$$\frac{972l.\ 5s.\ 10d. \times 100l.}{102l.\ 17s.\ 0d.} = 945l.\ 7s.\ 0d.,$$

the interest on which for one year at 3*l.* per cent. (less tax) amounts to 26*l.* 18*s.* 10*d.*

The result is as follows:—

Capital - - - - - - - -				£945 7 0
Interest on 945*l.* 7*s.* 0*d.*				
capital at 3 % for one year is - - -	£28	7	2	
Less tax - -	1	8	4	
			£26 18 10	
Capital - - -	- £945	7	0	
And interest - -	26	18	10	
Interest on - -	- £972	5	10	
At 3 % for one year is -	£29	3	4	
Less tax - -	1	9	2	
			27 14 2	
				54 13 0
				£1,000 0 0

The reversion has already been entered in the schedule, and there can now be added the particulars of the property received in respect thereof (see Item 26, p. 209), and afterwards the cash

(*h*) See note (*e*), p. 99.

and investments will be debited in the capital account in the ordinary way (see Item 34, p. 224), and there will therefore be transferred to income 54*l*. 13*s*. 0*d*. (See Item 33, p. 223.)

The same principle was applied in a case where the testator had sold his business for a consideration to be paid by ten half-yearly instalments. The testator by his will bequeathed his residuary estate upon trust for conversion with power to postpone. The testator's widow was tenant for life of the residue. It was decided that each instalment ought as from the testator's death to be apportioned between corpus and income by ascertaining the sum which, put out at interest at four per cent. on the day of the testator's death and accumulating at compound interest at that rate with yearly rests and deducting income tax, would, with the accumulations of interest, amount on the day when the instalment was or should be received to the amount actually received, and the sum so ascertained must be treated as capital and the difference between it and the sum actually received as income It by no means followed that in every case where the outstanding estate was represented in part by a right to receive purchase or other moneys by deferred instalments or included a terminable annuity, the tenant for life would be entitled to insist on apportionment (*i*).

The Rule in Allhusen v. Whittell (*k*)

RULE (6).—Where assets which are applied in paying debts funeral and testamentary expenses or legacies have, previously to such application, produced income, the tenant for life of the residue is not entitled to such income, insomuch as the assets in question have never become part of the residue. And the strict and proper rule is that, whenever a capital asset is applied in payment of debts, funeral and testamentary expenses or legacies, and such capital asset has produced income between the death and the application thereof for any such purpose, the income so produced should also be applied in like manner, so that when the debts, funeral and testa-

---

(*i*) *In re Hollebone*, (1919) W. N. p. 144.

(*k*) The rule mentioned in this and the following pages was approved by Sargant, J., in *Re McEuen, deceased, McEuen* v. *Phelps*, (1913) 2 Ch. 715, 716. In the later case of *Re Wills*, (1915) 1 Ch. 769, where there was a trust for sale and power to postpone, with a direction that the whole interim income was to be applied as income, the average return from the estate was taken as regulating the contribution of income towards the debts, &c.

mentary expenses or legacies have been fully discharged, there may remain in the estate no income which has arisen from assets applied in discharge thereof, and no capital from which any income so applied has arisen.

Wherever, in fact, the debts and funeral and testamentary expenses are paid otherwise than in accordance with this rule, the tenant for life or remainderman, as the case may be, is entitled to an adjustment so as to give effect to this rule. (*Allhusen* v. *Whittell* (1867), L R. 4 Eq 295.)

In cases where the rule applies it may be given effect to in the accounts as follows:—

(1) Ascertain the total sum paid in debts, funeral and testamentary expenses and legacies; carry all receipts of capital to the capital account and all receipts of income to the income account, as if there were no debts, funeral and testamentary expenses or legacies to be paid, and in the first instance charge all debts, funeral and testamentary expenses or legacies as paid on capital account.

(2) Ascertain the income produced by such of the authorised investments as were actually realised for the purpose of paying debts, funeral and testamentary expenses or legacies, and also so much of the income produced by the unauthorised investments realised for the like purpose as is carried to income from the suspense apportionment account as representing pure income.

Wherever the income arising from any asset applied in paying debts, funeral and testamentary expenses or legacies is itself, in fact, exhausted in paying debts, funeral and testamentary expenses or legacies, the income so applied should be carried over to the capital account with explanatory entries, and to this extent the rule will have been fully complied with and no further adjustment will be necessary.

(3) Wherever debts, funeral and testamentary expenses or legacies have been, in fact, paid out of a capital fund or a mixed fund otherwise than as above mentioned, the amount of the debts, funeral and testamentary expenses and legacies so paid must be divided between the

capital and income of the fund out of which the same have been paid in the proportions which the respective amounts of such capital and income bear to one another, treating as capital such part of the income of unauthorised assets comprised in the fund as according to the foregoing rules ought to be treated as capital. Then (insomuch as in the meantime capital will have been charged with the whole of such debts, funeral and testamentary expenses and legacies) a readjustment will be made by transferring from income to capital the apportioned sum which ought to have been borne by income, such transfer being made in addition to the transfer of the capitalised portions (if any) of the income of unauthorised investments.

It is submitted that substantial justice will be done between the parties by working out the apportionment as indicated above. This rule is frequently disregarded and often very difficult to apply, especially where debts are paid at different times, yet executors cannot safely neglect it, although in most well-drawn wills the necessity of applying the rule is excluded by express provision. It becomes necessary in the administration of every estate to consider whether the rule applies, and if so, how it is to be complied with.

Example:—

In the accounts worked out in the Appendices, it will be seen that on the 1st November, 1903 (p. 221), the total payments amounted to . £2,501 10 4
That figure included the following items, none of which represented debts, &c., viz. (Items 12, 20, 26, 27 and 28) 1,098 13 11
——————— £1,402 16 5
Then ascertain the capitalised portion of income from unauthorised investments (Items 2 and 4 ex column 12, p. 249) . . 2 9 11

Total capital involved.. ... £1,405 6 4

Income from authorised investments sold for the purpose of paying debts, &c., In this case . . . Nil
Pure income from unauthorised securities sold (Items 2 and 4 ex column 11, p. 249) . .. 6 13 9

Total income involved £6 13 9

Therefore it becomes necessary to divide 1,402*l*. 16*s*. 5*d*., the amount paid for debts and other charges, in the proportion that 1,405*l*. 6*s*. 4*d*. capital bears to 6*l*. 13*s*. 9*d*. income.

The result is that—

$\frac{1,405l.\ 6s.\ 4d.}{1,412l.\ 0s.\ 1d.} \times 1,402l.$ 16*s*. 5*d*. = 1,396*l*. 3*s*. 7*d*. is the amount to be contributed by capital, and $\frac{6l.\ 13s.\ 9d.}{1,412l.\ 0s.\ 1d.} \times 1,402l.$ 16*s*. 5*d*. = 6*l*. 12*s*. 10*d*. is the amount to be contributed by income, and as the debts and other charges were, in the first instance, paid exclusively out of capital, there must be transferred from income to capital the sum of 6*l*. 12*s*. 10*d*. (Item 27, p. 220.)

The following propositions have been established as to the applicability or non-applicability of the foregoing rules in the particular classes of cases to which such propositions apply, viz.:—

(1) Where there is a simple gift of residuary personal estate to persons in succession with a power for the executors or trustees to postpone the realisation of the estate or any part of it the rule in *Howe* v. *Lord Dartmouth* is wholly or *pro tanto* excluded, and the tenant for life is entitled to the whole net income of the estate or of the part retained, pursuant to the power, whether consisting of authorised securities or not.

The same result follows, even in the absence of an express power of postponement, when there is anything else in the will which shews clearly that the testator does not intend the estate to be converted at his decease, *e.g.*, a trust to convert it after the death of the tenant for life, or words clearly recognising that the estate will not in fact be converted before the death of the tenant for life.

(2) Where there is a trust for sale, but the trustees have *no express power* to postpone conversion, and the proceeds of sale are settled upon trust for persons in succession, the foregoing rules apply in the same manner as they apply to the "simple case."

APPORTIONMENTS 107

(3) Where there is a trust for sale *with a power* for the trustees to postpone the sale, but there is no disposition in the will amounting to an express gift to the tenant for life of the interim income from unauthorised assets pending the sale thereof, such interim income is ordinarily subject to the same rules as apply to the "simple case," except that instead of "Consol interest" 4 per cent. interest (*l*) is allowed on value as at death: but the will may be such as to shew that the power to postpone is not merely ancillary to the trust for sale, but it is intended to authorise a permanent retention of the investments, and in that case the tenant for life will take the whole income. (*In re Inman*, (1915) 1 Ch. 187.)

(4) Where there is a trust for sale with a power for the trustees to postpone such sale and some disposition amounting to an express gift of the interim income in favour of the tenant for life, the foregoing rules, except Rule 6, are entirely displaced, and Rule 6 is, or is not, displaced according to the other terms of the will. It must, however, be remembered that a discretionary power to postpone the sale is one that must be exercised by all the trustees, and if the trustees do not in fact exercise their discretion, or if any one or more trustees dissent, the result is the same as if the power of postponement had not been given. (See *Re Rowlls*, (1900) 2 Ch. 107, and *Re Hilton*, (1909) 2 Ch. 548.)

Insufficient Mortgage Security

In cases in which trustees hold an authorised mortgage security under which the mortgagor makes default in payment of interest and the security is ultimately sold for a sum insufficient to pay capital and interest in full, under these circumstances the sum realised must be divided between capital and income in the proportion which the amount due for arrears

(*l*) See note (*e*) on p. 99, *ante.*

of interest bears to the amount due in respect of the capital debt. (*Re Atkinson*, (1904) 2 Ch. 160 (*m*).) If default is made before the death of a testator the interest to death is capitalised in the usual way.

Example.—Assume a mortgage for 1,000*l.* at 4 per cent. which has been settled upon a tenant for life and then upon remaindermen, assume also that interest is paid for some years, then that the interest falls into arrear and that at the date of sale when 800*l.* is realised for the security the interest has been in arrear for ten years, here we have 400*l.* due to the tenant for life, 1,000*l.* due to the remaindermen, and only 800*l.* with which to pay the whole 1,400*l.* The rule is to divide that 800*l.* in the proportion that 400*l.* bears to 1,000*l.*, and to do this the following fraction must be worked out :—

$$\frac{1,000}{1,400} \times 800l. = 571l.\ 8s.\ 7d.$$ represents capital, and 228*l.* 11*s.* 5*d.*

belongs to income subject to deduction of tax.

It will be noticed that the difference in the rule here and that in the *Earl of Chesterfield's case* is, that in the latter the calculation is made upon the basis of compound interest, whilst in this case simple interest only is computed

Where the investment is an unauthorised security, in other words, where there is a breach of trust, and loss ensues, then the rule is to throw the loss on income and capital rateably; to do this the aggregate must be divided in the proportion which the total amount of dividends that the tenant for life would have received if the money had been invested in Consols from the date of the wrongful investment to the death of the tenant for life, bears to the value of the Consols at his death, his executor bringing into hotchpot any income actually received, but the executor is not liable to refund any over-payment if the tenant for life was not responsible for the breach of trust (*n*).

(*m*) The law here seems somewhat illogical. The tenant for life has received part of his interest, but the remainderman has received none of his principal money, and yet the tenant for life receives on the balance due to him the same dividend that the remainderman receives upon the capital sum The result is that, counting in the interest already recovered by the tenant for life, the latter obtains a much larger proportion of his total claim than does the remainderman.

(*n*) *Re Bird, Re Evans, Dodd* v. *Evans*, (1901) 1 Ch. 920

APPORTIONMENTS 109

Covenant to pay an Annuity

Where a testator has covenanted to pay an annuity and gives his residue to one for life with remainder over, each future instalment of the annuity must, as it accrues, be apportioned between capital and income. This has in some cases been done by calculating what sum with 4 per cent. simple interest from the testator's death to the day of payment would have met the particular instalment and charging that sum to capital, the balance to income. (*Re Perkins*, (1907) 2 Ch. 596; *Re Poyser*, (1910) 2 Ch. 444 (*o*).)

This is the converse of the method employed in the *Earl of Chesterfield's case* and is not of frequent occurrence. Therefore it has not been included in the accounts contained in the Appendices, but it may be useful to give an example of the application of the rule here.

Example.—A testator covenanted to pay his sister an annuity of 500*l*. during her life. Here we have to ascertain what sum set aside at his death with interest thereon at 4 per cent. for the year would have met the particular payment.

(*o*) The method employed in *Re Perkins* is fair and produces the correct result if the annuity comes to an end during the first life tenancy of the residue, but would throw an undue proportion on the second tenant for life or remainderman if the annuitant outlived the first tenant for life. Other methods have been adopted (see *In re Dawson*, (1906) 2 Ch. 211.) No doubt the Court retains full discretion to direct a method of apportionment suitable to the facts of each case. The method adopted in *Re Perkins* should not be regarded as a rule of law. To meet the case of one or more annuitants surviving the first tenant for life, it is thought that the trustees could not greatly err if they were to set aside on the death of the testator such a sum as with the interest to accrue thereon would be sufficient to provide for the annuities if the annuitants were to live for the longest period of human possibility, and to pay the annuities out of the income of this fund so far as it would extend, drawing on its capital as required for the balance; the amount of the fund set free on the death of each annuitant, or remaining unexhausted at the death of the last annuitant, being distributed on the basis of the rule in *Chesterfield's case*, between tenants for life and capital, as if it had been a reversion then falling into possession. The tenant for life in this way receives no more than the income of true residue. If the instalments were provided for as they ripened, without regard to future instalments, and the first tenant for life should die before the annuities had ceased, he would have received more income than he was entitled to, as he would have had the whole income of the fund required for meeting the future instalments. (See the argument of Mr. Ingpen in *Re Bacon* (1893), 62 L. J. Ch. 445.)

Thus 100*l.* invested at the death at 4 per cent. would, at the expiration of one year, when the first payment of the annuity becomes due, produce 104*l.*, so that in order to ascertain the amount required to produce 500*l.* the following fraction must be worked out, viz.:—

$$\frac{100}{104} \times \frac{500}{1} \; l. = 480l. \; 15s. \; 5d.$$

The result is that the sum of 480*l.* 15*s.* 5*d.* so ascertained is chargeable against capital and the balance of 19*l.* 4*s.* 7*d.* (less income tax) against income. This calculation must be made every year during the currency of the annuity, and although the amount attributable to income is not large, yet it is an increasing quantity, and if the life upon which the annuity depends is of long duration the effect of the application of this rule is to throw upon income a burden which steadily increases each year.

A jointure rentcharge in a settlement in the absence of any covenant is not apportionable and must be borne by the tenant for life. (*Re Popham,* (1914) W. N. 247.)

All annuities are subject to a deduction in respect of income tax. So much of the annuity as falls upon income has been taxed at the source, *e.g.*, rents and dividends, and the tenant for life upon paying his contribution will deduct the tax in respect thereof. So much as is payable out of capital will be paid less tax, and the trustees will make a return to the Government in respect of which an assessment will be made upon which they will pay the tax. (8 & 9 Geo. V. c. 40, Income Tax Act, 1918, rule 19 of the rules applicable to all the schedules.)

The Suspense Apportionment Account

Appendix D. (see p. 247).—It will now be possible more fully to appreciate this account. The balances, after deducting the proportion due to capital, of dividends and rents accruing due at the death in respect of all unauthorised investments the income of which has not been given to the tenant for life, are brought down from the dividend and rent apportionment accounts respectively (Appendices B. and C.), and constitute the first entries in the suspense apportionment account. On to this account must also be brought all other income derived from each unauthorised investment, whether leaseholds, stocks or shares, received since the death of the testator down to the sale of the asset.

In the third column of the account a description of such unauthorised investment will be entered. In the same column will also be entered any particulars of a single deduction or the total of two or more deductions. There can be no deductions except income tax in the case of dividends and interest; in other cases there will be the property tax, with the additional deduction for ground rent in the case of leaseholds let on lease. Where, however, leaseholds are let at rack rents, involving the trustees in the obligation to repair, then the agent must be instructed to render his rent account shewing the gross rent received, the total payments made or allowed, and the net amount produced from each property, for reasons which will presently transpire.

During the first year columns 4 and 5 will remain blank, unless within that time any of the unauthorised investments are sold. In such cases the amount produced by the sale will be entered in column 4. The pen will be drawn through the next column 5, the appropriate rate of interest will be entered in column 6, the gross income in respect of the investment in question in column 8, any deductions in column 9, and the net income in column 10, which last three figures will be taken from the agent's account, then interest at the appropriate rate from the death of the testator to the sale of the investment will be calculated at intervals, upon the value set forth in column 4, and the amount of such interest will be entered in column 11. The difference between the amounts in columns 10 and 11 will be entered in column 12. If, under the rules above set forth, 3 per cent. (*a*) is payable to the tenant for life upon the value as at the death, then the figure to be inserted in column 4 will be altered accordingly, and, subject thereto, the working out of the figures will proceed as already explained.

If Consol interest is payable, then the value of the property mentioned in column 3 as of the first anniversary of the testator's death will be entered in column 4; the price of Consols on that

(*a*) See note (*e*) on p 99, *ante*

day is given at the head of the account, and the amount of Consols which the value, if realised, would have purchased will be inserted in column 5. Then in column 6 the rate of interest will be entered at $2\frac{1}{2}$ per cent., and all the other entries will follow as already described, except that the interest will be calculated at $2\frac{1}{2}$ per cent. upon the notional sum of Consols instead of 3 per cent. (*a*) upon the value.

It is an essential consequence of these arrangements that, strictly speaking, no payment can be made to the tenant for life during the currency of the first year after the death out of income derived from such an unauthorised investment, except in the case of a sale, because the events will not have transpired which fix the data upon which the calculations have to proceed.

As soon as one year has passed, the apportionments should be worked out and the total of columns 11 and 12 transferred to the income and capital accounts respectively. If in any of these cases the net income should happen to be less than the interest, then the tenant for life can only receive the net income —the deficiency he must forego.

After the first year the unauthorised assets still remaining unsold will be repeated in the account and no new unauthorised investment can be involved. On the second and subsequent occasions when income is received the fewest words possible will be used to describe the property producing the income, because it will have been fully described on the first occasion. The figures in the 4th, 5th and 6th columns will be repeated, but there may possibly be slight variation in the figures to be entered in the remaining columns. This suspense apportionment will continue until the last unauthorised investment has been converted, and it is obvious that the trustee must always receive all income which is subject to apportionment; in other words, he cannot allow the tenant for life to collect it.

(*For specimen Apportionment Accounts, see pp.* 239—251.)

(*a*) See note (*e*) on p. 99, *ante*.

CHAPTER VIII

HOTCHPOT

It often happens that in the distribution of an estate or fund, a beneficiary is required to "bring into hotchpot" an advance previously received by him, *i.e.*, to bring its value into account as part of his share of the estate or fund, so that he cannot receive anything further in respect of his share until the other beneficiaries have received countervailing payments. This is the effect of section 3 of the Statute of Distribution (1670), 22 & 23 Car. 2, ch. x, whenever a father dies intestate having in his lifetime made settlements upon any of his children, or made advances to any of them by way of portion (except that land given to his heir-at-law is exempt), and a will often contains similar provisions directing that advances made by the testator in his lifetime to beneficiaries (or perhaps benefits received by them from other sources, *e.g.*, from grandparents) are to be brought into hotchpot by them in the distribution of his estate.

Again, where a fund is settled (whether by will or settlement) and powers of appointment are given among any class of persons or their children, with a trust for all the members of the class in equal shares in default of appointment, there is commonly a direction that where any appointment has been made in favour of any member of the class or his children, the appointed share (whether appointed to him or to his children) is to be brought into hotchpot by him on the distribution of the unappointed part of the fund.

The general method for giving effect to a "hotchpot" provision is to add to the estate or fund for the purpose of computation a sum equal to the amount which has to be brought into hotchpot, and to ascertain the amount of each beneficiary's share on this basis, and then to deduct the amount brought into hotchpot from the share of the corresponding beneficiary. Thus, if a fund worth £10,000 is divisible into two equal shares, but one of the beneficiaries has to bring a sum of £2,000 into hotchpot, the £2,000 would be added to the £10,000, and the total of £12,000 would be divided into two equal shares each of £6,000; thus the sum of £2,000 brought into hotchpot would be deducted from the share of the beneficiary bringing it into hotchpot, leaving his net share at £4,000.

If it is found that the amount required to be brought into hotchpot exceeds the beneficiary's share he is (*a*) not required to make any repayment, but is merely treated as having had his whole share, and the remaining estate or fund is distributed among the other beneficiaries on that footing.

In the absence of any express direction to the contrary a beneficiary is not required to bring into hotchpot any interest upon the amount of his advance until the moment at which the beneficial interests of himself and his co-beneficiaries fall into possession. (*Re Rees* (1881), 17 C. D. 701.)

This moment (which may be the death of a testator or intestate, or of a tenant for life, or the determination of a trust for accumulation, or any other event) is usually described as the "period of distribution," though it is in the ordinary course impossible for the actual distribution to be then effected—time being required for such preliminary steps as clearing off death duties and other liabilities, realising the fund or passing accounts; and sometimes owing to the settlement of shares or charges for annuities or for other reasons the actual distribution is postponed for many years.

Usually interest is charged upon the amount to be brought into hotchpot at the rate of £4 per cent. per annum (see *Re Davy*, (1908) 1 Ch. 61; *Re Cooke*, (1916) 1 Ch. 480; *Re Rees* (1881), 17 C. D. 701), as from the "period of distribution" until actual distribution of the fund, when the countervailing amounts are actually paid or transferred to the other beneficiaries, or appropriated for their benefit, the interest

(*a*) But a direction that a debt due from the beneficiary to the testator is to be brought into hotchpot does not release the beneficiary from the obligation of the debt if it exceeds his share. (See *Re Young*, (1914) 1 Ch. 581; *Re Barker*, (1918) 1 Ch. 128)

charged upon the advance being brought into account on any periodical payments of income

A different method of procedure, however, applies in the cases referred to below, where the amount brought into hotchpot is treated as a proportion of the fund and not (as is commonly the case) as a sum of money.

It will have been observed from the foregoing observations that there are two distinct classes of cases in which questions of hotchpot may arise: (a) cases where in the distribution of the estate of a testator or intestate amounts have to be brought into hotchpot which have strictly formed part of the estate, but were either advanced by the deceased in his lifetime or arose from some quite outside source, and (b) cases where funds appointed or advanced originally out of an estate or fund have to be brought into hotchpot on the distribution of the residue of the estate or fund.

In cases of the second type the amount advanced or appointed may either take the form of a sum of money or a particular asset, the value of which has to be brought into hotchpot, or it may take the form of a definite proportion of the whole fund. Thus out of a fund consisting of a mixed list of investments, a sum of £1,000 cash or a sum of £1,000 consols may be appointed or advanced; in which case there would be no doubt that the amount to be brought into hotchpot would be a sum of £1,000 or the value of the consols as the case might be Or, on the other hand, an appointment might be made of $\frac{1}{10}$th of the entire fund, in which case the beneficiary would not bring into hotchpot a pecuniary sum but a share of the whole; thus if his share, apart from the appointment, would have been $\frac{1}{4}$th of the whole, he would have in fact already received $\frac{1}{10}$th of the whole, and would thus have only $\frac{1}{4}-\frac{1}{10}$ $(=\frac{6}{40}$ths) of the whole still to come to him, and this would be equivalent to $\frac{6}{8}$ths of the sum remaining for division after taking out the $\frac{4}{10}$ths already taken by him.

Cases may occur in which it is uncertain whether the beneficiary ought to be called upon to bring into hotchpot a proportion or a pecuniary sum Thus if out of a fund consisting of £10,000 consols a sum of £1,000 consols were appointed to a beneficiary, it might be a question whether he should be required to bring into hotchpot $\frac{1}{10}$th of the fund or the value of £1,000 consols. It is apprehended that in such a case the former alternative should be adopted. The distinction might be very important if (for example) between the date of the advance and the period of distribution the remaining £9,000 consols were invested in a speculative security which either gained or lost greatly in value, as would readily appear by working out the two methods in an imaginary case

Where the beneficiary brings into hotchpot a proportion of the fund he is not, of course, charged a percentage interest on its value; he merely takes a reduced share of the income of the residue of the fund corresponding with his reduced share in the corpus.

It may happen (as already pointed out) that an advance has to be brought into hotchpot many years before the actual distribution of the fund; for example, where shares of the fund are settled or annuities are charged thereon, and the actual realisation or distribution of the fund are indefinitely postponed on that account; and in some such cases the plan of bringing the advance actually into hotchpot only when the fund is actually distributed, and in the meantime charging the advanced beneficiary with fixed interest thereon at the rate of £4 per cent. per annum as from the theoretical period of distribution has been rejected, and in lieu thereof a preliminary process of hotchpot has been effected at the moment of the theoretical period of distribution whereby the amount to be brought into hotchpot has been converted from a sum of money into a proportion of the fund; thus the estate itself and the amount to be brought into hotchpot have both been valued as at the theoretical period of distribution, and it has been found what proportion the latter is of the total value; and from that time on the beneficiary has been treated as bringing into hotchpot that proportion of the whole in lieu of a sum of cash with interest.

According to this method if the fund remaining for division is found to be worth £12,500, and the sum to be brought into hotchpot is £1,000, the beneficiary would be treated as having received $\dfrac{1000}{12500+1000}$ or $\frac{2}{27}$ths of the fund, and would bring this proportion into hotchpot instead of the sum of £1,000 on the principles already explained. (See *Re Hargreaves* (1903), 88 L. T. 100; *Re Gilbert*, (1908) W. N. 63; and *Re Hunt* (1913), 107 L. T. 757.)

This appears at first sight to be fairer than the ordinary method and is no doubt fairer where reasonably applicable, but it is a comparatively recent innovation and liable to cause much difficulty, and it has been treated as being only of very exceptional application. (See *Re Tod*, (1916) 1 Ch. 567.) It would often result in a very elaborate fractional division (*e.g.*, suppose the estate to be worth £12,453 : 12s. 6d., and the sum to be brought into hotchpot was £461 : 2s. 1d.), and it depends upon a valuation at the theoretical period of distribution, which may be in some cases (*e.g.*, when the shares of a private family company are concerned) highly speculative.

The innovation, however, shews that the Court is prepared to adjust the precise method of giving effect to a hotchpot provision to the special circumstances of individual cases where a strict construction of the instrument or a fair and reasonable method of accountancy so required. Cases in which the method of *Re Hargreaves* has been considered and rejected as inapplicable, are (*Re Poyser* (1888), 1 Ch. 828; *Re Craven*, (1914) 1 Ch. 358; *Re Forster Brown*, (1914) 2 Ch. 584; *Re Cooke*, (1916) 1 Ch. 480; *Re Tod*, (1916) 1 Ch. 567), and speaking generally the method would appear to be applicable only where the estate and fund can be valued with some approach to accuracy, and the will shews an intention that the distributive shares should be treated as ascertained at the earlier date. It is thought that (unless the will is very clear upon the point) the method in question should not in the present state of the authorities be applied to any case, except under a direction of the Court.

Where pending distribution the estate is subject to the payment of annuities, and the surplus income after paying the annuities does not enable the unadvanced beneficiaries to receive payments balancing interest at the rate of £4 per cent. per annum upon the advances which have to be brought into hotchpot, there appears to be a conflict of authority as to whether the deficit is to be added to the sum which the advanced beneficiary is required to bring into hotchpot, or whether it is simply cancelled. (See *Re Lambert*, (1897) 2 Ch 169; *Re Hargreaves* (1903), 88 L. T. 100, on the one side, and *Re Forster Brown*, (1914) 2 Ch. 584, on the other.) The editors respectfully prefer the latter decision, on the ground that interest is charged on advances for the purpose of adjusting the distribution of the interim income of the fund, and not for the purpose of adding to the capital amount ultimately brought into hotchpot.

Where specific assets have been appointed or advanced, the question will arise at what date they should be valued. For example, if the testator has in his lifetime given to a son a block of mining shares or a house, or a sum of consols which he directs to be brought into hotchpot, on the distribution of the estate, or if like assets are appointed out of a settled fund, should the sum brought into hotchpot be the value of these assets at the date of the gift or appointment, or at the death of the donor, or at the period of distribution? The value may be very different at the different dates.

This question may of course be answered by a careful consideration of the exact terms of the direction under which the hotchpot is made, and if it is made pursuant to the Statute of Distribution on the division of an intestate's estate, the date of the gift appears to be designated as the critical moment (see *Watson* v *Watson* (1864), 33 Beav. 574; *Hatfield* v. *Minet* (1878), 8 C. D. 136, at p. 146); where, however, the terms of the direction give no decisive help, resort must be had to general principles. On general principle, where the asset is taken out of a trust fund, the proper time to value it would in theory seem to be the moment when it passes out of the trust into the control of the beneficiary, whether directly or through a release of a life interest, because at that moment it passes out of the purview of the trust, and is at the absolute disposal of the beneficiary. If any other view were taken (a) the trust might have to bear the loss arising from the retention of the asset by the beneficiary, after the trustee had ceased altogether to approve of the retention of the property as an investment; (b) in many cases the value at a later date could not be effectively ascertained, *e.g.*, shares of a company where there had been a rearrangement of capital, reconstruction, or amalgamation, or a winding up and distribution of assets or land developed by subsequent building, and (o) the beneficiary might between the gift and the period of distribution have sold the asset and used the proceeds for his own purposes, and the value of the asset at the period of distribution (if ascertainable) might bear no relation to the value at the date of the gift or the amount realised by the sale.

Of course, if the asset is appointed to a beneficiary, but subject to a life interest, so that during the life interest the asset remains a part of the trust fund and in the control of the trustee, the proper time to value it would be the death of the tenant for life, when for the first time it becomes at the disposal of the appointee, and if in the meantime the trustee has sold the asset, in order to make a change of investments, it is the substituted investment that would be valued.

Similar principles undoubtedly apply where a gift has been made by a testator or intestate which has to be brought into hotchpot as a part of a share of his estate, the gift passing absolutely out of the donor into the donee when the gift is completed. (See *Watson* v. *Watson* (1864), 33 Beav 574 ; and *Re Prockter*, (1916) 1 Ch. 25.)

In one case, however, under a settlement, where a mother appointed to her daughter on the occasion of her marriage a specific sum of stock subject to the trusts of her own marriage settlement, and at the same time released in favour of her daughter her own life interest in the same sum of stock, so that it became immediately vested in and transferable to her daughter, it was held that the amount to be brought into hotchpot by the daughter in respect of the stock at the subsequent period of distribution was its value at that time and not its value at the time of the daughter's marriage. (*Re Kelly's Settlement*, (1910) 1 Ch. 78.) In that case the appointed asset had in fact been made subject to the daughter's marriage settlement, and had been retained unaltered until the period of distribution, and no doubt the decision was affected by that consideration. The case, however (if correctly decided).

shews that no absolute rule can be laid down as to the date at which an appointed asset is to be valued where the appointee in fact receives it before the period of distribution.

Where an advance is made shortly before the death of the testator or intestate, so that it becomes subject to the payment of estate duty, the duty is deducted from its value for the purposes of hotchpot. (*In re Beddington*, (1900) 1 Ch. 771; and *Re Crocker*, (1916) 1 Ch. 25.)

Great care is necessary in ascertaining the true effect of a hotchpot clause when more than one fund is involved.

The same settlement often deals with a husband's trust fund, a wife's trust fund, and a third fund representing additional assets brought in by the wife in compliance with her covenant to settle after-acquired property. Or a testator by his will distributes his property amongst such of his children as attain twenty-one, and goes on to provide that the share of those dying under twenty-one shall accrue to the other shares. In all these cases it is necessary to be very careful to see what funds are affected by the clause. Ought advances in such cases out of one fund to be brought into hotchpot upon the distribution of the other fund, where the advance or appointment to be brought into hotchpot by any beneficiary exceeds his share of the particular fund, out of which the advance or appointment has been taken?

This appears to turn upon the answer to two questions:—

(1) Is the set of words which settles the additional fund really a separate settlement of the additional fund, the words being merely words of reference so as to operate by way of compendious introduction of the earlier trusts? If so, *primâ facie*, the two funds constitute separate settlements.

(2) Does the second set of words operate as an amalgamation of the second fund with the first fund, so as to make it an augmentation of or accretion to the first fund, so that the two funds really constitute one settlement? If so, they are one fund for purposes of hotchpot (*Re Fraser*, (1913) 2 Ch. at 232—3; for other instances see *Re Perkins* (1892), 67 L. T. 743; *Re North* (1897), 76 L. T. 186; *Re Marquis of Bristol*, (1897) 1 Ch. 946, 949; and *Re Cavendish*, (1912) 1 Ch. 794).

In order that the two funds may be treated for hotchpot purposes as a single fund, you must find upon the construction of the documents an intention to amalgamate the two funds. There is no presumption one way or the other, but its result depends upon the true meaning of the document as a whole. If there is any difference in the trusts at any stage, the doctrine of accretion cannot apply. A useful test is to see whether the provisions must be regarded as independent trusts: could separate trustees have been appointed of each of the funds?—if so, there would be no coalescence—one could not be deemed to be an accretion to the other.

If separate trustees had been appointed, then one set of trustees could not be required to hand over the funds to another set for the purpose of giving effect to a hotchpot clause although the beneficiaries might be the same. (*Re Wood*, (1913) 2 Ch. D. at 583-4.)

The following summary statement is taken from the judgment of Cozens-Hardy, M.R., in *Re Willoughby*, (1911) 2 Ch. 597:—

" 1. That no interest is charged against an advanced child prior to the
  " testator's death.
" 2. That where the period of distribution of the testator's property is
  " at the testator's death, interest is charged against an advanced
  " child from the death and not from the subsequent date at
  " which in fact the distribution takes place.
" 3. That if the period of distribution is at the expiration of a period of
  " accumulation or of a prior life estate, interest is charged not
  " from the death but from the period of distribution.
" 4. That the effect of a charge upon the residue, such as a life
  " annuity secured by a fund set apart to meet it, does not alter
  " the period of distribution."

Difficult questions of construction arise under hotchpot clauses in cases where it is doubtful whether some particular benefaction constitutes an advance for the purposes of the clause, and in cases where advances are directed to be brought into hotchpot by a life tenant of a settled share, the difficulty being to decide whether the advance is to be charged against the life interest or against the corpus of the shares, but such questions lie beyond the scope of this work. (See Jarman on Wills, ed. 6, p. 1175, &c.)

CHAPTER IX

THE BANK ACCOUNT

A SEPARATE account should be opened at a bank in the names of all the executors (which term in this chapter includes trustees and administrators as well) as soon as possible. If, as is probable, the testator had a banking account, then the most convenient course will be for the executors to open their account with the same bank, and after registering the probate there to give instructions for the transfer of the testator's balance to the credit of their account. Some banks allow the executors before probate is granted to draw upon the deceased's balance for Estate Duty, thereby saving interest involved in borrowing. If the testator had no banking account, then one should be opened in the names of the executors with the first sum of cash which comes to their hands.

Every sum of money received by the executors in connection with the trust should be paid, without delay, to the credit of the trust account at the bank. All agents of the executors should be instructed to pay the balance of moneys in their hands belonging to the estate to the credit of this special account. Companies having to pay dividends or interest to the executors upon stocks, shares and debentures belonging to the trust estate should, as soon as possible after the death, be authorised to send such dividends and interest until further order direct to the bank for the credit of the trust account.

When this arrangement prevails, then each executor will feel safe in knowing that all the trust moneys stand to the credit of the joint account, and each will know in what way the money is disposed of, in that he with his co-executors will have to sign every cheque drawn upon the account.

In the event of one of two or more executors dying, the

separate account will be found to be of the greatest advantage, as the surviving executors can draw on the account immediately after the death of their colleague has been proved at the bank. On the other hand, if one executor dies with some of the trust moneys in his own account, then the surviving executors will not be able to recover those moneys until the will of the deceased executor has been proved, or letters of administration have been granted to his estate, and if he dies insolvent moneys in his hands may be lost to the estate.

No separate entries will be made in the account of moneys paid to the bank or of cheques drawn upon the bankers, as such entries are of no permanent importance to the trust estate, and if at any time they are wanted the bank pass book is the best quarter in which to look for them. Further, a very clear distinction must be drawn between the account which a trustee will keep as between himself and the beneficiary and any account which he will have to keep as between himself and a stranger to the trust. One of the best examples of the latter is the trust banking account, which is one between the trustee and his banker, and, of course, may shew a very different balance to that which may appear to be due to or from the trustee on the trust accounts. It is true that the whole of the balance on the capital account should be included in the balance due on the banking account, but still the balance on the former account is that by which the trustee is bound, and if the whole amount is not at the bank, then all the moneys may not have passed through that account. The fact is that the bank, with regard to cash, somewhat resembles a safe with regard to documents—it is a secure and convenient receptacle for any cash which may be in hand, out of which from time to time will be taken so much cash as may be necessary to discharge trust liabilities.

Particulars of all moneys received, and of all payments made will, of course, be entered in the accounts, and if, in addition to the entry of those particulars, the book-keeper enters every cheque drawn and every sum of money paid into the bank, such latter entries will be a surplusage.

The pass book and the counterfoils of the cheques and payment-in slips will therefore be alone relied upon for all records appertaining to the bank account pure and simple; consequently no specimen of any bank account will be found in the estate book as contained in the Appendices.

It is, however, essential, when all moneys have been paid into the bank, to examine the bank pass book frequently, to see that the balance of cash at the bank and the balance on the cash accounts agree To do this the entries on each side of the pass book should be checked against the entries in the accounts. In the event of an entry appearing in the accounts which cannot be traced in the pass book, it may not unlikely be accounted for as follows, assuming that the practice of paying all moneys received into the account has been strictly followed. If under such circumstances the entry in question is on the receipt side of the account, it is probably a country cheque which has been paid into the bank, and not yet credited by the bank; if on the payment side, it is probably a cheque which has been drawn by the executors and not yet presented to the bank for payment.

To ascertain whether the balance of cash at the bank is correct, the following plan may be adopted: to the cash balance shown on the pass book add the amount of any payments in not yet credited, and deduct the amount of any cheques not yet presented for payment; such ultimate balance should equal the net balance on all the open cash accounts in the estate book.

The facility of detecting an error in the accounts, when it is known that all moneys received or paid have passed through the bank, is obvious.

It is true that there is no statutory obligation upon an ordinary trustee to keep a separate banking account for each trust estate, but it is a grave dereliction of duty for any executor or trustee to mix trust funds with his own. Neither should one executor or trustee allow trust money to be held by a co-executor or co-trustee, but if there is no bank account then any cash belonging to the estate must, of necessity, pass into the hands of one of the executors, or an agent must hold it. The bank account avoids the necessity of this happening, and further, saves every executor from the invidious task of having to take exception to money passing into the hands of any one person, whether a co-executor, co-trustee, or an agent. Again, the separate account avoids innocent confusion of moneys.

If trust money is paid into a separate account and the bank should fail, the executors would not be answerable for the loss unless the money had been allowed to remain there for an unreasonable length of time, but if the trust money had been mixed with an executor's own money when such eventuality occurred, then he would be liable to be called upon to replace the lost fund. Moreover, if he happened to have a large balance of trust money in his account and should have overdrawn his own money in the bank, he would, instead of simply overdrawing his banker, be drawing upon the trust money, which might subject him to interest at 5 per cent. upon all balances in his hands at the time or give a claimant an option to share the profits of his business. (*Docker* v. *Somes* (1834), 2 My. & K. 655.)

The view of the legislature on the subject of trustees' separate banking accounts may be gathered from the fact that when a judicial trustee is appointed a separate account for receipts and payments on behalf of the trustees has to be kept in the name of the trustee at some bank approved by the Court, and there is an imperative duty imposed upon the judicial trustee to pay all moneys coming into his hands on account of the trust, without delay, to the trust account at the bank, and if he keeps any such money in his hands for a longer time than the Court considers necessary he is liable to pay interest upon it at such rate not exceeding 5 per cent. as the Court may fix for the time during which the money remains in his hands. The obligations imposed by statute upon a trustee in bankruptcy are more severe: such a trustee is required to pay into a local bank, to be appointed by the committee of inspection, all sums from time to time received by him—failing such appointment, into the Bank of England. Further, if such trustee at any time keeps in his hands for more than ten days any sum exceeding 50*l*., he must pay interest on the same at the rate of 20 per cent. per annum, and is liable, moreover (unless he can satisfy the Board of Trade as to the retention), to be dismissed his office without remuneration. (4 & 5 Geo. 5, c. 59, s. 89 (5).) He must not pay any sums received by him as trustee into his private banking account (sect. 88). An agent (judicial factor) when appointed by the Scotch Courts to manage a trust is not allowed to retain in his hands a sum exceeding 50*l* at any time for a period longer than ten days, and if he breaks this rule it is obligatory on the Court accountant (an officer whose duty it is to examine the factor's account annually) to debit him with penal interest at the rate of 20 per cent per annum. (12 & 13 Vict c. 51, s 5.)

Separate accounts must be kept by the Public Trustee and all payments of money to or from the capital of the trust property shall be made through the banker to the trust. (The Public Trustee Rules, 1912, rr. 19 and 20.)

The judges of the High Court have continually in recent years condemned the practice of paying trust moneys into the same banking account with other moneys.

CHAPTER X.

FINAL STATEMENT FOR THE BENEFICIARIES

THE preparation of the statement to be rendered to the parties ultimately entitled to the capital in any trust is a matter of considerable importance, and it should be prepared in such a way as will disclose to the beneficiary in the simplest manner possible—

    (a) The original assets of the trust estate.
    (b) The dealings with those assets and with the investments which from time to time represented the proceeds of any which have been sold.
    (c) The property, whether investments or cash, to which the beneficiaries are entitled, and the mode in which it is proposed to make the distribution.

On the death of the last tenant for life it is necessary to decide to whom accounts must be rendered, and for this purpose an examination of the document (if any) creating the trust and the memoranda must be made.

If it is found that the trustees have received notice of any dealings by the beneficiaries with their reversionary interests, either by way of mortgage, assignment or settlement, the parties who gave the notice must be informed of the death of the tenant for life and required to prove their title, which is done by delivery of abstract and production of deeds in the ordinary way.

Wherever it is found that an *absolute* assignment has been executed, the assignees, whether they be purchasers or trustees of a daughter's settlement, will be the persons to whom the accounts should be rendered, but in the case of a mortgage the accounts should be rendered to the mortgagor in the first instance, if there is an obvious balance coming to him.

Where a remainderman mortgages his interest, the Court will only pay to such mortgagee so much money, out of the mortgagor's share, as may be sufficient to discharge the principal, interest, and costs, the balance being paid to the remainderman direct, and this notwithstanding that the mortgagor's whole interest in the trust estate has been included in the security (*Hockey* v. *Western*, (1898) 1 Ch. 350), and the Court supports a trustee in doing that which the Court would order. (*Seagram* v. *Knight* (1867), 2 Ch 630.) The trustee will, however, obtain a good receipt from a mortgagee by assignment if for any reason he prefers to transfer the whole mortgaged fund to the mortgagee, leaving the mortgagee to settle with the beneficiary. (Item 2, p. 231.)

When it is decided on distribution to divide between the beneficiaries any stocks or shares in *specie*, it is sometimes convenient to divide only so much as will enable each beneficiary to receive a round sum of stock, say, an exact multiple of 10*l*. (nominal value), and to sell any odd amount and distribute the proceeds in cash In the example in the Appendix A., p. 225, the sum of 18*l*., the odd amount of the Lancashire and Yorkshire Railway Stock, was sold and the balance was divided equally between the children, so that each child received 200*l*. of this stock. (See p. 227.)

When preparing the final statement for the beneficiaries there should be set forth, in the first place, particulars of the original assets. Those particulars are ready at hand; indeed, nothing here is wanted save a copy of the original schedule.

Having thus shewn the beneficiary what the estate consisted of at the commencement of the trust, it becomes necessary, in the second place, to prove to him in what way the trustees have dealt with the items mentioned in the schedule. This second requirement is satisfied by rendering a cash account verified by the vouchers which the trustees have kept throughout the administration of the trust. The cash account which will be wanted in order to satisfy this second requirement is the existing cash and investment account, omitting the entries appertaining to investments. The entries in this account are in chronological order, with receipts and payments under every heading scattered promiscuously through the account. In order, therefore, to present the account in such a form that the result of the administration can be readily comprehended by the beneficiary, it will be desirable to classify the receipts as well as the payments.

Instead, therefore, of merely copying the account as it stands, with items arranged in chronological order, the account will be arranged in classes or sections, the details of each class being entered in an inner column and the total carried out; and now will be experienced the advantage of having prefaced every entry with the name of the appropriate class to which the receipt or payment belongs. The cash headings in the account as set forth in the index should be examined, and the order in which they are to be brought on to the final statement must be decided upon. Regard should be had to the subject-matter of each heading, and the headings must be arranged in their order of importance and their relation the one to the other, because neither the alphabetical order nor the numerical order is for this purpose of any consequence whatever; indeed, the original numbers given to the classes should be omitted in this final statement. All the items under each heading on the debit side will be collected together in the order of date, the amounts being entered in an inner column and the total carried out The items appearing on the credit side of the account will be treated in an exactly similar manner. The result will be that in the statement prepared for delivery to the beneficiaries the items constituting each class of expenditure and receipt will be grouped together, the details appearing in the inner columns and the totals carried out.

Care must be taken to see that the various classes of items on the debit and credit sides of the account which have relation the one to the other are as far as possible set opposite one another in the statement, so that the net result may be apparent; for instance, all the receipts in respect of securities sold for re-investment are on one side, then on the other, and immediately opposite should be set forth the corresponding payments made for securities purchased.

The number given to each item in the account will be repeated in this statement, to facilitate reference, and the various items under each heading will be entered in chronological order. Finally the items will be numbered consecutively throughout, so that each item will have two numbers—the original number in the cash and investment account and the new number in the statement—for the purpose of facilitating reference

The cash balance on the whole account will finally be brought down to shew the amount in hand for division amongst the beneficiaries. This is important, because the book-keeper will remember that, until the balance is brought down for division, the general account must not be charged with any payment to a beneficiary without debiting the payment as an investment. Then, when the time comes to make a distribution all such payments appearing in the list of investments will be brought into account and deducted from the share of the beneficiary to whom or on whose account such payments were made.

The advantage of thus classifying the receipts and payments is that the perusal and checking of the account is simplified, and the beneficiary will be able to see at a glance not only the details of each class of receipts and payments, but also the total of each class; for instance, he will see in one figure what the real estate produced; in another, what the general personal estate produced; in a third, what was the total amount produced by the sales of investments. Then on the other side of the account he will have before him in one figure the total of the executorship expenses; in another, the total of the debts due at the death; in a third, the total of the legacies; in another, the total cost of realising the real estate, and so on. A summary of the total of each class of receipts and payments may usefully be added as a supplement which will give a nicely condensed view of the result of the administration (See pp. 276, 277.)

The items appertaining to investments will be copied from the cash and investment account, and will constitute a separate account The chronological order of these items, with the original consecutive numbering, will be preserved, and if they all belong to one class there will be no sections into which the entries can be divided (See pp. 278, 279.) But in cases in which existing investments have been transferred to beneficiaries those taken over by each beneficiary would be separately classified; the rest being included in one class

The balance of investments and the particulars of which the balance consists will be brought down for division, and then those investments will be divided between the parties entitled in accordance with the terms of the trust   (See p. 226.)

It is obviously necessary that the schedule should accompany the account, as without it the legatee would merely have before him particulars of the receipts—the moneys come to the hands of the executors—and of the payments made by them; but these particulars in themselves would not be sufficient to prove that the balance on the account represented the residue of the whole estate; therefore, when the schedule is added to the Final Statement the residuary legatee has before him the whole of the material necessary for ascertaining the true residue   Further, the fact may be recalled that neither the Chancery Division, the Masters in Lunacy, nor the Bankruptcy Department of the Board of Trade, ever attempt the investigation of an account without having a schedule to work upon

Upon the determination of any trust the trustee is entitled to have the accounts of his administration of the trust property examined and settled by the beneficiary, and to receive an acknowledgment in writing, discharging him from any further liability in respect of the trust property thus accounted for. If the beneficiary refuses to grant such a discharge, the trustee is entitled to have his accounts taken by the Court

Trustees and executors usually ask for, and very often obtain, upon the final distribution of the estate, a release under seal from the beneficiaries who are *sui juris*, but as to releases, see Chapter XIII.

So far as the dealings with the estate are recorded in the accounts, then for a discharge to that extent the trustees can have nothing better than a copy of the final statement signed by the beneficiaries under a footnote as indicated in the precedent, p. 282, which in the event of a release also being taken will be referred to therein.

A copy of the income account from the death of the tenant for life, in which will be contained, by reference to an apportionment account, all income current at his death, will accompany this statement. Particulars of the apportionments will be supplied if called for.

In a statement for the beneficiaries such as that above described, the history of the trust is nicely focussed, and after there has been sent to the residuary legatee copies of (1) the will, (2) the schedule, (3) a statement for beneficiaries or the capital account and the summary thereof, together with the investment account, and the income account, as before described, it is difficult to see what further information can reasonably be asked for.

When income accounts have to be rendered periodically, they should be so arranged that the result of one year may readily be compared with that of any preceding year; the form of such accounts has been fully dealt with in Chap. VI. p. 69 *et seq*.

(*For specimen Final Statement, see pp.* 261—283.)

CHAPTER XI

A MARRIAGE SETTLEMENT TRUST

It will be found that the system which has been worked out in detail in the previous pages is one which is as appropriate for an estate subject to the trusts of a settlement as it is for one subject to the trusts of a will.

In the event of the practitioner having to keep the accounts of a marriage settlement trust, which includes personal estate and real estate conveyed upon trust for sale, he will proceed upon exactly similar lines to those which have been explained in the foregoing pages concerning the personal estate of the testator William Roberts, because the real estate has been converted, and in equity the whole property is deemed to be personalty, which avoids the necessity of keeping accounts of the real estate separate from those of the personal estate. On the other hand, if the marriage settlement trust, as is more often the case, does not include any real estate, then again the system already explained will be applicable. At the risk of some repetition, but in order to give another example involving the same system, a specimen of a marriage settlement trust account (in which no real estate is included) has been set forth in Appendix I.

It is not uncommon in practice to delay opening a marriage settlement trust account until long after the settlement has been perfected, but this practice is irregular and should be avoided. The husband is often a man of affairs, and very naturally manages the whole of the family business, arranging with the trustees what investments are to be made and deciding upon any changes in the existing investments which may become desirable. This, however, does not relieve the trustees of the obligation to keep strict accounts and to have them always ready for inspection; accordingly, as soon as the settlement has been perfected, an estate book should be prepared which will consist of—

(1) An Epitome of the settlement.
(2) The Memoranda.
(3) The Schedule.
(4) The Accounts.

There will be set forth in the epitome the parties to the deed, the short effect of any recital bearing upon the estate, the trusts in the fewest words possible, the powers of investment *verbatim*, the substance of the power to appoint new trustees, and any other extracts from the settlement which it may be thought desirable to include. It is better not to set forth in the epitome the particulars of the property settled, but in the appropriate place in the epitome reference should be made to the schedule for the particulars of the trust estate.

The memoranda will be utilised in a manner similar to that already explained in the case of a will, but no opportunity should be neglected of recording any events which may hereafter be useful in the administration of the trust as soon as they transpire and are discovered or notified: for instance, the place where and the date when the marriage of the settlor takes place, the name of each child born, and the place where and the date when the birth takes place. Similar entries might be made with regard to every death and every marriage of every person who could by any possibility become interested in the estate. It is impossible to mention all the occasions on which entries will be made in the memoranda: sufficient has been stated here and in Chapter III. to indicate the nature of the facts which should be recorded, and the details must be left to the discretion of the practitioner in each case.

There is but little to add to what has already been stated with regard to the preparation of the schedule: the form of it will be the same as that used for the testator's estate, the items will be taken from the settlement, and where each of the contracting parties brings property into settlement the schedule must be divided into two parts, the one being devoted to the "Husband's Trust Fund" and the other to the "Wife's Trust Fund." This is important, because at the beginning it is impossible to say which of the trusts in the settlement will ultimately take effect; but even after children of the marriage have been born and it has become highly probable that the ultimate trusts will never take effect, yet it is still necessary to keep separate records of the one fund and the other, as these will be wanted on the death of the respective settlors for the purposes of aggregation when ascertaining the rate at which duty is payable, and also for the purpose of determining the property in respect of which a claim for duty has then arisen

The items in the schedule will be numbered as before, and those which have a nominal pecuniary denomination will be entered in the accounts and discharged on the schedule as soon as they have been vested in the trustees.

The way in which reversionary interests and covenants to settle after-acquired property should be entered has already been fully described in Chapter IV., p. 39. Sooner or later the Revenue will want to be satisfied that duty was paid in respect of each legacy which accrued to the trust under the covenant, and for this reason there should be entered in the memoranda such particulars of the Inland Revenue accounts under which those duties were paid as will enable the Inland Revenue authorities to refer to their own entries and so satisfy themselves that the claim has been discharged.

With regard to the capital account. It would indeed be a surplusage to do more than direct attention to the fact that there will be opened a cash and investment account, divided into two parts, the one for the husband's trust fund and the other for the wife's trust fund, and the assets brought into settlement will be entered in the account in the same way as those of the testator, as already explained in Chapter V , those brought in by the husband being kept distinct from those brought in by the wife. These two funds must never be mixed for the reasons already explained.

Income, of course, will accrue, and in all probability will be received by the tenant for life direct. No question can arise as to any apportionment of a first dividend, because here there is a contract between the parties, whilst in the case of a will there is no such contract, neither can any question subsequently arise with regard to the apportionment of income under the rule in *Howe* v. *Earl of Dartmouth*, which does not apply in the case of a settlement by deed. (See *Re Van Straubenzee*, (1901) 2 Ch. 779.)

On the death of a tenant for life, an apportionment will become necessary, in order to ascertain the amount due to the executors of the deceased, and if there is no second tenant for life, the balance will be divided between those entitled in remainder. No account or apportionment of this income is included in Appendix I., because similar examples have been fully worked out in the earlier Appendices.

There should be a separate banking account for the trust, and the pass book with the counterfoils of the payment-in and cheque books will from time to time be examined and the balance at the bank (after allowing for all payments-in which have not been entered and all outstanding cheques which have not been charged) ascertained to agree with the balances on the accounts.

The epitome, the memoranda, the schedule and the accounts will be put together in the order mentioned, and made into an estate book in manner already described in Chapter II.

When a marriage settlement trust comes to an end and the fund has to be divided, the account should be submitted to the beneficiaries, and no better discharge can be taken by the trustees in respect of the receipts and payments mentioned in that account than that set forth in the precedent in Appendix I , pp 314, 315; but as to a release, see Chapter XIII.

(For specimen Marriage Settlement Estate Book, see pp. 289—315.)

CHAPTER XII

INVESTIGATION AND AUDIT OF TRUST ACCOUNTS

By virtue of the provisions contained in the 13th section of the Public Trustee Act, 1906, a solicitor may at any time be appointed to investigate and audit the condition and accounts of any trust.

Prior to the 1st January, 1908, when the above-mentioned Act came into operation, the only way in which an official investigation of a trust and audit of the accounts thereof could be obtained was through the instrumentality of the Courts. Now under this Act an official investigation and audit can be enforced without having to resort to the Court at all.

There is a very substantial difference in the final result which ensues after an account has been taken and certified by the Court and an audit of that account has been held and reported upon under the Act. In the former case the work proceeds in pursuance of an order made in some action, when the account is taken by one of the Masters of the Chancery Division, or by a Registrar of a County Court in the presence of the parties to the action, which include all those liable to account and some or all of the beneficiaries. Every question which arises is decided in the first instance by the master or registrar after hearing the parties, any of whom may appeal and require that every such decision should be referred to the judge himself. On the appeal the judge re-hears the case, and then gives his decision. After all questions have thus been disposed of, the master or registrar certifies the result, and in cases in the High Court, after eight days have expired since the certificate was filed the payment of any sum which is certified to be due can then be enforced, or in proper cases relief granted.

When an account is audited under the Act the Report is in the nature of an expert's report upon the trust accounts and the condition of the trust generally, after having examined all books, documents, and vouchers, and having been supplied with all necessary information and explanation at the hands of the accounting parties. If the auditor reports that any particular sum of money is due from the accounting party, there is no means of enforcing immediate payment or obtaining any relief without a substantive application to the Court.

The Provisions of the Act considered

It will now be well to carefully consider the provisions of the Public Trustee Act, 1906, and the rules made thereunder so far as is material for the present purpose.

The whole of the machinery in connection with the investigation and audit of trust accounts is contained in sect. 13 of the Act and Rules 31 to 37 and 40 and 41 of the Public Trustee Rules, 1912, made under the Act. This section and those rules are as follows :—

SECT. 13.—(1) Subject to rules under this Act and unless the Court otherwise orders, the condition and accounts of any trust shall, on an application being made and notice thereof given in the prescribed manner by any trustee or beneficiary, be investigated and audited by such solicitor or public accountant as may be agreed on by the applicant and the trustees or, in default of agreement, by the Public Trustee or some person appointed by him:

Provided that (except with the leave of the Court) such an investigation or audit shall not be required within twelve months after any such previous investigation or audit, and that a trustee or beneficiary shall not be appointed under this section to make an investigation or audit.

RULE 31 —Any application under sect. 13 (1) of the Act shall be made to the Public Trustee, and notice thereof shall (unless

INVESTIGATION AND AUDIT OF TRUST ACCOUNTS

the Public Trustee otherwise directs) be given by the applicant to every other person being a trustee or beneficiary under the trust

This obligation to give notice to every other person being a beneficiary under the trust unless the Public Trustee otherwise directs, will occasion applications for directions under Rule 41, *post*, *e.g.*, when it is not known where a beneficiary is, and indeed who he is and when infants are concerned. The notice may be served as provided by Rule 40, *post* (p. 147)

RULE 32 —(1) Upon receiving any such application the Public Trustee may in his absolute discretion by notice to the applicant require that before a day to be specified in the notice such security (by deposit of a sum of money) as he shall deem sufficient shall be given to him by the applicant for the payment of any expenses of the investigation and audit which may be ordered by the Public Trustee to be paid by the applicant personally.

(2) Where any such requirement is made no further proceedings shall be taken upon the application until the security has been given, and if the same is not given before the day specified in the notice the application shall be disallowed unless under special circumstances the Public Trustee thinks fit to extend the time for giving the security or to dispense therewith.

(3) Any sum so deposited shall be kept by the Public Trustee on deposit in his name and to a separate account at a bank until all proceedings in connection with the investigation and audit have been concluded, and thereupon the deposited sum and the interest (if any) allowed thereon by the bank shall be applied in or towards payment of any expenses of the investigation and audit which may be so ordered to be paid by 'the applicant personally and the balance (if any) shall be paid to the applicant

As to what expenses of the investigation and audit the Public Trustee may order to be paid by the applicant see sect 13 (5) of the Act and Rules 35 and 36 (2), *post*, and as to the fees of the Public Trustee see the Public Trustee (Fees) Order, 1912, *post* (p. 146).

RULE 33 —The Public Trustee may in his absolute discretion upon the application of any trustee or beneficiary direct that the investigation and audit shall extend only to a specified period of time or to a specified part of the trust property or shall be otherwise restricted.

The applicant should carefully consider over what period of time and in respect of what part of the trust property he asks for an audit and investigation. The Public Trustee now has power to limit the investigation and audit, but if on the report it shall appear to have been unnecessarily wide the applicant may find that an order is made against him personally to pay the whole or some part of the costs which have been incurred.

RULE 34 —If within one month from the date of the application under sect. 13 (1) of the Act no solicitor or public accountant shall have been appointed by the applicant and the trustees to conduct the investigation and audit, there shall be deemed to be a default of agreement within the meaning of the said sect. 13 (1) and the applicant may apply to the Public Trustee accordingly.

This limit of time was three months by the Rules of 1907.

Any beneficiary or trustee can apply for an investigation and audit of the condition and accounts of any trust at any time whatever in which he is interested, subject to the limit that except with the leave of the Court the application cannot be made within one year after there has been a prior audit. There is no limit backwards beyond which the audit is not to be extended, and therefore in a trust which has lasted thirty or forty years it is open to a *cestui que trust* to go back to the beginning unless the Court or Public Trustee otherwise orders, which means that the audit can only be prevented by an application to the Court or Public Trustee to stay the exercise of the *primâ facie* right conferred upon the beneficiary. The penalty for insisting improperly upon an investigation of the trust accounts is that to which the applicant is liable under the jurisdiction vested in the Public Trustee, to order the applicant to pay the costs of the audit (sect. 13 (5), and *Re Oddy*, (1911) 1 Ch. at 536), but the Public Trustee may have exercised his jurisdiction under Rule 33 of limiting the enquiry.

An application for an investigation and audit must be addressed to the Public Trustee, and may be sent to him by post at his office in London, or if the trust is being adminis-

INVESTIGATION AND AUDIT OF TRUST ACCOUNTS 141

tered in a branch office then at that branch office. It should state :—

(a) Particulars of the document (if any) creating the trust.
(b) The interest which the applicant has in the trust, and
(c) That a previous investigation and audit has not been required *and* made within a year from date.

At the same time as application is made to the Public Trustee notice thereof shall (unless the Public Trustee otherwise directs) be given by the applicant to every trustee and to every beneficiary under the trust.

The notice must also contain a request to the trustees or cotrustees, as the case may be, to join the applicant in appointing a solicitor or public accountant, not being a trustee or beneficiary, to conduct the audit and investigation. The service of this notice may also be effected through the post (preferably the registered post), addressed to the person to be served at his last known place of abode or place of business.

If within one month from the date of the application no solicitor or accountant shall have been appointed by the applicant and the trustees to conduct the investigation and audit, then the applicant may apply to the Public Trustee to do the work himself or appoint some solicitor or public accountant to undertake the work on his behalf.

Once the auditor has been appointed there is no authority vested in the parties to enter into any agreement limiting his powers or duties. He has statutory duties to perform, one of which is that at the conclusion of the investigation and audit he has to give a certificate that the accounts exhibit a true view of the state of the affairs of the trust, or that such accounts are deficient in such respects as he may specify.

The applicant himself, however, may, when making his application, place a limit on what he wants the auditor to do, but in the absence of any such limitation by the applicant or by the Public Trustee, or by order of the Court, the auditor must

,examine the whole matter from the beginning. (*Re Oddy,* (1911) 1 Ch. at 536.)

If the audit involves an account under which the applicant has no longer a beneficial interest on the ground of laches, or in consequence of the Statute of Limitations, then it would appear to be a case in which application should be made to the Court or the Public Trustee to limit the extent of the audit; or, again, when a reversioner applies for an audit, it might reasonably be limited to the capital account, as he could have no interest in the income. (*Re J. Williams, deceased* (1910), 26 Times Rep. 604, and Rule 33, *ante.*)

Suitable forms of application and notice under the Act will be found on pp. 148 and 149.

RULE 35.—The remuneration of the auditor and the other expenses of the investigation and audit shall be such as may be determined by the Public Trustee. Provided that the Public Trustee may refer the costs of any solicitor (being part of such expenses) for taxation to a Taxing Master of the Supreme Court, and in such case the amount of the said costs when taxed shall be included in such expenses.

This power to refer the solicitor's costs for taxation is new.

SECT. 13.—(2) The person making the investigation or audit (hereinafter called the auditor) shall have a right of access to the books, accounts, and vouchers of the trustees, and to any securities and documents of title held by them on account of the trust, and may require from them such information and explanation as may be necessary for the performance of his duties, and upon the completion of the investigation and audit shall forward to the applicant and to every trustee a copy of the accounts, together with a report thereon, and a certificate signed by him to the effect that the accounts exhibit a true view of the state of the affairs of the trust and that he has had the securities of the trust fund investments produced to and verified by him or (as the case may be) that such accounts are deficient in such respects as may be specified in such certificate.

By this sub-section the auditor is vested with all necessary authority to enable him properly to discharge his duties. He not only is to have access to all books of account and documents of the trust, but he may demand information and explanation from the trustees. (*Re J. Williams, deceased* (1910), 26 Times Rep. 604.) The details as to how the audit and investigation should be conducted and the contents of the report and certificate are all dealt with later on in this chapter

RULE 36.—(1) Where any investigation or audit has been made, copies of the report and certificate of the auditor under sect. 13 (2) of the Act and such copies of accounts and other documents as the Public Trustee may require shall be forwarded to him by the auditor, and shall be considered by the Public Trustee before giving any direction or making any order under sect. 13 (5) of the Act.

(2) The expense of making and forwarding any such copies as aforesaid and the fee of the Public Trustee (within the limits prescribed by or in pursuance of any order relating to the fees of the Public Trustee for the time being in force) shall for the purpose of sect. 13 (5) of the Act be part of the expenses of the investigation and audit.

This is new, and is a supplement to sect. 13 (2) of the Act.

SECT. 13.—(3) Every beneficiary under the trust shall, subject to rules under this Act, be entitled at all reasonable times to inspect and take copies of the accounts, report and certificate, and, at his own expense, to be furnished with copies thereof or extracts therefrom.

The auditor (under sect. 13, sub-sect. 2, of the Act, *ante*) has to forward to the applicant and to every trustee a copy of the accounts, together with a report thereon and a certificate. By sub-sect. 3 it would appear that every other beneficiary is entitled to inspect and take copies of " the accounts, report and certificate ": this apparently means that such a beneficiary is entitled to inspect and take copies of the originals, of which copies had been furnished to the trustees.

The right to inspect is merely declaratory of the existing law. The right to demand copies is new, because except under this section a beneficiary's right is generally to take copies.

The auditor has also, under Rule 36 (1), to forward to the Public Trustee copies of the report and certificate and such copies of accounts and other documents as the Public Trustee may require.

Sect. 13.—(4) The auditor may be removed by order of the Court, and if any auditor is removed, or resigns, or dies, or becomes bankrupt or incapable of acting before the investigation and audit is completed, a new auditor may be appointed in his place in like manner as the original auditor.

The Court alone has power to remove an auditor, but the power to fill up every vacancy, whether created by removal, death or otherwise, is vested in the same persons or person who had the power to make the original appointment.

Sect. 13.—(5) The remuneration of the auditor and the other expenses of the investigation and audit shall be such as may be prescribed by rules under this Act, and shall, unless the Public Trustee otherwise directs, be borne by the estate; and, in the event of the Public Trustee so directing, he may order that such expenses be borne by the applicant or by the trustees personally or partly by them and partly by the applicant.

INVESTIGATION AND AUDIT OF TRUST ACCOUNTS

RULE 37.—(1) Before making any order under sect. 13 (5) of the Act the Public Trustee shall, if any of the parties interested so desire, hear the said parties in such manner as he shall think fit

(2) Any such order shall specify the person by or to whom any sum is to be paid and the amount of such sum Provided that such an order may direct payment of the taxed costs of any solicitor employed in connection with the investigation and audit, and such costs shall be taxed by a Taxing Master of the Supreme Court, and the amount of such costs when taxed shall be paid as if such amount had been specified in the Order.

(3) Any such Order may be enforced in the same manner as a judgment or order of the Court to the same effect.

The rule by which trustees and the parties had power to agree the auditor's fee has been rescinded.

In the Public Trustee is now vested the power to direct how the costs of the investigation and audit shall be borne.

In the first place, the remuneration of the auditor and the expenses of the investigation and audit shall be such as may be determined by the Public Trustee (Rule 35), and the expenses of copies of the report, certificate and accounts supplied to him by the auditor are included in the term " expenses " as well as the fee of the Public Trustee   (Rule 36 (2).)

Secondly, the expenses shall, unless the Public Trustee otherwise directs, be borne by the estate. (Sect. 13 (5))

Thirdly, the Public Trustee can, in the exercise of his discretion, order the expenses to be borne by the applicant or by the trustees personally, or partly by the trustees and partly by the applicant (sect. 13 (5)), but before making any such order he shall hear any of the parties interested who desire to be heard. (Rule 37 (1).)

Lastly, any order which the Public Trustee makes shall specify the person by or to whom any sum is to be paid and the amount of such sum. It may also direct payment of the costs of the solicitors employed in connection with the investigation and audit. (Rule 37 (2), and Public Trustee (Fees) Order, 1912.) In case the applicant is ordered to pay the expenses, the deposit made by him, with any interest thereon, shall be applied in or towards payment of such expenses. (Rule 32 (3).)

The order is enforced in the same manner as a judgment or order of the Court. (Rule 37 (3).)

In a proper case the expenses will come out of the estate, but upon an unnecessary and vexatious application, the Public Trustee was upheld in ordering the applicant to pay the expenses of the audit. (*Re Oddy*, (1911) 1 Ch. 532; and *Re Utley, Russell* v. *Cubitt*, (1912) W. N. 147.)

The order of the Public Trustee can be appealed under sect. 10 of the Act, and he is not made a respondent. (*Re Oddy*, (1911) 1 Ch. 532.)

Audit fee in respect of the duties of the Public Trustee under sect. 13 of the Act.

Upon the performance of any duty under that section such fee not being less than 5s. or more than 5l. as the Public Trustee shall determine in each particular case, regard being had to the time and trouble involved, the value of the estate and the other circumstances of the case. (The Public Trustee (Fees) Order, 1912.)

SECT. 13.—(6) If any person having the custody of any documents to which the auditor has a right of access under this section fails or refuses to allow him to have access thereto or in anywise obstructs the investigation or audit, the auditor may apply to the Court, and thereupon the Court shall make such order as it thinks just.

Reference must be made to sub-sect. 2, *ante*, to ascertain what documents the auditor has a right of access to.

Any application by the auditor under this section is made to the Chancery Division by an originating summons (*Re J. Williams, deceased* (1910), 26 Times Rep. 604), and any order then made would be enforced by a subsequent application for leave to issue a writ of attachment or for an order of committal for contempt of Court. (See Ord. XLIV. of the Rules of the Supreme Court.)

INVESTIGATION AND AUDIT OF TRUST ACCOUNTS

SECT. 13.—(7) Subject to Rules of Court, applications under or for the purposes of this section to the High Court shall be made to a judge of the Chancery Division in Chambers.

SECT. 13.—(8) If any person in any statement of accounts, report, or certificate required for the purposes of this section wilfully makes a statement false in any material particular, he shall be liable on conviction on indictment to imprisonment for a term not exceeding two years, and on summary conviction to imprisonment for a term not exceeding six months, with or without hard labour, and in either case to a fine in lieu of or in addition to such imprisonment.

These provisions in sub-sect. 8 are new, and the consequence of a wilfully false statement in any material particular, either in an account, report or certificate, is most serious. Under this section a guilty trustee or auditor can be punished.

RULE 40.—(1) Any notice or application required to be given or made for the purposes of the Act or these Rules to the Public Trustee may be addressed to the Public Trustee at his office in London, or if the same relates to a trust or estate in course of administration or proposed to be administered from a branch office, then at that branch office.

(2) Any notice or application required to be given or made for the purposes of the Act or these Rules to any person other than the Public Trustee may be addressed to that person at his last known place of abode or place of business.

(3) Any such notice or application may be delivered at the place to which it is addressed or may be served by post.

RULE 41.—Where any person who (if not under disability) might have made any application, given any consent, done any act, or been party to any proceeding in pursuance of these Rules is an infant, idiot or lunatic, the guardian or (as the case may require) the committee or receiver of the estate of such person may make such application, give such consent, do such act, and be party to such proceedings as such person if free from disability might have made, given, done, or been party to, and shall otherwise represent such person for the purposes of these Rules. Where there is no guardian or committee or receiver of the estate of any such infant, idiot or lunatic, or where any person is of unsound mind or incapable of managing his affairs but has not been found lunatic under any inquisition, it shall be lawful for the Court to appoint a guardian of such person for the purpose of any proceedings under these Rules, and from time to time to change such guardian.

Proposed Form of

Application for an Audit

IN THE MATTER OF THE TRUSTS OF Mr. and Mrs. A. B.'s marriage settlement, dated the   day of   , 19 , *or* the will of A. B., late of   , in the county of   , proved on the   day of   , 19 , in the   registry at   , the testator having died on the   day of   , 19 (*a*)

and

IN THE MATTER OF the Public Trustee Act, 1906.

I,   , of   , in the county of   , being [one of the trustees of the property subject to the above-mentioned trusts, *or* a beneficiary under the above-mentioned trust entitled to   (*b*)] Do HEREBY APPLY that the condition and accounts of the above-mentioned trust may [so far as . . . . (*c*)] be investigated and audited by such solicitor or public accountant as may be agreed upon by me and the present trustees of this trust within one month from the date of the receipt of this notice, or in default of agreement by you or some person appointed by you in accordance with the provisions and in pursuance of the powers in that behalf in the above-mentioned Act contained.

AND I DECLARE that such an investigation or audit has not been required and made within twelve months from the date hereof, and that the present trustees of the settlement (*or* will)

(*a*) Adapt to circumstances, but identify the trust.
(*b*) Adapt to circumstances.
(*c*) If a general audit is not demanded, here define clearly the limitations thereof. (See *ante*, p. 141.)

are   upon whom notice of this application has been served by posting the same on the day of the date hereof.

Dated this   day of   , 19 .

To   (d),

The Public Trustee.

(d) This notice must be addressed to the Public Trustee at his office in London, or if the same relates to a trust being administered from a branch office, then at that branch office. The notice may be delivered at the place to which it is addressed, or may be served by post.

Proposed Form of
Notice of Application

IN THE MATTER OF THE TRUSTS OF Mr. and Mrs. A. B.'s marriage settlement, dated the   day of   , 19 , (or) the will of A. B., late of   , in the county of   , proved on the   day of   , 19 , in the   registry at   , the testator having died on the   day of   , 19 (a)

and

IN THE MATTER OF the Public Trustee Act, 1906.

PLEASE TAKE NOTICE that I,   , of   , in the county of   [one of the trustees of the property subject to the above-mentioned trusts, *or* a beneficiary under the above-mentioned trusts entitled to   (b)] have this day made application to the Public Trustee that the condition and accounts of the above-mentioned trust may (*any limitation contained in the application will here be noticed*) be investigated and audited in accordance with the provisions in that behalf in the above-mentioned Act contained.

And take further notice that I DO HEREBY REQUEST you to join with me in appointing a solicitor or public accountant, not being a trustee or beneficiary under the trust, to conduct the aforesaid investigation and audit, and that in default of our being able to agree upon the person to be appointed I shall after the expiration of one month from the date hereof apply to the

Public Trustee to act himself or appoint someone in his stead to conduct the investigation and audit pursuant to the powers in that behalf which will then become vested in him.

Dated this   day of   , 19   (c).

To   (d).

(a) Adapt to circumstances, but identify the trust.
(b) Adapt to circumstances.
(c) To bear same date as the application to the Public Trustee.
(d) If the applicant is a beneficiary this notice must be addressed to and served upon every trustee and other beneficiary; if the applicant is a trustee this notice must be addressed to and served upon each co-trustee and upon every beneficiary under the trust. The notice may be delivered at the place to which it is addressed, or may be served by post.

The following may be taken as a precedent for an auditor's report:—

Proposed Form of
Report and Certificate

IN THE MATTER OF   .

I   , of   , in the county of   , the solicitor appointed in this matter on the   day of   , 19 , by   , in pursuance of the powers in that behalf contained in sect. 13 of the Public Trustee Act, 1906, do hereby report that I have completed the investigation and audit of the condition and accounts of the above-mentioned trust (*any limitation of the general audit will here be noticed*), and hereby certify that the account set forth in the first schedule hereto exhibits a true view of the state of affairs of the trust (*any limitation of the general audit will here be noticed*).

(*Or*, I have to report that the accounts are deficient in the following respects (*here the deficiencies must be specified*).

And I certify that the securities of the trust fund investments which are specified in the second schedule hereto have been produced to and verified by me (or that such securities are deficient in the following respects) (*here the deficiencies must be specified*).

Dated this   day of   , 19   .

                                                                    Auditor.

The First Schedule above referred to.

The Second Schedule above referred to.

The Audit

It will have been noticed that sect. 13 (1) of the Public Trustee Act, 1906, provides for the investigation of the condition as well as for the audit of the accounts of a trust. The principles underlying such an audit will next be considered and the investigation subsequently, because the accounts must be audited before the condition of the trust can be ascertained.

Audits of commercial accounts are quite general at the present day, and, indeed, in the case of limited companies they are obligatory.

The object of a commercial audit is to ascertain that just and true accounts have been kept in accordance with the custom of the particular trade; that all partnership regulations (if any) have been complied with, and then finally to ascertain the profit or loss made or sustained during the period of account.

The duties of an auditor of a limited company have been defined by sect. 113 of the Companies (Consolidation) Act, 1908, and explained in *Cuff* v. *London & County Land & Building Company*, (1912) 1 Ch. 440, and in *Republic of Bolivia, &c., Ltd.*, (1914) 1 Ch. 139.

The principles upon which a commercial audit is to proceed have not been defined by the legislature, neither have they been precisely determined by the Courts; but in two cases at least judges have indicated certain duties which devolve upon auditors of commercial accounts. In those cases they have laid down the following principles as applicable to the facts then under review, which principles would presumably apply (*mutatis mutandis*) to an audit under the Public Trustee Act :—

(a) It is the duty of an auditor not to confine himself merely to the task of verifying the arithmetical accuracy of a balance sheet, but to inquire into its substantial accuracy and see that it was properly drawn up, so as to contain a true and correct representation of the state of the affairs of the business under audit. (*Leeds, &c. Co.* v. *Shepherd* (1887), 36 C. D. at p. 802.)

(b) It is not the duty of an auditor to consider whether a business is prudently or imprudently conducted, yet it is his duty to consider and report whether the balance sheet of such business exhibits a correct view of the state of affairs and the true financial position at the time of the audit. He must ascertain this by examining the books, and must take reasonable care that what he certifies as to the financial position is true, and, except in very special cases, it is his duty to place before the parties interested the necessary information as to the true financial position, and not merely to indicate the means of acquiring it. He must be honest, *i.e.*, he must not certify what he does not believe to be true, and he must take reasonable care and skill before he believes that what he certifies is true. (*London, &c. Bank*, (1895) 2 Ch. at p. 673.)

(c) " I do not subscribe to the doctrine that his (the auditor's) " sole duty is to see whether there are vouchers, appa- " rently formal and regular, justifying each of the " items in respect of which the authority seeks to get " credit upon the accounts put before the auditors for " audit. I think that is an incomplete and imperfect " view of the duties of the auditors. I think an " auditor is not only entitled, but justified and bound " to go further than that, and by fair and reasonable " examination of the vouchers to see that there are not,

INVESTIGATION AND AUDIT OF TRUST ACCOUNTS 153

"amongst the payments so made, payments which are
"not authorised by the duty of the authority or con-
"trary to the duty of the authority or in any other
"way illegal or improper. If he discovers that any
"such improper or illegal payments appear to have
"been made, his duty certainly will be to report to
"the authority." (Lord Russell, L.C.J., *Thomas* v.
Devonport Corporation, (1900) 1 Q. B at 20 and 21.)

(d) It is not the duty of an auditor to take stock. It had been said that an auditor was not a detective; it was his duty to exercise what was reasonable care in the circumstances. (*Re Kingston Cotton Mill* (No. 2), (1896) 2 Ch. 284.) The most that could be said was that he must make a reasonable and proper investigation of accounts and stock sheets, and if a reasonably prudent man would have concluded on that investigation that there was something wrong it was his duty to call his employer's attention to the fact. In making his investigation he would be entitled to rely on documents vouched by servants of the business at whose accounts he was looking, unless there were some reason for believing those servants to be dishonest. (*Henry Squire, Cash Chemist (Limited)* v. *Ball, Baker & Co.*; *Mead* v. *Same*, Times, 17th February, 1911. See also *Republic of Bolivia, &c., Ltd.*, (1914) 1 Ch. 139.)

The audit of a trust account is not yet general, but is becoming more common, and it is encouraged by the Public Trustee Act, 1906. In auditing the accounts of a trust there is no question of profit or loss ; accordingly no balance sheet is involved.

Whenever a business forms part of the trust estate there must be supplemental accounts of that business kept in the usual commercial form, and the resultant figures will be brought into the trust account when ascertained.

The duty of an auditor of a trust estate may be thus summarized :—

He must ascertain all the items of property which have at

any time been subject to the trust, see that all have been dealt with in a due course of administration, that all necessary apportionments have been made, that all capital and income have been duly accounted for, and that for these purposes all proper accounts have been kept and entries made therein.

The objects of a trust audit are:—To ascertain all assets which at any time formed part of the trust estate, to see that all such assets have been dealt with in a due course of administration, to discover any devastavit, and to see that all capital and income have been paid at due dates to the parties entitled.

No doubt the principles which should guide the auditor in commercial cases as laid down in the judgments already referred to apply to all auditors alike, but the chief point of difference between a commercial and a trust audit is that in the former case the auditor is concerned to ascertain what profit has been made or loss sustained, whilst in the latter case he is not concerned with profit or loss, but his duty is to see whether the administration has proceeded in accordance with the rules of equity as modified, if at all, by the trust instrument. The estate takes any profit that may have been earned, and is liable to bear any loss that may have been sustained in a due course of administration. Thus it is quite immaterial whether any stocks belonging to the trust have risen or fallen in value while they were standing in the trustees' names, provided that the investments in the origin were properly made by the trustees. But if the trustee has made an illegal investment a material distinction arises between investments which are illegal because they are unauthorised and those which are illegal because they were not made with due caution, although otherwise coming within the class of securities authorised by the trust. (*Re Salmon* (1889), 42 Ch. D. 351.)

In the former case, that is, a wholly illegal investment, the *cestui que trust* must accept or reject it, and if he rejects it, the trustee upon making good the trust fund is entitled to have the investment returned to him, but if in fact he has realised it at a profit before the *cestui que trust* makes his election, then he must bring the profit into account, and if at a loss he must make good the loss.

In the case in which the money was invested according to the terms of the trust, though without due care, the investment was from the first a part of the trust estate; the trustee's liability here is to make good the loss occasioned by the improper investment, which liability may be enforced by making him pay the deficiency after realising the security. But where the investment is that of a mortgage, made without due care, there the trustee is entitled, by virtue of sect. 9 of the Trustee Act, 1893, to insist upon the mortgage being taken for such smaller sum as would have constituted a good security, and thereupon he becomes liable only to make good the sum advanced in excess of such smaller sum. Before, however, this section can be applied the security must be found to have been a proper investment in all other respects.

Payments made in respect of an unauthorised security, *e.g.*, expenses incurred in respect of an unauthorised leasehold mortgage security, cannot be charged against the trust estate.

The Conduct of the Audit

It will now be useful to explain in some detail how the audit of a trust account should be conducted, but before proceeding the auditor is reminded to keep two facts constantly before him: the one is that when he has completed his work he will have to render an account to the trustees and certify that it exhibits a true view of the state of affairs of the trust (subject to any named exceptions); the other is that he must take reasonable care and skill to verify the statements and figures of the trustee before he accepts and certifies them to be true.

Analysis of the Trust.—In the first place the auditor must make himself thoroughly familiar with the terms and provisions of the trust instrument, and for that purpose he will examine the probate or deed of settlement and prepare a careful analysis thereof.

The following points should be noted:—

(a) The beneficial interests, the legacies and duties (if any) to be paid out of the estate.
(b) Who have been and who are now the duly appointed trustees.
(c) Any special powers given to the trustees, *e.g.*, to carry on a business.
(d) The terms of the investment clause (if any).
(e) Any difficulties of construction.
(f) Any apportionments which may be involved.
(g) The death duties payable and the persons or estates respectively liable to pay or bear them.
(h) Any advancements which may have to be brought into account, and
(i) Any other special matters to be borne in mind.

As the audit proceeds memoranda should be made of any and every devastavit, irregularity, omission, or other mistake discovered in the administration of the estate, which will have to be satisfactorily explained by the trustees and in default reported upon.

The Different Kinds of Accounts.—Having made an analysis of the trust, the auditor will in the next place direct his attention to any accounts which the trustees may have kept. These must now be examined generally in order to thoroughly understand the system adopted.

If the system prescribed in this work prevails there will be a schedule of original assets and a cash and investment account.

In other systems, besides the account of cash receipts and payments, a separate account is opened in a ledger for every investment.

In yet other cases a cash account only is kept without any schedule, and no attempt is made to preserve a continuous record of the investments which from time to time may have been held by the trustees.

Again, the auditor will sometimes find, particularly in the case of settlements, no account whatever, but a history, more or less complete, of all dealings with the trust estate contained in recitals in appointments of new trustees, releases and other such-like documents, and sometimes in memoranda endorsed on the settlement itself.

In the cases in which there is no account, or no sufficient account, the auditor must prepare his own from the commencement of the trust.

The Original Assets.—If no schedule is supplied by the trustee, then a schedule of all the original assets brought into trust must be prepared.

Little or no difficulty will generally be experienced in preparing the schedule of assets included in a settlement, because the deed itself usually describes them. If any estate or succession duty accounts have been passed under the settlement, such accounts must be examined in order to see what then were the trust assets

More difficulty may be experienced in preparing the schedule of assets constituting a testator's or an intestate's estate. To discover these resort must, in the first instance, be had to the original draft affidavit or corrective affidavits filed with the Inland Revenue; then, in order to make certain that nothing has been omitted from those affidavits, further search may have to be made through the deceased's ledgers and his other books in which any trace of property or investments is likely to be found. When examining these books, search should be made for records of any advances made to any child of the deceased or to any other person to whom he had placed himself *in loco parentis*, which may have to be brought into account. The deceased's pass book will often contain entries relating to his income, and thus afford a clue to some assets. It may also be necessary to refer to bankers, estate and other agents to obtain information on the subject.

A list of all property and investments held by the deceased at any time during the twelve months prior to his death should be prepared. This can easily be done by adding to the copy schedule (referred to on p. 156) any necessary items. Having such a complete list, it remains for the auditor to ascertain what has become of the added items—most likely they were sold by the deceased; but whatever may be the fact, the auditor must find it out and satisfy himself that the executors have no right to or interest in any of such added items

It should be borne in mind that a trust estate may be increased—

    (a) In the case of a settlement by the operation of a covenant to settle after-acquired property.
    (b) In the case of a will or an intestacy, by further property falling into the estate.

The possibility of these events happening must not be lost sight of; indeed, in the former case, specific enquiry should be made of the covenantor whether, since the date of the settlement, any property has accrued which could be caught by the covenant. In cases where further property falls in it is often necessary to prepare a separate account of such, because duties, hotchpot clauses, appointments and expenses different from those in the original trust will often attach. In each of the cases above mentioned where additional property is said to have accrued the auditor must satisfy himself that such is the fact, and in these and all other cases he must be quite sure that property is not in the hands of the trustee which does not strictly form a part of the capital of the trust fund.

As soon as the auditor is satisfied that he has a perfect schedule of original assets to work upon, then a copy with a wide margin should be made for use in the course of the audit. A note may be inserted in this margin against every asset which the trustees have no power to hold. Specifically devised or bequeathed property mentioned in the schedule will be marked off as soon as the auditor is satisfied that the executors have consented to the gift. He will also see that there is evidence to shew that the trustees hold such property upon the trusts of the will or settlement in question.

Enquiry should be made as to any incumbrance affecting the trust estate, and in the case of a mortgage created since the death, it should be seen that there was power to create it.

Capital Cash Receipts.—All moneys received on account of the trust by or on behalf of the trustees must appear in the accounts, and the auditor must satisfy himself that the items have been carried to the appropriate accounts, and that the sums entered represent the full amounts receivable, in a due course of administration. He will call for and examine such evidence as can be supplied in support of each item of receipt, and judge for himself as to the sufficiency of such evidence. On the sale of land all necessary evidence will generally be obtained from the contract and particulars of sale. In the case of debentures, stocks and shares, the information will be obtained from the broker's notes. When farming stock, furniture, stock-in-trade, &c., have been sold by auction, the auctioneer's account and his marked catalogue must be examined. In the case of a mortgage being paid off the draft mortgage with draft reconveyance or transfer may be called for.

Sometimes trustees have to receive a share in another trust. This is most common under marriage settlements; in such cases the auditor must examine that trust, so far as he may deem necessary, in order to satisfy himself that the cash and securities taken over represent the whole of the interest accruing to the trust under audit. In every case the best evidence procurable of the sufficiency of the amounts received must be obtained.

In cases where a net amount only is received, as, for instance, when an agent has paid tradesmen's bills out of money belonging to the trust in his hands, and then pays over the balance, all the deductions must be justified and properly vouched.

If the deceased died possessed of a business, a separate set of books belonging exclusively to that business will probably be found, but the auditor must, at the outset, see whether the business was insolvent, and whether it was carried on merely for the purposes of realisation, which should be the case in the absence of any special directions in the instrument of trust. In these cases the executors' receipts and payments in connection with the business would in principle be treated in the same way as any other of their receipts and payments, although the entries may have been kept in a separate cash book. Here in the absence of such authority the auditor must see that the business was not carried on for a longer time than was necessary in order to realise it to the fullest advantage. If, on the other hand, the business was left to trustees to be carried on for the benefit of a *cestui que trust*, then if the executors have consented to the gift the books of the business will be kept upon the ordinary commercial basis and audited accordingly; but in this case care must be taken to see that no fresh capital has been embarked in the business in excess of that (if any) expressly authorised by the trust.

In the event of the deceased having been a partner in a business at the time of his death, then the rights of the executors in that business will probably be regulated by the articles of partnership, and subject thereto they will be controlled by the Partnership Act, 1890.

If by inadvertence any item of income has been entered in the capital account, it must, of course, be transferred, and so *vice versâ*.

Apportionments.—It must be ascertained that all income accruing at the death, and the due proportion of income subsequently received in respect of securities the income of which has not been given to the tenant for life has been duly apportioned as between capital and income, and the amounts due to capital brought into account. For this purpose particulars of all such rents, interest and dividends must be prepared from the tenancy agreements, mortgage deeds and counterfoils of the dividend warrants, as the case may be, and the income on any such properties apportioned according to the principles explained in Chapter VII.

If regular apportionment accounts exist, it will still be necessary for the auditor to ascertain for himself what amounts are in fact apportionable, and then to agree the items in the accounts with his own list of what ought to be included. All these apportionments must be worked out in order to approve the results.

Where no apportionment account has been kept the auditor will generally find it useful to compose one for himself.

It will be found convenient to deal with all the items in the capital and income accounts which involve apportionment at one and the same time, picking them out wherever they appear, checking and marking them off.

Capital Cash Payments.—All moneys paid or allowed on account of the trust by or on behalf of the trustees must also appear on the accounts, and the auditor must satisfy himself that such moneys are properly payable or allowable out of that part of the estate against which they have been charged. Special attention should be directed to the payment of death duties, the liability in respect of which was ascertained when preparing the analysis of the trust, and a note must be made of any duties remaining undischarged. This is most important, because often the trustees, executors and administrators are personally liable in this behalf.

A stamped receipt must be produced for every separate payment of 2l. or over. Sums under 40s. should also be evidenced by vouchers as far as possible. When accounts are taken by the Court an item of 40s. or under is allowed without a voucher if the executor has sworn positively, and not as to his belief only, that the money was paid, giving the name of the person to whom and for what purpose it was so paid, but of course it is impracticable to obtain vouchers for some small payments. All vouchers when examined should be marked by the auditor as having been produced to and examined by him.

Evidence of the correctness of the amounts charged should be called for in some cases; for instance, when Stock Exchange investments have been purchased, the production of the broker's bought note should be required.

With reference to payments in connection with the deceased's business, see the observations concerning his business under Capital Cash Receipts, *ante*.

In the case of tradesmen's bills, full particulars of the work done or goods supplied must be furnished, and it should be seen that nothing has been included in respect of a period subsequent to the death of the deceased, and the deceased's account book should be examined in suitable cases to see that the bill has not been already paid, as accounts sometimes are by inadvertence rendered again after they have been paid.

The auditor should constantly keep before him the analysis which he made when reading the probate or settlement, and see that all the points then raised are being satisfactorily disposed of as he goes through the account.

Assuming that the examination of both sides of the capital cash account has now been perfected, reference in the next place must again be made to the schedule, and it must be seen that every item of cash mentioned therein has been duly brought into account, or sufficient reason given for those remaining on schedule which have not been so brought in. The extreme importance of this will be obvious.

If a separate banking account has been kept for the trust, the pass book must be examined, and it must be seen that all capital moneys paid into the bank, and all capital moneys paid by cheques drawn on that account, have been duly brought into account. Often an item in the pass book will be represented by several items in the accounts, some of which will appear in the capital and others in the income account, and sometimes in a separate loan account, but with the assistance of the counterfoils of cheques and payment-in slips the details of such an item in the pass book can generally be discovered, otherwise enquiry must be made.

Balancing.—It remains to ascertain and verify the amount of any cash in hand belonging to the trust. When one separate and continuous capital account has been kept, and assuming that account is not overdrawn, the balance on such account, together with that on any income or other open trust account, will represent the cash in hand. If the trustees have borrowed money the amount of any such loans still due and owing will be found in the list of incumbrances, and must be taken into account. In cases in which ledger accounts have been opened a balance must be struck on each trust account. Then all such balances shewing money in hand will first be added together, afterwards any remaining trust balances will be added together and the one total deducted from the other, when the result of such subtraction will represent the cash in hand.

A letter should now be obtained from the bank manager certifying the cash balance standing to the credit of the trustees' separate account on the day on which the books were closed for the audit. If any cheques had been drawn and entered in the accounts but not yet paid, the particulars thereof should be entered on the face of the bankers' letter, and the total amount of such outstanding cheques will then be deducted from the certified balance; the net result will be the same as the cash balance appearing on the trustees' capital and income accounts.

If no separate banking account has been kept, and if the trustees have not placed the cash balance on deposit, the auditor should report what balance is due from the trustees.

Sales, Purchases, Mortgages and Transfers of Investments.—Attention must now be directed to the investments as distinguished from cash. If the accounts have been kept upon the system prescribed in this work the face value of all securities belonging to the trust will have been debited and credited in chronological order in the account. In these cases it will be necessary in the first place to trace from the schedule to this part of the account every original investment having a pecuniary denomination received by the trustees.

Where, however, this system has not been adopted, it will be found convenient to prepare an investment account, entering in it at their face value all investments having a pecuniary denomination mentioned in the schedule, and which have been received by the trustees.

On the appropriate side of the cash and investment account, or in the investment account, as the case may be, every security purchased or otherwise acquired will be entered at face value; and in a similar manner every investment sold or transferred will be discharged.

If for any reason accounts such as those above described are not kept, then the auditor may work upon his copy of the schedule by striking off the items sold or transferred, putting against each the date of the sale or transfer, and adding at the end of the schedule of original assets particulars of all new investments. The items remaining at the finish should be those in hand at the date of audit.

When Stock Exchange securities have been purchased or sold, the brokers' bought and sold notes should be called for, to see that the amount of stock has been correctly entered in the accounts, and in the former case that the trustees had power to purchase the investment in question.

It must now be ascertained that all the unauthorised investments marked in the copy schedule were sold within twelve months from the death, and if not so realised the auditor must satisfy himself that there was no market or there was some other sufficient reason for the delay in realisation.

Where money is lent upon mortgage it should be seen that the valuation shewed at the date of advance at least the statutory margin of one-third, and that the advance was recommended by the valuer, and in the case of leaseholds that no underlease has been accepted as security.

When dealing with investments the auditor must see that they are authorised by the general law or the terms of the trust.

The Verification of Inscribed Stocks.—In cases in which no certificates for stocks are issued, as in the case of Consols, it must be ascertained that the stock stands solely in the names of the present trustees; this is done by one of the stockholders authorising the Bank of England, or other bank keeping the register of stockholders, to answer the auditor's enquiry.

Conversion of Stocks and Shares.—If stocks or shares have been converted, the terms and conditions of that conversion should be examined and the original investment discharged, the new investment being entered in lieu thereof. Any money receivable on conversion must be traced into the capital account, and if any options were granted to take new shares of which the trustees did not avail themselves, then such options should have been sold and the proceeds brought into account. Sometimes the investment is of a character different from that surrendered in exchange, so that on every conversion the invest-

INVESTIGATION AND AUDIT OF TRUST ACCOUNTS 165

ment clause must be referred to in order to see that there is power to hold the new stocks, shares or debentures, as the case may be, which otherwise must be sold and the proceeds reinvested in authorised securities.

Production of Deeds, Scrips, &c.—All deeds of the property subject to the trust must be ascertained to be in proper custody. All debentures, certificates of stocks and shares, bonds, mortgage deeds, bills, notes or other obligations, and all other securities or evidence of trust assets must be examined. It should be seen that all these are properly vested in the duly appointed trustees for the time being, and that bearer securities are deposited in the joint names of such trustees. If the examination of these securities and original documents cannot be completed at one appointment, then those which have been examined should be placed under the joint control of the trustees and auditor until the examination has been completed; after which everything will be restored to the original custodians at one and the same time.

Nothing short of the originals of these deeds, certificates, &c., can satisfy the auditor, and if they are not produced by the trustees themselves the auditor should see that they are held on behalf of the trustees by the individual producing them.

It is well to ascertain that all buildings are sufficiently insured, and that the policies stand in the names of the trustees alone, except in special circumstances, as, for instance, when the name of a lessor or mortgagor has to be included. For this purpose the policies, with the receipts for the current premium, must be produced. This is most important in the case of leaseholds, and in these cases the receipt for the last ground rent due should also be produced.

All furniture, plate, pictures, jewels, and other chattels should be scheduled, and it should be ascertained that all these chattels are in the custody of the person entitled thereto.

They should also be insured in the names of the trustees

The trustees have power, under sect. 18 of the Trustee Act, 1893, to insure against fire any building or other insurable property up to not exceeding three-fourths of the value thereof, and pay the premiums out of income or out of the income of any other property subject to the same trusts. (See *Re Earl of Egmont*, (1908) 1 Ch. 821)

Capital Payments and Transfers to Beneficiaries —It must be ascertained that every beneficiary has received all the cash, capital and investments due to him or her, or that the same are now available and that the beneficiaries to whom payments or transfers have been made were of full age at the respective dates. In the case of married women, enquiry must be made as to whether any settlement or agreement for settlement affecting the lady's interest in the trust is in existence, and in all cases every notice of incumbrance received by any trustee must be examined and enquiry made to see that the assignees have been satisfied

Advances to beneficiaries under a power must be enquired into, and it must be seen that the power has been strictly exercised in favour of the right person and the payment made out of the proper fund duly charged against the beneficiary in the accounts.

Appointments.—When cash or investments are paid or transferred in pursuance of appointments, the documents must be examined to see that the power was strictly exercised in all respects and proper entries traced into the accounts. Unless the fund is appointed "clear" or "net" or "free from all deductions," or in some other similar terms, the fund must bear its own legacy or succession duty, estate duty and share of trustees' costs, charges and expenses.

Outstanding Assets.—These remain to be considered A line must be drawn at the foot of the schedule, and every item examined Those which have been discharged by transfer or otherwise will be marked off ; the rest must be brought down and re-entered under the line drawn at the foot. Then a balance must be struck on the investment columns of the capital account, and details added shewing of what that balance consists. It must be seen, as already explained, that all the deeds of the properties remaining in schedule and all the documents of title relating to the trust investments included in the balance have been produced by the trustees or by the agent holding these documents on their behalf, and that any cash balances are in hand as already explained.

Income Account.—The examination of the capital account having been completed, the auditor will at this stage direct his attention to the income account

Particulars now exist of all assets which at any time have been subject to the trust. The first step will be to ascertain that all income accruing due at the death has been duly apportioned between capital and income, and the proportion belonging to income has been brought into account. Further, that the due proportion only of any income subject to the rule in *Howe* v. *Earl of Dartmouth* has also been brought into this account. All this will be accomplished in the manner already described in Chapter VII.

The rents payable for the houses and lands held in trust and the repairs falling on the landlord will be found from the leases and tenancy agreements.

The amounts of the dividends payable from time to time in respect of stocks and shares and other such like investments will generally be evidenced by the counterfoils of the dividend warrants, but in the case of Government securities the amounts payable are too well known to require proof; in other cases where no counterfoils are issued some other evidence must be procured. The rate of interest on mortgages, bonds, &c., will be ascertained from the securities or other obligations to pay.

It will now have to be ascertained that all rents, dividends and interest which have accrued due have been either collected and brought into account, or have been carried forward or discharged for sufficient reason. For this purpose the auditor will take the copy schedule and see that the income accruing in respect of every item has been duly accounted for in each year, bearing in mind to correct the schedule from time to time as sales are effected, new investments purchased, or other alterations made in the trust estate.

The ground rents, rates, taxes, repairs, insurances, expenses of collection and management will now be enquired into, and the vouchers appertaining to each examined and marked. The auditor must satisfy himself that all such are proper to be paid or allowed. Vouchers, where possible, must be produced for all deductions.

Evidence must be furnished that the balance of all such income has been duly paid to the parties entitled if *sui juris*, or has been properly invested, if held over in trust for an infant or other person under disability.

Generally.—The auditor must realise that it is his duty to detect any error of omission or commission which may exist, and to satisfy himself, as far as he possibly can, that the estate has been duly and properly administered in accordance with the general law as modified or enlarged by the trust instrument (if any).

The Investigation of the Condition of the Trust

The duties of an auditor when acting under the provisions of the Public Trustee Act are not at an end when he has completed his audit and ascertained and brought down the balances, because he has also to investigate the condition of the trust.

For this purpose he will again approach the trust as a whole, bearing in mind the cash balances and the trust assets and securities, which he has satisfied himself are in existence.

Any outstanding queries raised in the analysis of the trust and in the memoranda of the audit must be enquired into, and if there are any which cannot be satisfactorily explained, or which have not been satisfied, the same must be reported upon. If any breach of trust or devastavit has been discovered the irregularity may be made good by the trustee, but, where that is impossible, it must be reported upon.

Care should be taken to see that all duties, particularly estate duty, succession duty, legacy duty, and the old settlement estate duty when it applies, have all been paid out of the proper funds; that interest has been paid on legacies in cases where interest is payable. A common error in this respect is with regard to legacies given to infants, who are, on attaining majority and in the absence of special direction to the contrary, entitled to the capital sum bequeathed, together with interest at 4 per cent. per annum from the expiration of one year from the death to date of payment. They are not bound to accept any investment with the dividends thereon as representing such legacy.

Sometimes an executor or administrator is guilty of a devastavit by (1) paying excessive sums for a funeral; (2) carrying on a business, (3) neglect in compelling payment of a debt; (4) neglect in realising assets; (5) neglect to invest moneys in hand; or (6) by allowing an agent to retain moneys for too long a period of time (a).

It does not, however, follow that every breach or devastavit must be made good by the trustee, for he may be entitled to the protection of the Statute of Limitations, or sect 8 of the Trustee Act, 1888 (*Re Blow*, (1914) 1 C. D. 233); or he may be entitled to relief on the ground that he had acted honestly and reasonably (sect 3 of the Judicial Trustee Act, 1896).

It is, of course, impossible to anticipate all that the auditor may be called upon to do when investigating the condition of the trust. It is only possible to speak generally by reminding him that he must do whatever is necessary to enable him at the finish to certify that the accounts which he renders to the trustees exhibit a true view of the state of affairs of the trust, subject to any exceptions which he may have to report upon.

The notes which the auditor should have made in the course of his audit under this section as already suggested will, in most cases, have supplied the bulk of the material for the investigation ; indeed, seldom will an auditor when making the investi-

---

(a) As to the liability of an executor or administrator for his tortious acts, see Ingpen on Executors and Administrators, 2nd edit., chap. xlv., p. 654.

gation come across an irregularity which he might not have discovered in the course of the audit, but it may be useful to look over the auditor's reminders on pp. 171 to 191, *post*.

The Auditor's Report, Certificate and Account

Upon completion of the investigation and audit the Act requires the auditor to forward to the applicant and to every trustee—(1) A copy of the accounts; (2) a report thereon; (3) a certificate signed by him to the effect that the accounts exhibit a true view of the state of the affairs of the trust, and that he (the auditor) has had the securities of the trust fund investments produced, and that they have been verified by him, or (as the case may be) that such accounts are deficient in such respects as may be specified in such certificate.

The auditor must also forward to the Public Trustee copies of the report and certificate and such copies of accounts and other documents as he may require.

The accounts to be forwarded will first claim attention. The Act does not define what accounts are to be forwarded, but it cannot mean that copies of all the books of account are to be sent. Probably no great detail is contemplated by this section, and it is thought that the requirements of the statute would be fulfilled by a copy of the schedule, together with such an account as in the opinion of the auditor will present a true summary view of the dealings with and state of the trust; and the auditor should if necessary prepare such an account, the amount of detail involved depending upon the circumstances of each case

The preparation of the report will follow that of the account, and here the general condition of affairs must be described, and any breach of trust or deficiency in the accounts must be reported upon.

The report must conclude with a certificate that subject to the exceptions named, the accounts exhibit a true view of the state of affairs of the trust, and that the auditor has had the

INVESTIGATION AND AUDIT OF TRUST ACCOUNTS

existing securities of the trust fund investments produced to and verified by him; but if any security is wanting or unauthorised, or otherwise defective, that fact must be specially mentioned.

At the end of Chapter XIII. will be found a list of points which frequently arise in the administration of trusts. It is thought that this list may be useful to those engaged in investigations or audits.

CHAPTER XIII

RELEASES

WHEN an executor or administrator has paid the debts and legacies (if any) of the deceased and contemplates a distribution of the residue, or when trustees are in a position to hand over the trust funds to the persons ultimately entitled, the advisers of the executor, administrator or trustee must consider what discharge should be asked for on payment or transfer of the trust assets.

Before any discharge can be asked for the executors, administrators and trustees must render to their *cestui que trust* an account of the nature and origin of the trusts, and of their dealings with the trust property (*Lloyd* v. *Attwood* (1858), 3 De G. & J. at 649) For this purpose it is necessary to furnish complete accounts with full details, shewing what assets have been involved, how they have been dealt with, and what remain for distribution Further, it is the duty of these accountable parties to make their beneficiaries fully acquainted with their rights, and any irregularities or breaches of trust must be disclosed before they can be released. (*Cole* v. *Gibson* (1750), 1 Ves. Senr. 507; *Walker* v. *Symonds* (1818), 3 Swans. 58 et seq.; *Collyer* v. *Dudley* (1823), Turn. & R. 421; *Overton* v. *Banister* (1844), 3 Hare at 507.) Sufficient time must be given to these beneficiaries to investigate the accounts furnished and information supplied. (*Wedderburn* v. *Wedderburn* (1838), 4 My. & Cr. at 50.) The trustees should see that the beneficiaries have competent and independent advice during the investigation (*Lloyd* v. *Attwood, ante,* at p. 650; and *Rhodes* v. *Bate* (1866), 1 Ch. at 257), and this is particularly necessary when the relationship is that of parent and child (*Turner* v. *Collins* (1871), 7 Ch. 329), or a person *in loco parentis* (*Kempson* v. *Ashbee* (1874), 10 Ch. 15), or solicitor and client (*Wright* v *Carter*, (1903) 1 Ch. 27).

When the beneficiary has thus been fully informed as to his rights, the nature of the discharge which he should be called upon to give will have to be considered.

Here a distinction has been drawn in judgments of the Court between the right of an executor (and an administrator would appear to be on the same footing) and the right of a trustee. Thus in *King* v. *Mullins* (1852), 1 Dr. 308, Vice-Chancellor Kindersley is reported as saying:—

"It is true that in the common case of executors where the executor-ship is being wound up it is the practice to give executors a release. An executor has a right to be clearly discharged and not to be left in a position in which he may be exposed to further litigation; therefore he fairly says, unless you give me a discharge on the face of it protecting me I cannot safely hand over the fund, and therefore it is usual to give a release."

The practice so spoken of appears to have been confined to executors acting strictly in the capacity of executors, *i.e.*, where the estate was given direct to the legatees, and not through the medium of an express trust; for in *Chadwick* v. *Heatley* (1845), 2 Coll. 130, where the subject-matter under discussion was a reversionary estate given through the medium of a trust, it was held that a release under seal could not be required, Vice-Chancellor Knight Bruce saying as follows:—

"Upon the proposal being made to transfer the fund a release was required, that is a general release in respect of the estate, having the effect of closing the account, and discharging the then sole surviving trustee from all accountability in the matter, so far as it could be done: to this one beneficiary acceded. The deed was prepared for both, and might have been executed by both, and supposing both disposed to execute it, it seems to me unobjectionable The other beneficiary, however, did not avail himself of the opportunity of executing it, but declined to do so; and I, as at present advised, am not of opinion that it was competent to the surviving trustee to insist upon having that deed executed in the circumstances of this case or of any such case. Whether to execute such a deed would not have been a perfectly harmless and a reasonable course is a very different thing. But though it may not have been the right (and possibly

"it was not the right) of the trustee to require a deed, I think it
"was his right to require that his account should be settled, that is to
"say, that he and his family should be delivered from the anxiety (a)
"and misery attending unsettled accounts; the possible ruin which
"they who are acquainted with the affairs daily litigated in the Court
"of Chancery well know to be a frequent result of neglect in such a
"matter. . . . The trustee had a right to have his account gone through,
"examined and settled. Now this is what he did not require; he required
"a release. . If the matter were confined to the single question
"as to the balance of right or wrong in the institution of this suit . . .
"I should say that although in strictness a release by deed could not be
"demanded, yet there was nothing out of the ordinary course of busi-
"ness—nothing unreasonable in asking for it But what is the
"course taken on the other side? There is not only a refusal to
"execute the deed, which in my opinion was justifiable, but a state-
"ment that the plaintiff (the beneficiary) will execute no release,
"express or implied, and give nothing but a receipt for a particular
"sum. I think that was positively unreasonable If he was satisfied
"upon the account as sent in that nothing more was coming to him
"he should have expressed his willingness to close the accounts, on
"the other hand, if he was dissatisfied with it he should have asked to
"have the accounts taken."

Possibly at the date of the decisions quoted above a stronger claim to a release under seal was recognised on the part of an executor than on the part of a trustee by reason of the fact that the executor was liable to be sued in the common law courts, where equitable defences would have been of no avail, whereas the trustee could only be sued in equity If that be so, the reason of the distinction has ceased with the fusion of the legal and equitable jurisdictions, and certainly at the present time there appears to be no logical ground for any distinction between the two cases, the execution of a trust being often more complicated and difficult than the mere administration of an estate,

---

(a) The Trustee Act, 1888, sect. 8, has greatly alleviated the hardships alluded to by the learned Vice-Chancellor by extending to an honest trustee the protection of the Statute of Limitations. This enactment has reduced the importance of a release, insomuch as the lapse of time now to a great extent automatically releases an honest trustee Further, under sect 3 of the Judicial Trustees Act, 1896, the Court may now in a proper case release a trustee who has acted honestly and reasonably from the consequences of a breach of trust.

and it is thought very doubtful whether at the present time the Courts would recognise a stronger *primâ facie* claim to a release under seal on the part of an executor than on the part of a trustee.

The position at the present time may, it is thought, be summarised thus:—

(1) Apart from proved or admitted breaches of trust, trustees, executors and administrators alike, on handing over the fund to beneficiaries, are entitled to a full discharge in respect of all dealings with the trust estate that have been properly disclosed to the beneficiaries.

(2) In a simple case this discharge may take the form of a memorandum of approval written at the foot of the trustee's account, and signed by the beneficiaries, *e.g.*

"I, &c., approve and agree this statement of "account and agree to accept the sum of £ "thereby shewn to be due to me in discharge of "all claims upon the assets thereby disclosed."

(3) In a case where any difficulty or complication has arisen in the administration of the estate or execution of the trust, more particularly where the trust funds are large, it is thought that the trustees may properly require from the beneficiaries a more formal discharge with proper recitals setting forth the facts giving rise to the difficulty or complication or otherwise occasioning the proposal for a more formal discharge; and it is thought that in such a case a beneficiary willing to accept the position disclosed by the document could not reasonably refuse to execute the document as a release under seal, and it has always been and still is the custom in such cases to give a release under seal

If, however, an adequate discharge is offered in any other shape it is doubtful whether a deed could be insisted upon; but if no such alternative discharge were offered and a release were refused, the accounting parties would be entitled to have their accounts taken by the Court at the expense of the fund. (*Re Wright* (1857), 3 K. & J. 419; and *Chadwick* v. *Heatley* (1845), 2 Col 137.)

The authorities appear in some particular cases to be somewhat inconsistent in dealing with the rights of a trustee to a discharge on distributing the trust estate; for where the beneficial interest had become vested in other trustees, *e.g*, the trustees of a sub-settlement (*Re Cater's Trust* (No. 2) (1858), 25 Beav. 366), or in executors of an appointor under a general power (*Re Hoskin* (1876), 5 C D. 229), or even in an ordinary beneficial assignee (*Re Foligno's Mortgage* (1863), 32 Beav. 131), it was held in the cases cited that nothing more could be claimed from the sub-trustees, executors or assignees than a simple receipt, it was, however, said by Lord Romilly, M.R., in *Cater's Trusts* (*supra*) that on payment to the trustees of a sub-settlement the head trustees would be entitled to a discharge from the original beneficiary. This may well have been the case at the date of the decision, insomuch as before the Judicature Act the original beneficiary would have been required to be made a party to any action to recover the trust fund from the trustee or to complain of a breach of trust, so that a discharge from him to the trustee may well have been effective; but since the Judicature Act (sect. 25 (6)) the original beneficiary drops out completely after an assignment of his share, so that any discharge to the trustee by him would be wholly inoperative; and if the trustee cannot ask for more than a simple receipt from the sub-trustee or assignee he could obtain no discharge from anyone; and having regard to the altered position of an assignee since the Judicature Act, and to the wide powers of trustees under sect. 21 of the Trustee Act, 1893 (which enables trustees to settle accounts, make compromises and give releases), it may be that the Courts would now treat the decisions in the cases cited above as open to reconsideration.

At all events it would *primâ facie* be the duty of a trustee of a sub-settlement, upon taking a transfer or payment of his settled share, to examine the accounts of the head trustee in order to satisfy himself that he is getting all that he is entitled to under his assignment; and there would appear to be no hardship in requiring him, when he has done so, to exercise for the benefit of the head trustee his power of settling the account so as to relieve the head trustee from liability to future attack. Failing this the head trustee would, where there has been an assignment, obtain no adequate protection unless he takes the risk of applying to the Court to take his accounts, when he would be only too likely to be called upon to pay the costs.

On the whole it is the editors' opinion that the sub-trustee or assignee ought to examine the account of the head trustee, and ought in a straightforward case to give a proper discharge if, when he has done so, he has found the account correct (being completely protected in giving such a discharge by sect. 21 of the Trustee Act, 1893), but in any case of doubt, difficulty or complexity it is thought that a sub-trustee could not ordinarily be required to take the responsibility of giving a release, though if he regards it as a proper case for a release and decides to give one he will not expose himself to any liability to his new beneficiaries. If no adequate discharge is offered the head trustee may be driven in such case to choose between foregoing his discharge or taking the risk of an application to the Court, and in most cases the former alternative would be the proper one to choose, but in the editors' opinion an ordinary assignee of a beneficial interest ought to be treated as on precisely the same footing as the original beneficiary.

In conclusion, it may be stated that it is the duty of beneficiaries and trustees to be reasonable, and that the Court would be apt to look with disfavour upon a trustee who held out for a release under seal when an adequate discharge was offered in some other form, or upon a beneficiary who obstinately refused a release under seal where the trustees on any reasonable ground desired it. The net substance of the matter is that the trustees should have a clear deliberate admission that the beneficiary has agreed to accept the sum offered him in discharge of his claims, and that he has had before him all material facts before deciding so to agree.

When preparing a release the principles to be observed have thus been described in Davidson's Precedents, 2nd ed., Vol. V., Part II., p. 624: " Great care is requisite in framing the recitals in a release, and the recitals should explain in detail the origin of the claims to be released, and all the circumstances which have arisen in connection with them, and the manner in which they have been satisfied, or why it is intended to release them, and the title of the persons to give the release. In doing this, it is proper to set out, as concisely as practicable, every trust or clause under which the claims have arisen, or which in any way may affect them, and to state the subsequent material facts exactly as they have occurred, and where breaches of trust have been committed, they should be stated and treated as such. In short, every circumstance should be stated, to put the releasors in possession of every material fact, so that it cannot be said that they acted in ignorance of their rights, or were not aware of what they were doing," otherwise they will subsequently be entitled to enforce those rights when they are discovered, and the release will be no bar to the claim then put forward.

No general words, however sweeping, will extend to release any other claims than those specified or indicated in the deed (*Pritt* v *Clay* (1843), 6 Beav. 503).

Releases often contain covenants of indemnities against doubtful or possible claims, and the necessity of such a covenant is frequently the primary reason for giving the release. The accounts which have been agreed should be scheduled or identified.

AUDITOR'S REMINDERS

ACCOUNT RENDERED is an altogether insufficient voucher. Such a document, if receipted, would be evidence that a sum of money had been paid on a certain day to a person named, but would not shew on what account or for what purpose the money had been paid, to do that full details with dates must be given

ACCUMULATION OF INCOME, limit of, but excess only is bad, unless the rule against perpetuities is also infringed. (Thellusson Act, 1800 (39 & 40 Geo. 3, c. 98). See also Accumulation Act, 1892 (55 & 56 Vict. c. 58).)

ADEMPTION of a specific legacy of debentures may ensue in consequence of a conversion of the debentures into debenture stock or of a contract for sale.

ADEMPTION OF LEGACIES. Any such must be verified and noted.

ADVANCES must be deducted with interest at four per cent. from death. (*Re Davy*, (1908) 1 Ch. 61.) See also "Hotchpot," Chap. VIII.
What constitutes such (See *Re Scott*, (1903) 1 Ch. 1.)

ADVERTISEMENTS FOR CLAIMS—STATUTORY. Inquiry should be made as to what were issued.
Protection afforded by. (See 22 & 23 Vict. c. 35, s. 29.)

AFTER-ACQUIRED PROPERTY, Covenant to settle The moment the wife receives the money it becomes subject to the equity and can be followed. (*Pullan* v. *Koe*, (1913) 1 Ch 9.)

ALLHUSEN v. WHITTELL, rule in. (See Chap. VII, p. 103.)

ANNUITANT is not liable for estate duty, which will be paid out of capital, but interest on the amount of the duty will be charged against the annuitant. (*Re Parker-Jervis*, (1898) 2 Ch. 643; and in *Re Duke of St. Albans*, (1900) 2 Ch. 873)

ANNUITIES given by will are generally charged on capital in aid of income when deficient. (*Re Howarth*, (1909) 2 Ch. 19; *Re Young*, (1912) 2 Ch. 479.)

Arrears do not ordinarily carry interest (*Mansfield* v. *Ogle* (1859),

4 De G. & J. 38); *secus*, after judgment in administration action. (*Re Salvin, Worseley* v. *Marshall*, (1912) 1 Ch. 332.)

Annuity, arrears of, charged on corpus of personal estate, do not carry interest (*Torre* v. *Browne* (1855), 5 H. L. C. 555, and *Wheatley* v. *Davies* (1876), 35 L. T. R. 306), but arrears since an administration action has been commenced carry interest at 4 per cent. from the judgment. (*Re Salvin*, (1912) 2 Ch. 332.)

ANNUITY commences at death, and first payment is at end of the year from testator's death, unless otherwise directed. (*Gibson* v. *Bott* (1802), 7 Ves. 89.)

Annuity, deficiency of assets to meet. Value the annuity according to Government scale and treat arrears and valuation as a legacy of that amount (*Re Cottrell, Brickland* v. *Bedingfield*, (1910) 1 Ch. 402), except where annuitant a married woman restrained from anticipation or otherwise not absolutely entitled. (*Re Ross*, (1900) 1 Ch. 162.)

Any annuity which the deceased was personally liable to pay must be provided partly out of income and partly out of capital, as in *Re Perkins*, (1907) 2 Ch 596, and *Re Poyser*, (1910) 2 Ch. 444. See also pp. 109–110, *ante*.

ANNUITY. Funds set aside to meet and then proving to be insufficient —resort may be had to other estates originally charged. (*Evans' Contract*, (1910) 2 Ch. 438.)

ANNUITY of which the deceased died possessed must (apart from special directions) be sold and proceeds invested, and the interest of such investment will alone be paid to the tenant for life. (*Re Whitehead*, (1894) 1 Ch. 678.)

APPOINTMENT OF STOCK by life tenant subject to life tenancy. See p. 119, *ante*.

APPORTIONMENTS. See Chapter VII.

Rule in *Howe* v. *Lord Dartmouth* does not apply in the case of a settlement by deed. (See *Re Van Straubenzee*, (1901) 2 Ch. 779.)

APPROPRIATION. Whenever an executor appropriates any part of the estate in satisfaction of a particular legacy, the fund so appropriated becomes the property of the legatee, together with any accretions, and, subject to any losses, it ceases to form part of the testator's estate

APPROPRIATION, Power to postpone. Trustees cannot appropriate unauthorised securities to settled shares (*Re Craven, Watson* v. *Craven*, (1914) 1 Ch. 358), but they can appropriate to legatees being *sui juris* and sell the rest.

APPROPRIATION, without special power in the trust. Securities not authorised cannot be appropriated to settled shares. (*Re Beverly*, (1901) 1 Ch 681 and 688; and *Re Craven*, (1914) 1 Ch. 359.)

BONUSES ON LIFE POLICY are usually added to capital (*Macdonald* v. *Irvine* (1877), 8 C. D. 101); but it should be seen that they have not been specifically excluded.

BUSINESS, carrying on. Where executors in accordance with the provisions of the will and with the assent of the testator's creditors properly carry on his business, they are entitled to a complete indemnity out of his estate. (*Dowse* v. *Gorton*, (1891) A. C. 190—203.)

BUSINESS, PROFITS OF In addition to all sums actually expended in repairs and renewals, there should be written off a proper sum for depreciation of the machinery used in the business (*Thomas* v *Crabtree* (1912), 106 L T R 49)

CHARITY, gift to, is for the general purposes of the charity unless otherwise directed (*Society of the Deaf and Whittle's Contract*, (1907) 2 Ch. at p. 493.)

CHESTERFIELD'S CASE, rule in. (See Chap. VII., p. 110.)

COMPENSATION. Where licensed premises are settled and compensation paid for the extinguishment of the licence, the cash paid represents capital money of the estate. (*Re Bladon, Dando* v. *Porter*, (1912) 1 Ch 45)

CONVERSION OF REAL ESTATE. Shares of persons *sui juris* at the date of order for sale are converted by that order into personalty—all cases in which there is no conversion are cases of persons under disability. (*Herbert* v. *Herbert*, (1912) 2 Ch. 268.)

CONVERSION OF STOCKS AND SHARES BY RECONSTRUCTION, &c. The substituted investment, if not within the powers of the investment clause, must be sold, and the proceeds re-invested. (*Re New*, (1901) 2 Ch. 534, at p. 547.)

CONVERSION, trust for—with power to postpone—the power must be exercised by all the trustees or the trust prevails. (*Re Hilton*, (1909) 2 Ch 548)

COSTS OF ADMINISTRATION. If these have been increased by the administration of the real estate, the increase must be borne by the real estate accordingly, the costs of the inquiry as to an heir-at-law must be borne by the realty, and this is so notwithstanding a general direction in the will that the testamentary expenses should be paid out of personalty. (*Re Betts*, (1907) 2 Ch. 149.)

COSTS OF ASCERTAINING LEGATEES or next of kin come out of the general fund before residue can be arrived at. (*Re Giles* (1886), 34 W. R. 712; *Re Gibbons* (1887), 36 C. D. 486.)

DEATH DUTIES are now mainly regulated by:—
The Legacy Duty Act of 1796.
The Succession Duty Act of 1853.
The Finance Act of 1894, and
The Finance (1909-10) Act of 1910.
The Finance Act, 1914.

DEBTS AND LEGACIES charged on mixed fund. Each fund (real and personal) has to bear proportionately. (*Re Moore, Strickland* v. *London*, (1907) W N., p. 181.)

DEBTS, PRIORITY OF,
Crown Debts.
Friendly Society, sums due from officer of. (59 & 60 Vict. c. 25, s. 35.)
Judgments. If estate is insolvent and being administered in Chancery.

DEEDS, CUSTODY OF. See Title Deeds, *post*.

DEVASTAVIT or waste in an executor or administrator is when he doth misemploy the estate of the deceased and misdemean himself in the managing thereof against the trust reposed in him. (Sheppard's Touchstone, 485.)

DILAPIDATION money recovered from a lessee who holds from a tenant for life without impeachment of waste belongs to the tenant for life to use as he thinks fit (*Re Lacon's Settlement*, (1911) 2 Ch. 17; and *Re Dealtry*, (1913) W. N. 138); but money recovered by trustees for sale must be treated as *corpus* of the estate. (*Re Pyke*, (1912) 1 Ch. 770.)

DIRECTION TO PAY DUTIES may include settlement estate duty and estate duty on specifically devised real estate. (*Re Pimm, Sharp* v. *Hodgson*, (1904) 2 Ch. 345.) Also estate duty on deaths subsequent to that of the testator.

DISTRIBUTION OF ASSETS. Widow of a man dying intestate without a child is entitled to 500*l*. to be raised rateably out of his real and personal estates. (Intestates Estates Act, 1890.)

DOMICILE. If the domicile of the deceased was foreign, then generally estate duty is only payable in respect of real and personal estate situate in Great Britain or Ireland. Again, the validity of a gift of foreign movable property depends on the law of such domicile.

DONATIO MORTIS CAUSÂ takes effect only in the event of death, and must have been accompanied by actual delivery. (*Powell* v. *Hellicar* (1858), 26 Beav. 261.)

EMBLEMENTS pass to the executors.

ESTATE DUTY is payable out of capital. (Finance Act, 1896, s. 13.)
Interest thereon is payable out of income. (*Earl Howe* v. *Kingscote*, (1903) 2 Ch. 83.) But see *Re Wills*, (1915) 1 Ch. 769, in cases to which the rule in *Allhusen* v. *Whittell* applies. (See p. 103, *ante*.)
Estate duty on real estate is not a testamentary expense within the meaning of a direction for payment of testamentary expenses out of personalty. (*Re Sharman*, (1901) 2 Ch. 280.)
Estate duty on a fund appointed by will under a general power has now been held by the House of Lords to be payable out of the appointed fund. (*O'Grady* v. *Wilmot*, (1916) 2 A. C. 231, overruling *Re Hadley*, (1909) 1 Ch. 20.

EXECUTORS have power to compound or compromise debts. (Trustee Act, 1893, s. 21.)

EXECUTORSHIP EXPENSES. (See "Testamentary Expenses.")

FIRE INSURANCE Where trustees insure under sect 18 of the Trustee Act, 1893, or the tenant for life is under an obligation to insure, the insurance forms part of the settled property.
If tenant for life insures voluntarily, then—apart from the Fires Prevention Act of 1774 (14 Geo 3, c. 78, s. 83), which gives certain interested persons power to insist upon the buildings being reinstated—he is alone entitled to the policy money· and that would also be so in the case of chattels (*Re Bladon, Dando* v *Porter*, (1911) 2 Ch at 354.)

FIXTURES of a deceased person may be removed by his executor as against the landlord but not as against the heir of the deceased. (*Bain* v. *Brand* (1876), 1 A. C 767, 768)

FRIENDLY SOCIETY members over 16 may nominate in writing the person to receive money up to 100*l* payable on member's decease. (Provident Nominations and Small Intestacies Act, 1883, ss. 3—5; Industrial and Provident Societies Act, 1893, s. 25)

FUNERAL expenses should be reasonable having regard to the ostensible position of the deceased Those of a deceased known to be insolvent are generally fixed at a sum not exceeding 20*l.* (*Hancock v. Podmore* (1830), 1 B. & Ad. at 264.)

FURNITURE, should be insured by the trustees. The premiums may be charged against any income from property subject to the same trusts. (See *ante*, p. 165.)

GIFT OF RESIDUE, to convert and invest after payment of testamentary expenses. In such cases the expense of ascertaining persons entitled to a legacy falls upon residue, but any increase of such expense by legatee incumbering his share falls upon the legacy to the extent of the increase. (*Re Vincent*, (1909) 1 Ch. 810.)

GIFTS must vest within a life or lives in being and twenty-one years afterwards (*Cadell v. Palmer* (1832-3), 1 Cl & Fin. 372.)

HOTCHPOT. Advanced children must bring their advances into hotchpot with interest at four per cent. up to the actual distribution of the estate, such interest to be computed from the time when the estate vests in the children in possession whether by the death of testator or by death of life tenant or otherwise (*Re Rees* (1881), 17 C. D. 701. See also Chap. XIII.)

HOUSEKEEPING. Executors are allowed a reasonable time for breaking up a testator's domestic establishment and discharging his servants. (*Field v. Peckett* (No. 3) (1861), 29 Beav. 576.)

HOWE V. EARL OF DARTMOUTH, rule in. (See Chap. VII. p. 98.) Has no application to settlement by deed. (*Re Van Straubenzee*, (1901) 2 Ch. 779.)

INCOME TAX on annuity. See "Annuity."

INCOME TAX, RETURN OF. If the beneficiary is an infant, any return of income tax to which he may be entitled should be recovered by the trustees and brought into account.

INCREMENT DUTY. (Finance (1909-10) Act, 1910.)

INFANT'S LEGACY. A legacy given to an infant without the intervention of a trustee cannot be paid until majority, when he will be entitled to the legacy with interest at 4 per cent. from one year after the death until payment unless the legacy has been previously paid into Court under sect. 43 of the Trustee Act, 1893. (See also *Re Salaman*, (1907) 2 Ch. 46, (1908) 1 Ch. 4.)

INSOLVENT ESTATE. Power given to a solicitor-executor to make charges is not binding on creditors. (*Re White*, (1898) 2 Ch. 217; and *Re Shuttleworth* (1911), 55 S. J. 366.)

INSURANCE. Trustees may insure against fire up to three-fourths of value, and pay premiums out of income of any property subject to the same trusts. (Trustee Act, 1893, s. 18.) As to who is entitled to the money, see *Dando* v. *Porter*, (1911) 2 Ch. 354; but in the case of a voluntary insurance by the tenant for life then apart from 14 Geo. III. c. 78, he is entitled to the money and not the trustees.

INTEREST ON LEGACIES. Where no time is fixed the legacy is payable at, and therefore bears interest from, the end of a year after the testator's death, even though the testator directs payment of the legacy at an earlier date. The rate is 4 per cent. per annum. (R. S. C., Order 55, r. 64; *Lord* v. *Lord* (1867), 2 Ch at p. 789) But if payable at a future date, it carries interest only from the time fixed for its payment. (*Lord* v. *Lord*)

Exceptions:—When a father or one *in loco parentis* gives a legacy to his child, and there is no other fund provided for maintenance, then the legacy will carry interest from the testator's death. (*Wynch* v. *Wynch* (1788), 1 Cox, 433, 29 Eng Rep. 1236.) Of course, if the will contains any express direction as to interest, effect will be given to it, *e.g.* a payment to be made as soon as convenient

INTEREST ON CONTINGENT LEGACIES is not payable while they are in suspense (*Re George* (1877), 5 C D. 837 and 843), except in the case of a legacy from a person *in loco parentis* (*Re Bowlby*, (1904) 2 Ch. 685 and 712); but the exception will not apply when the testator has provided another fund for the maintenance (*Re George, ante*); neither does it apply in the case of a legacy contingent upon events other than the legatee attaining full age or previous marriage. (*Re Abrahams, Abrahams* v. *Bendon*, (1911) 1 Ch. 109.)

INTEREST. The general rule is that interest is payable upon a legacy from the end of one year from the death or other the date fixed by the testator for payment thereof. (*Lord* v. *Lord* (1867), 2 Ch. 782 and 789; *Kenyon* v. *Walford*, (1912) 1 Ch. 219.) But in the case of a legacy given to a person to whom the testator was *in loco parentis* interest is payable from the death. (*Raven* v. *Waite* (1818), 1 Swans. 553.)

INTESTATES ACT, 1890. When a man dies intestate after 1st September, 1890, leaving a widow but no issue, the widow takes before any division 500*l.* which is raised rateably out of the real and personal estates. (53 Vict. c. 29.)

INVESTMENTS. Where an investment is purchased on which dividends had been earned and declared, though not paid, the tenant for life is not entitled to such dividends   (*In re Sir Robert Peel*, (1910) 1 Ch. 389.)

JUDGMENTS against executors are entitled to payment in order of date out of the legal assets   (*Dollond* v. *Johnson* (1854), 2 Sm. & G. 301.)

LAPSE. A legacy falls into residue if legatee dies in testator's lifetime, unless the legatee is a child or other issue of the testator and leaves issue capable of inheriting, when the legacy is payable to the personal representatives of the legatee. (1 Vict. c 26, ss. 25 and 33.)

LAPSE   Residue cannot fall into residue, so a lapsed share passes as on an intestacy.

LEASEHOLDS. Administrators are personally liable, but limited to the annual value of the property, for the proportion of rent due in respect of leaseholds for the period during which they were actually in possession. (*Whitehead* v. *Palmer*, (1908) 1 K B. 151.) The estate, however, is liable for the whole.

LEGACIES, INTEREST ON, as from the end of one year from the testator's death at 4 per cent., unless ordered to be invested, then from the end of such year to actual investment.

LEGACY. A fund set aside to meet it does not release other estate in the hands of beneficiaries when the fund proves to be insufficient   (*Re Evans' Contract*, (1910) 2 Ch 438)   See also "Annuity," *ante*.

LEGACY BY TESTATOR *to his infant child*, or other infant to whom he has placed himself *in loco parentis*, carries interest at 4 per cent. from testator's death.

LEGACY DUTY, ACCOUNTS. Costs of passing are part of the expenses of administration, and payable out of the general estate. (*Earl Cowley* v. *Wellesley* (1866), 1 Eq. 656.)

LEGATEE who has mortgaged his legacy must bear any increase of costs occasioned thereby, which increase comes out of the legacy in respect of which they have been incurred. (*Re Vincent*, (1909) 1 Ch. 810.)

LEGATEE ABROAD. Costs of paying comes out of legacy.

LEGATEE'S debt must be set off against the legacy or share, and only the balance paid. This applies to a statute-barred debt (*Courtney* v. *Williams* (1844), 3 Hare, 539), but not to a debt owed by a partnership of which the legatee is a member. (*Turner* v. *Turner*, (1911) 1 Ch. 716.) The same principle applies where a next of kin is indebted to the intestate. (*In re Cordwell's Estate* (1873), 20 Eq. 644)

LOAN by a widow to her husband for the purposes of his trade is postponed to other creditors (Married Women's Property Act, 1882, s. 3; *Re Leng*, (1895) 1 Ch. 652), but if widow is executrix she can retain. (*Re Ambler*, (1905) 1 Ch. 697.)

LOCKE KING'S ACTS. Charges on real and leasehold estates must be raised in the first place out of the property charged. But the Acts do not apply to other personal property. (17 & 18 Vict c 113; 30 & 31 Vict. c. 69; and 40 & 41 Vict. c 34)

MAINTENANCE (See Conveyancing Act, 1881, s. 43.)

MARSHALLING testator's secured debts. Note that personal estate is not within the Act, so that where a mortgage debt is charged upon land and personal estate not being leasehold property, *e g.*, a life policy, the debt must be apportioned and the proportion charged on the policy paid out of residue
See Locke King's Acts (*ante*).

MIXED FUNDS Charged with debts and legacies, then the realty and personalty contribute proportionately, and the legatees, in the absence of directions to the contrary, must bear their own estate duty upon so much of the real estate as goes to make up the amount due to each. (*Re Spencer Cooper*, (1908) 1 Ch. 130.)

MORTGAGEE is not entitled to insist upon trustees of a reversionary interest, when it falls in, paying over the whole share to him, but only sufficient to satisfy his principal, interest and costs. (*Re Bell*, (1896) 1 Ch. 1; *Hockey* v *Western*, (1898) 1 Ch. 350)

MORTGAGES which prove to be insufficient upon sale to pay capital and interest. It must be seen that the tenant for life, if any, has received his due proportion of proceeds of sale, under the rule in *Re Atkinson* ((1904) 2 Ch. 160).

MORTMAIN. Land may be given by will for charitable purposes by testators dying after the 5th August, 1891 (54 & 55 Vict. c. 73).

MOURNING for members of the deceased's family is not chargeable against the estate. (*Johnson* v. *Baker* (1826), 2 Car. & P. 207.)

NEXT OF KIN. If none, executors are entitled to undisposed of residue of personal estate (*Attorney-General* v *Jefferys*, (1908) A. C. 411.)

.NOTICE to all trustees need not be renewed (*Re Wasdale, Brittin* v. *Partridge,* (1899) 1 Ch. 163); but it is otherwise if not given to all. (*Re Phillips*, (1903) 1 Ch 183)

PARTNERSHIPS are regulated by the Partnership Act, 1890, subject to the terms of the articles (if any). (53 & 54 Vict. c. 39.)

PAYMENT OF LEGACIES cannot be enforced until after the expiration of twelve months from testator's death.

PERPETUITIES, rule against. Property must vest during a life or lives in being, and twenty-one years afterwards. (*Cadell* v. *Palmer* (1833), 1 Cl. & Fin 372)

POSSESSION OF THE TITLE DEEDS other than bearer securities Only in special circumstances will the Court interfere to make one trustee hand over possession to his co-trustees. (*Sisson's Settlement*, (1903) 1 Ch. 262.) See also " Custody of Deeds."

POWER FOR TRUSTEE-SOLICITOR to make charges is not binding upon creditors. (*Re White*, (1898) 2 Ch. 217; and *Re Shuttleworth* (1911), Sol. J., 25th March.)

PREMIUMS payable in respect of policies of assurance of any description are not apportionable under the Act of 1870. (See sect. 6.)

PROFITS OF A BUSINESS are not apportionable. (*Jones* v. *Ogle* (1872), L. R. 8 Ch 192.)

RATES are not apportionable. (*Re Wearmouth Co.* (1882), 19 C. D. 640.)

RENTS are apportionable. (Apportionment Act, 1870, s. 2.) Chap. VII., p 75, *ante.*

REPAIRS. Subject to the terms of the trust instrument a legal tenant for life is not liable for repairs to freeholds (*Re Cartwright* (1889), 41 C. D. 532); if the limitations are equitable the tenant for life is similarly free (*Powis* v. *Blagrave* (1854), Kay, 496; *In re Freeman*, (1898) 1 Ch. 28); but in those cases the Court has on occasions authorised the expenditure of capital money in repairs on the principle of salvage (*Re de Teissier's Settled Estates*, (1893) 1 Ch. 153; *Re Willis*, (1902) 1 Ch. 15; *Legh's Settled Estates*, (1902) 2 Ch. 74); in the case of leaseholds he is liable for rent and performance of covenants from the death (*Re Courtier* (1886), 34 C. D. 136, and *Gjers*, (1899) 2 Ch. 54), but as between tenant for life and remainderman he is not liable for repairs due at the testator's death. (*Re Courtier, ante; Re Betty*, (1899) 1 Ch. 821.)

If there are trustees, and they have powers of management, they probably have power to repair. (*Re Fowler* (1881), 16 C. D. 723.)

RESTRAINT on anticipation can only be removed by the Court. (Conveyancing Act, 1911, s. 7.)

RETAINER. The executor has a right to retain debts due to him out of legal assets (*Re Rhoades*, (1899) 2 Q. B. 347, 354); and this is so although the debt is statute-barred (*Trevor* v. *Hutchins*, (1896) 1 Ch. 844); and there is no distinction between specialty and simple contract debts (*Re Samson*, (1906) 2 Ch. 584, and *Re Harris*, (1914) 2 Ch. 395.)

Executor's right, of, cannot be exercised against equitable assets. (*Re Allen*, (1896) 2 Ch. 345; *Re Jones*, 31 C. D. 440; *Re Rhoades*, (1899) 2 Q. B. at p. 354.)

RETAINER. Creditor administrator is, since 1st January, 1900, deprived of right of retainer by the terms of his bond

REVERSION DUTY. (See Finance (1909-10) Act, 1910.)

REVERSIONARY INTEREST. It should be seen that any tenant for life has received his share of income upon the falling in of the reversion under the rule in *Earl of Chesterfield's Case*.

SATISFACTION of debts by legacies and of portions by legacies.

SECURITY which depreciates in value. Trustees are not liable to make good if authorised in the origin. (Trustee Act, 1893, s. 14.)

SET-OFF. Beneficiary who is also a debtor to the estate must account for his debt before he can participate, and the debt is outside the Statute of Limitations. (*Re Akerman*, (1891) 3 Ch. 212.)

SETTLED LAND ACTS, 1882 to 1890, should be borne in mind.

SETTLED LAND ACTS. A deposit forfeited under a contract for sale is capital under sect. 31, sub-sect 1 (ii) of the Settled Land Act, 1882. (*Re Ward's Settled Estates*, (1919) W. N. 51.)

SETTLEMENT ESTATE DUTY was payable, in the absence of contrary instructions, out of the settled property where deceased died after 1st July, 1896. (Finance Act, 1896, s. 19 (1).) But by 4 & 5 Geo. 5, c. 10, s. 14, that duty was abolished in the case of persons dying after the 11th May, 1914, and there is a right of set-off in respect of the settlement estate duty paid when subsequently paying estate duty under the settlement.

SIMPLE CONTRACT AND SPECIALTY CREDITORS Executors may pay one in preference to another. (*Re Samson*, (1906) 2 Ch. 584.)

SOLICITOR-TRUSTEE'S CHARGES. See "Power for Trustee-Solicitor," &c., *ante*.

SPECIFIC BEQUESTS. Expenses incurred since testator's death in connection with these are payable by the specific legatee. (*Re Pearce*, (1909) 1 Ch. 819.)

SPECIFIC LEGACY. Dividends and other accretions belong to the specific legatee as from the testator's death.

Expenses incurred in the upkeep thereof between death and

delivery are payable by the legatee, and not out of residue. (*Re Pearce*, (1909) 1 Ch. 819.)

Expenses of warehousing fall on the legatee. (*Sharp* v. *Lush* (1879), 10 C. D. 468.)

SPECIFIC LEGATEE OF SHARES pays the brokerage, stamps and expenses involved in transferring to him the bequest. (*Re Grosvenor*, (1916) 2 Ch. 375.)

STATUTE-BARRED DEBTS. Executor may pay these until a beneficiary interferes. (*Lowis* v. *Rumney* (1867), 4 Eq. 451)

STOCK AND SHARES OF TESTATOR. Executors, like trustees, are entitled on demand to have their names entered on the register of a limited company without any statement that they hold the shares in a representative capacity and to have their names inserted in such order as they choose. (*Re T. H. Saunders*, (1908) 1 Ch. 415.)

STREET PAVING. A tenant for life is entitled to a charge on premises for sums applied in defraying street paving charges. (See sect. 257 of Public Health Act, 1875; and *Re Pizzi*, (1907) 1 Ch. 67.)

SUCCESSION DUTY is a first charge on the interest of the successor. (16 & 17 Vict. c. 51, s. 42.)

SUCCESSION DUTY ACCOUNTS. Costs of passing fall upon the beneficiary's income. (*Earl Cowley* v. *Wellesley* (1866), 1 Eq. 656.)

SURVIVORSHIP. If one of several executors dies, the powers of the office pass to the survivors.

TENANT FOR LIFE, EQUITABLE. As to terms of possession when liable for repairs, see *Re Wythes*, (1893) 2 Ch. 369; also *Re Bagot*, (1894) 1 Ch. 177.

TESTAMENTARY EXPENSES. These include costs of administration of the personal estate and funeral expenses (*Re Middleton* (1881), 19 C. D. 552 , *Sharpe* v. *Lush* (1879), 10 C. D. 468), estate duty in respect of personal estate (*Barnes* v. *Chadwick*, (1903) 1 Ch 250); also in respect of real estate, if "duties" are directed to be paid (*Re Pimm, Sharp* v. *Hodgson*, (1904) 2 Ch. 345), but the costs of administration, so far as they are increased by administration of real estate, are borne by the real estate, unless otherwise directed.

Estate duty payable by the executor is a testamentary expense, and, the order of administration in respect of the payment of testamentary expenses being the same as that adopted for payment of debts, the duty must be met out of undisposed-of realty before resort is had to specifically bequeathed personalty, or devised realty.

Testamentary expenses are payable before debts. (*Re Pullen*, Solicitors' Journal, vol. 84, pp. 341, 355.)

Generally. (*Sharp* v. *Lush*, ante.)

TITLE DEEDS, POSSESSION OF. A legal tenant for life under S. L. Act is entitled to the custody of the deeds, but as to an equitable tenant for life, see *Re Wythes*, (1893) 2 Ch. 369.

In the absence of special circumstances a trustee is not entitled to have title deeds and non-negotiable securities removed from the custody of a co-trustee and placed at a bank in a box only accessible to the trustees jointly. (*Re Sisson*, (1903) 1 Ch. 264. But see also *Field* v. *Field*, (1894) 1 Ch. 425.) The same rule does not apply to bearer securities.

On the distribution of a trust fund the trustee has no right to require the delivery to him of mortgages, assignments, powers of attorney or other documents of title executed by a beneficiary. (*Re Palmer, Lancs , &c Co.* v. *Burke*, (1907) 1 Ch 486.)

TOMBSTONE AND MOURNING, expenses of, are not payable out of the estate without special direction

TRUST FOR SALE, of real and personal estate charged with debts, legacies, &c. , effect is, that so far as the legacies fall upon realty they have to bear estate duty upon so much of the realty as contributes to make up the legacy. (*Re Spencer Cooper*, (1908) 1 Ch. 130)

VOLUNTARY SETTLEMENTS. The provisions of sect. 42 of the Bankruptcy Act, 1914, must be borne in mind. (44 & 45 Geo. 5, c. 59.)

Estate duty attaches if the settlor dies within three years, or reserves any interest in the property settled, but if the gift is to a charity the limit is one year. (Finance (1909-10) Act, 1910, s. 59.)

VOUCHERS of payments made by solicitors or other agents on behalf of trustee out of trust money in their hands must be delivered to the trustee. (*In re Ellis & Ellis*, (1908) W N. 215.)

WITNESS Legacy or devise to a person who attests the will, or to his or her wife or husband, is void (Wills Act, 1837, s. 15); and a solicitor having power to charge who attests the will loses his right. (*Re Trotter*, (1899) 1 Ch 764)

APPENDICES

INDEX

APPENDIX "A."

	PAGE
Estate Book of Mr. William Roberts, deceased	195
Will	198
Probate Grant	204
Memoranda	205
Schedule	207
General Capital Account	211
Loan Account	232
Separate Account of the Share of Mrs. Alice Ford and her Children	235

APPENDIX "B."

Apportionment Account of Dividends and Interest accruing due at the death of the Testator 239

APPENDIX "C."

Apportionment Account of Rents accruing due at the death of the Testator 243

APPENDIX "D."

Suspense Apportionment Account 247

APPENDIX "E."

Income Account 253

APPENDIX "F."

	PAGE
Final Statement for the Beneficiaries	261
Schedule	263
Capital Account	266
Investments Account	278
Account of Mr. James Roberts' Share	282

APPENDIX "G."

Specimen Rent Account	285

APPENDIX "H."

Specimen Income Accounts	286

APPENDIX "I."

Estate Book for a Marriage Settlement Trust	289
Epitome of the Settlement	291
Memoranda	293
Schedule	296
General Capital Account	299
Husband's Trust Funds	300
Wife's do. do.	308

APPENDIX A

IN THE MATTER OF THE ESTATE

OF THE LATE

Mr. WILLIAM ROBERTS deceased

ESTATE BOOK

(*See Chap. II., p.* 31 et seq., *as to this Estate Book*)

IN THE MATTER OF THE ESTATE

OF THE LATE

Mr. WILLIAM ROBERTS deceased

INDEX TO ESTATE BOOK

	PAGE
Will	198
Probate Grant	204
The Memoranda	205
The Schedule. Part I. (Real Estate of which the Testator died possessed)	207
,, ,, Part II. (Personal Property of which the Testator died possessed)	208
,, ,, Part III. A.—Mortgages created by the Testator	210
B.—Mortgages created by the Trustees	210
The Capital Account	211
Account of Mr. James Roberts' Share	230
do. Mrs. Alice Ford's, &c. do.	232
Loan Account	232

Headings used in the Capital Account—
1. "West View."
2. General Assets.
3. General Investments.
4. Funeral Expenses.
5. Estate Duty.
6. Executorship Expenses.
7. Debts due at the Death.
8. General Expenses.
9. Legacies.
10. Apportionments.
11. Investments Sold.
12. Investments Purchased.
13. Miscellaneous.

The Income Account 253

This is the last Will and Testament

OF ME

WILLIAM ROBERTS of "West View" St. Albans in the County of Hertford Corn Merchant I REVOKE all Testamentary instruments heretofore executed by me and I APPOINT my son JAMES ROBERTS and my friend ALEXANDER RICHARDS Executors and Trustees of this my Will who are hereinafter referred to as "my Trustees" I GIVE to the said Alexander Richards a legacy of £100 as a slight acknowledgment of his trouble in acting as a trustee of this my Will I BEQUEATH to my Wife Margaret the household furniture plate linen china glass books pictures prints provisions and other household effects belonging to me at the time of my death and a legacy of £100 to be paid to her out of the first moneys coming to the hands of my Executors I BEQUEATH to my daughter Alice £500 of my London & North Western Railway Stock I ALSO GIVE the following pecuniary legacies To my nephew Edward Ford the sum of £400 and to my niece Ethel Roberts (Spinster) the sum of £400 I GIVE to Mrs. Susan Ross the sum of £26 per annum during her life to be paid quarterly from the day of my decease I DEVISE my Freehold farm known as "Stevenage" situate at St. Albans aforesaid to my said son James Roberts absolutely I DIRECT all the aforesaid legacies to be paid and transferred free of legacy duty as soon as conveniently may be after my decease And as to all the rest of my estate and effects both Real and Personal I DEVISE AND BEQUEATH the same unto

Marginal notes:
- Appointment of executors and trustees
- Legacy of 100l. to Alexander Richards
- Furniture &c. to wife
- 100l to wife
- Specific legacy
- 400l. to Edward Ford
- 400l. to Ethel Roberts
- Annuity of 26l to Mrs Ross
- Devise of Stevenage Farm to son James
- Legacies to be paid free of legacy duty
- Residue of real and personal estate to trustees

NOTE.—If the will is lengthy an epitome may be entered instead of a copy.

Observations on the Will

Upon trust to sell and invest the proceeds	my Trustees UPON TRUST to sell call in and convert into money my Real and Personal Estate AND UPON FURTHER TRUST out of the money arising from the sale calling in and conversion
Pay income to wife	thereof to pay the legacies bequeathed by this my Will and to invest the residue of such moneys in the names of my Trustees And to pay or permit my said wife to receive the annual income
On her death capital to be divided equally amongst the children	of such investments during her life And from and after her death as to the Capital and Income of the same investments UPON TRUST for my children in equal shares the respective shares of such children to be absolutely vested on my death
Settlement of the shares of daughters	I DECLARE that the share of each daughter of and in my Residuary Trust Estate shall be retained by my Trustees
—inalienable life interest	and held by them UPON TRUST to pay the income thereof to my daughter entitled thereto for her separate use during her life without power of alienation or anticipation And from and after the death of my same daughter as to as
—children and other issue of daughter as she shall appoint	well the Capital as the Income thereof UPON TRUST for all or any one or more of the issue of my same daughter in such proportions and for such interests to be absolutely vested within twenty-one years from her death as she whether covert or discovert shall from time to time by deed with or without power of revocation and new appointment
—hotchpot	or by her Will appoint But no child in whose favour or in favour of any of whose issue an appointment shall be made shall participate under the Trust next hereinafter contained in the unappointed portion of the said settled Fund without bringing the benefit of such appointment into hotchpot
—in default for children equally at twenty-one or marriage	And in default of appointment or subject to any partial appointment IN TRUST for the children of my same daughter who shall being sons attain the age of twenty-one years or being daughters attain that age or be married under that age such
—if no child attain twenty-one or marry	children if more than one to take in equal shares And if there shall not be any child of my same daughter who being a son

OBSERVATIONS ON THE WILL

shall attain the age of twenty-one years or being a daughter shall attain that age or be married then IN TRUST for such persons for such interests and generally in such manner in all respects as my same daughter shall by Will appoint And in default of appointment or subject to any partial appointment IN TRUST for the persons who at the death of my same daughter shall be of kin to her and who under the statutes for the distribution of intestates effects would be entitled to her personal estate if she were dead a spinster and intestate such persons to take in the proportions prescribed by the same statutes AND I EMPOWER my same daughter (notwithstanding the trusts herein contained subsequently to the trust in her own favour) by Deed executed either after or in contemplation of her marriage or by Will to appoint the annual income to accrue due after her death of the said settled fund or any part of such income to and for the life of any husband of my same daughter who shall survive her IN WITNESS whereof I have hereunto set my hand this 30th day of September 1902 WILLIAM ROBERTS SIGNED by the Testator in our presence and witnessed and attested by us in his presence and that of each other THOMAS GRESHAM Solicitor 100 Lincoln's Inn Fields H. BROOKS Clerk to Mr. Thomas Gresham

as daughter shall by will appoint
—in default for daughter's next of kin

Daughter empowered to appoint a life interest to a husband

NOTE.—A large portion of the above Will has been extracted from Hayes & Jarman's well-known book of precedents on the subject.

OBSERVATIONS ON THE WILL

EPITOME OF THE PROBATE GRANT

In His Majesty's High Court of Justice

THE PRINCIPAL PROBATE REGISTRY

BE IT KNOWN that William Roberts of "West View" St. Albans in the County of Hertford Corn Merchant died on the 1st day of November 1902 at "West View" St. Albans aforesaid

AND BE IT FURTHER KNOWN that the Will was proved by James Roberts son of the Testator and Alexander Richards the Executors named in the said Will

Gross Value of the Estate within the United Kingdom amounts to £7,294 : 11s. 8d.

Certificate that £183 : 2s 2d. for Estate Duty and Interest on such duty has been paid to the Inland Revenue at the rate of three per cent.

Dated the 15th day of November 1902

S. HOWARD

Registrar

L.S.

Extracted by Mr. THOS. GRESHAM
Solicitor
100 Lincoln's Inn Fields

THE MEMORANDA

No.	Particulars
1	*3rd January*, 1878. The testator was married once only, and then to Margaret Brown, at Brighton Parish Church.

2	There was issue of the marriage as follows:—
	  1. James, born at Brighton on 23rd of March, 1879
	  2. Alice, born at Shoreham, Sussex, on 10th of February, 1882; married at the Parish Church, Deal, on 20th February, 1900, to Mr. John Ford.
	  3. Frederick, born at Brighton on 30th of June, 1884; died at Brighton on 10th of December, 1889.

3	*1st November*, 1902. Testator died, leaving his widow and two children surviving.
4	*6th November*, 1902. Testator was buried at St. Albans Cemetery.
5	*26th November*, 1902. The furniture specifically bequeathed to the widow, handed to her, and receipt taken, being voucher No. 5.
6	*1st and 8th December*, 1902. Statutory advertisements for creditors inserted in "Times," "Telegraph" and "Hertford Post," and on 1st December, 1902, in the "Gazette." Claims to be sent in by 1st February, 1903, to Mr. Gresham, the Solicitor.
7	*24th February*, 1903. The mortgagee having released the estate from the covenant the executors consented to the devise of "Stevenage" to Mr. James Roberts.
8	*26th May*, 1903 "The Elms" sold by auction for £620. Auctioneers: Messrs. Jameson & Co.

(See Chap. III. as to The Mem^a.)

No.	Particulars
9	21*st March*, 1903. The annuitant, Susan Ross, died at Hatfield, Herts. Administration granted to John Ross on 6th April, 1903.
10	20*th April*, 1903. The addresses of the Trustees supplied to the brokers for registration in respect of all inscribed stocks are as follows:— James Roberts, of 29, High Street, and Alexander Richards, of 42, London Road, St. Albans, in the county of Hertford.

11	1*st May*, 1903. The accounts were examined on this day by Mr. James Roberts, one of the Trustees, assisted by Mr. Gresham, the Solicitor, and balances found to be correct. All the scrips for the various investments, the mortgage deeds, and other documents of title (which are now deposited in the names of the Trustees at the Hertford Bank, St. Albans Branch) were inspected and found to be in order.
	    (Sgd.) ALEX. RICHARDS
	                       (*Trustee*),
	    (Sgd.) THOS. GRESHAM
	                       (*Solicitor*).

12	10*th May*, 1903. Notice was received on this date of a mortgage, dated 8th May, 1903, executed by Mr. James Roberts, of his interest in this Estate to the British Reversionary Society to secure £700 with interest at 6 per cent.
13	1*st November*, 1904. Testator's father, Arthur Roberts, died at St. Albans.
14	16*th January*, 1906. Testator's widow died at St. Albans. Will proved by James Roberts and Arthur Ford in the Principal Registry on 10th Feb. 1906.
15	31*st March*, 1906. "West View" sold by auction for £600. Auctioneers: Messrs. Jameson & Co.

THE SCHEDULE

PART I

Real Estate of which the Testator died possessed

№.	Particulars of Property	References‡
1	A freehold house called "West View" situate at St. Albans in the Parish of Belmont in the County of Hertford with two acres adjoining in the Testator's occupation and assessed under Sch. A at £35 per annum Valuation for Land Duties £700	Carried down
2	A freehold farm known as "Stevenage" situate in the Parish of Hatfield in the County of Herts containing 12 acres Valuation for Land Duties £1,000 Mortgaged on the 7th October 1890 by the Testator in favour of Mr. Henry Bates to secure £500 and interest at 4½% which interest had been paid by the Testator down to the 7th October 1902 Subject to a tenancy particulars of which are as follows :—	Consent granted. See Memª Item 7

No	Description of Property	Nature of Tenancy	Name of Tenant	Amount of Rent
1	Stevenage Farm Hatfield	Annual from Michaelmas 1896	Henry Green	£60

(Specifically devised)

‡ The references are to the Items in the Capital Account unless otherwise stated
(*See Chap. IV as to The Schedule.*)

PART II

PERSONAL ESTATE OF WHICH THE TESTATOR DIED POSSESSED

No.	Nominal or Face Value (if any)	Particulars of Property	References‡
3	£ s. d.	A leasehold messuage and premises known as "The Elms" situate in Hertford Road St. Albans held for a term of 99 years expiring September 29th 1974 Granted by John England of 100 Pall Mall London at a ground rent of £6 per annum Valuation for Land Duties £600 Subject to a lease particulars of which are as follows*	Items 22 and 23, p. 218; also Mem^a Item 8, p. 205

No. of Lease	Property Leased	Name of Lessee	Date of Lease	Term	Last day of Term	Rent	References
1	The Elms Hertford Road St. Albans	W. Strong	3 Jan. 1901	21 years	25th Dec. 1921	£40	

No.	Nominal or Face Value	Particulars of Property	References
4	600 0 0	Consols............	Item 3, p. 212
5	3 11 3	One quarter's dividend due 5th October, 1902	,, 10, p. 214
6	1 1 1	Proportion of income to death	,, 18, p 216
7	500 0 0	London & N. W. Railway 4 % Guaranteed Stock (specifically bequeathed)	,, 4 (part), p. 212
8	6 9 1	Proportion of income on ditto to death......................	,, 18, p. 216
9	300 0 0	London & N. W. Railway 4 % Guaranteed Stock	,, 4 (part), p. 212
10	....	Proportion of income on ditto to death....	,, 18, p. 216
11	100 0 0	$500 St. Louis Bridge Railroad Company 1st Mortgage Gold Bond N^{od} 25 @ 4s. per dollar*	,, 5, p. 212
12	15 10	Proportion of income on ditto to death........	,, 18, p. 216
13	500 0 0	5 shares of £100 each in the Standard Bank of South Africa Limited*	,, 6, p. 212
14	12 15 1	Proportion of income on ditto to death	,, 18, p. 216
15	400 0 0	400 shares of £1 each in Golden Reef Mining Company Limited*	,, 7, p. 212
16	....	Proportion of final dividend on ditto to death................	,, 18, p. 216

‡ The references are to the Items in the Capital Account unless otherwise stated
* The rule in *Howe* v. *Earl of Dartmouth* applies to the income derived from these assets (see p. 98).

PART II—continued

Nominal or Face Value (if any)	Particulars of Property	References‡
£ s d. 50 0 0	50 shares of £1 each in the English Investment Trust Limited*	Item 9, p. 214
.. ..	Proportion of income on ditto to death	Valueless
12 5 6	Cash in the house	Item 1, p. 212
47 4 2	Cash at The Hertford Bank St. Albans on drawing account ...	,, 2, p. 212
500 0 0	Mortgage by Mr. Wilson to testator of "Weston Cottage" Hatfield Herts *	,, 8, p. 212
1 5 0	Interest thereon from the 8th October 1902 to death @ 4 %	,, 18, p. 216
200 0 0	Policy No. 10864 in the Equitable Assurance Company on the life of the Testator	
160 0 0	Bonuses thereon	,, 12, p. 214
100 0 0	Debt due from Mr Henry Wood (adjudicated bankrupt 29th September 1901) for money lent by Testator—proof admitted for	,, 13, p. 214 and ,, 32, p. 222
Produced:— £977 : 5s. 1d. Consols. £120 9s. 5d. Cash	The Testator's one-third share in the investments subject to the trusts of his parents' marriage settlement dated 21st January 1850†	,, 34, p. 224
....	Furniture (specifically bequeathed)	Mem* Item 5, p. 205
650 0 0	Testator's share in partnership of Messrs. Roberts, Wallis & Co. as per account to be stated by the surviving partners in accordance with the articles including interest on capital and share of profits to date of death*	,, 28, p. 222
5 8 6	Proportion of rent of freehold property current at the death as per separate apportionment account	,, 14, p. 216
3 1 5	Ditto in respect of leasehold property	,, 15, p 216
	BALANCE OF ASSETS remaining in Schedule on 1st November 1903	
....	PART I—REAL ESTATE The messuage and premises known as "West View" St Albans	Items 2 and 3, p. 228, and Mem* Item 15, p. 206
	PART II—PERSONAL ESTATE *Nil*	
	BALANCE OF ASSETS remaining in Schedule on the 16th of July 1906	
	PARTS I & II *Nil*	

he references are to the Items in the Capital Account unless otherwise stated.
he rule in *Howe* v. *Earl of Dartmouth* applies to the income derived from these assets (see p 98)
he rule in *Chesterfield's Case* applies in respect of this asset (see p. 101).

P

PART III

INCUMBRANCES

A.—Mortgages created by the Testator and other loans for which the Trustees are not personally liable.

No.	Particulars of Incumbrances	References
1	£500 with interest at 4½% is secured on Stevenage Farm being Item N^{od} 2 in Part I by mortgage of 7th October 1890 created by the Testator in favour of Henry Bates in which the Testator covenanted to pay the debt	This property was specifically devised subject to the mortgage
	NOTE.—There will be included in this part of the Schedule short particulars of any mortgages of Trust Assets created by the Trustees *involving no personal liability* on their part to repay the money borrowed	

B.—Mortgages created by the Trustees and other loans for which the Trustees are personally liable.

No.	Particulars of Incumbrances	References
1	£200 is secured on "West View" being Item N° 1 in Part I by deposit of the deeds on 9th November 1902 with the Hertford Bank including an obligation by the Trustees to repay the money	Discharged See Item 1, p 233
	NOTE.—There will be included in this part of the Schedule short particulars of any mortgages of Trust Assets created by the Trustees *involving a personal liability* on their part to repay the money borrowed	

The references are to the Items in the Capital Account unless otherwise stated.

IN THE MATTER OF THE ESTATE
OF
Mr. WILLIAM ROBERTS deceased

Executors and Trustees
1. Mr. JAMES ROBERTS
2. Mr. ALEXANDER RICHARDS

Int. Rev. Ref. R. 46,942—1902

GENERAL CAPITAL
(CASH AND INVESTMENTS)

Testator died	1st November 1902
Probate granted to both Executors .	15th November 1902

Gross personal estate . . .	£6094 11 8
Gross real estate . . .	1200 0 0
	£7294 11 8

PARTICULARS OF CORRECTIVE AFFIDAVITS.

As last previously shewn.	Increase	Decrease.	As corrected
£ s. d. 7,294 11 8	£ s d 200 0 0	£ s. d. —	£ s d. 7,494 11 8

The account of the Executors of the Will

GENERAL CAPITAL

Dr. RECEIPTS

No.	Date.	Name of Person from whom, and on what Account received.	Cash. £ s. d.	Investments. £ s. d.
1	1902 Nov. 2	GENERAL ASSETS (No 2). To cash in the house	12 5 6	
2	Nov. 16	To cash received from the Hertford Bank being balance of testator's drawing account	47 4 2	
3	Nov. 25	GENERAL INVESTMENTS (No 3) To amounts of the following investments belonging to the testator at the date of his death:— Consols	....	600 0 0
4		London and North Western Railway 4% Guaranteed Stock...	....	800 0 0
5		$500 St. Louis Bridge Railroad Co. 1st Mortgage Gold Bond N^{ed} 25 @ 4s per $	....	100 0 0
6		5 shares of £100 each in the Standard Bank of South Africa, Limited	....	500 0 0
7	·	400 shares of £1 each in Golden Reef Mining Co., Limited...	....	400 0 0
8		Mortgage by Mr. Wilson to testator of "Weston Cottage," at Hatfield, Herts, to secure	...	500 0 0
		Carried forward	£59 9 8	£2,900 0 0

Note.—Where a voucher exists for any receipt or payment
(See Chap. V as

of the late Mr. Wm. ROBERTS decd.

(PERSONALTY)

Payments and Transfers — *Cr.*

No.	Date	Name of Person to whom, and for what purpose paid or transferred.	Cash.	Investments.
			£ s. d.	£ s. d.

it bears the serial number as in the Capital Account to this Account.)

214

Dr.   Receipts   General Capital

No.	Date.	Name of Person from whom, and on what Account received.	Cash. £ s. d.	Investments. £ s. d.
	1902	Brought forward..................	59 9 8	2,900 0 0
9	Nov 25	GENERAL INVESTMENTS (No. 3). 50 shares of £1 each in the English Investment Trust, Limited.................................	....	50 0 0
10	Nov 25	GENERAL ASSETS (No. 2). To cash received being 1 quarter's dividend on £600 Consols @ 2½ % due 5th October, 1902, less 3s. 9d tax.	3 11 3	
11	Dec. 10	INVESTMENTS SOLD (No 11). To cash received of Messrs Bishop & Co., being proceeds of sale of £300 London and North Western Railway 4% Guaranteed Stock at 120 cum div. as per contract of 30th November, 1902 .... £360 0 0 Less · Brokerage and stamp 1 17 6	358 2 6	
12	Dec. 10	GENERAL ASSETS (No. 2). To cash received of the Equitable Assurance Co., being the amount payable under Policy No 10864 for.......................... £200 0 0 Bonuses on ditto 160 0 0	360 0 0	
13	Dec 10.	To cash received of the Trustee in Mr. Henry Wood's Bankruptcy being first dividend of 2s. 6d in the £ on £100 due to Testator	12 10 0	
		Carried forward	£793 13 5	£2,950 0 0

215

(PERSONALTY)—*continued.* PAYMENTS AND TRANSFERS   Cr.

No.	Date.	Name of Person to whom, and for what purpose paid or transferred.	Cash. £ s. d	Investments. £ s. d
	1902	Brought forward...............	....	....
1	Nov. 12	ESTATE DUTY (No 5) By cash paid Commissioners of Inland Revenue for Estate Duty	182 16 8	
2	Nov. 12	GENERAL INVESTMENTS (No. 3). By amount of 50 shares of £1 each in English Investment Trust, Limited (valueless) liquidated in 1900 ...	....	50 0 0
3	Nov. 15	GENERAL EXPENSES (No 8). By cash paid Mrs Roberts (testator's widow) for maintenance of "West View"	20 0 0	
4	Nov. 17	FUNERAL EXPENSES (No 4) By cash paid Messrs Hinton & Co. for testator's funeral.............................	33 10 0	
5	Nov. 17	LEGACIES (No. 9) By cash paid Mrs Roberts (testator's widow) being her legacy .... £100 0 0 *Less* Duty on real estate so far as it contributed to this legacy at, say ⅛th* . 0 10 0	99 10 0	
6	Nov. 30	GENERAL INVESTMENTS (No 3) By amount of London and North Western Railway 4% Guaranteed Stock sold on this date	...	300 0 0
7	Dec. 10	EXECUTORSHIP EXPENSES (No. 6). By cash paid Mr Gresham (Solicitor) for obtaining Probate.— Court fees .... £5 15 1 Costs 20 3 5	25 18 6	
		DEBTS DUE AT THE DEATH (No. 7) By cash paid the following debts due from testator:—		
8	Dec. 12	Dr. Thorpe (medical attendance)..............	17 10 6	
9		Mr. H. James (wines, &c.)	10 15 10	
10		Mr J. Walters (provisions)	7 3 4	
		Carried forward	£397 4 10	£350 0 0

* See p. 45.

Dr. RECEIPTS GENERAL CAPITAL

No.	Date.	Name of Person from whom, and on what Account received.	Cash.			Investments.		
			£	s.	d.	£	s.	d.
	1903	Brought forward...............	793	13	5	2,950	0	0
		APPORTIONMENTS (No 10).						
14	Jan. 6	To cash being proportion of rent of freehold property current at the death, as per Apportionment Account, Appendix C., Part I., p. 244	5	8	6			
15	Jan 11	To cash being proportion of rent of leasehold property current at the death, as per Apportionment Account, Appendix C., Part II, p 245	3	1	5			
		GENERAL INVESTMENTS (No. 3).						
16	Jan 12	To amount of cash on deposit with the Hertford Bank, St. Albans branch*...........	..			400	0	0
17	April 16	To amount advanced to pay Settlement Estate Duty on the share of Mrs Ford and her children†	....			26	15	0
		APPORTIONMENTS (No 10).						
18	April 15	To cash being proportion of dividends and interest current at the death, as per Apportionment Account, Appendix B., p. 239.............	22	6	1			
		MISCELLANEOUS (No. 13).						
19	April 16	To cash placed on deposit with the Hertford Bank, St Albans Branch, transferred to current account. ...	400	0	0			
		Carried forward	£1,224	9	5	£3,376	15	0

* See p. 53. † See p. 54.

(PERSONALTY)—*continued.*   PAYMENTS AND TRANSFERS   *Cr.*

No.	Date.	Name of Person to whom, and for what purpose paid or transferred.	Cash. £ s. d.	Investments. £ s. d.
	1903	Brought forward..........	397 4 10	350 0 0
		MISCELLANEOUS (No 13).		
11	Jan. 11	By cash transferred to income being proportion of property tax in respect of "West View" from 5th April to 1st November, 1902 (210 days), @ £2 per annum ...	1 3 0	
12	Jan 12	By cash placed on deposit with the Hertford Bank, St. Albans Branch............	400 0 0	
		GENERAL INVESTMENTS (No. 3).		
13	Feb. 1	By amount of London & North Western Railway 4% Guaranteed Stock transferred to Mrs. Alice Ford, being her specific legacy		500 0 0
14	April 16	By amount of cash on deposit with the Hertford Bank, St Albans Branch, withdrawn	....	400 0 0
		ESTATE DUTY (No. 5).		
15	April 16	By cash paid the Commissioners of Inland Revenue for further estate duty on corrective affidavit in respect of personalty	6 0 0	
		LEGACIES (No. 9).		
	April 16	By cash paid the Commissioners of Inland Revenue for legacy duty on the following legacies:—		
16		£100 to Mr. Alexander Richards (executor)	10 0 0	
17		£400 to Mr. Edward Ford (nephew)	12 0 0	
18		£400 to Miss Ethel Roberts (niece)...........	12 0 0	
19		Annuity of £26 to Mrs. Susan Ross	3 0 0	
		GENERAL ASSETS (No. 2)		
20	April 16	By cash paid Commissioners of Inland Revenue for settlement estate duty on share of residue bequeathed in trust for Mrs. Ford and her children Interest thereon was paid by the tenant for life	26 15 0	
		Carried forward..............	£868 2 10	£1,250 0 0

Dr.		RECEIPTS				GENERAL CAPITAL			
No.	Date.	Name of Person from whom, and on what Account received.	Cash.			Investments.			
			£	s.	d.	£	s.	d.	
	1903	Brought forward	1,224	9	5	3,376	15	0	
		INVESTMENTS SOLD (No. 11)							
20	May 1	To cash received of Messrs. Bishop & Co being proceeds of sale of $500 St. Louis Bridge Railroad First Mortgage Gold Bond @ 140, as per contract of 26th April, 1903 ....£140 0 0 *Less* Brokerage and stamp 0 15 0	139	5	0				
21	May 1	To ditto being proceeds of sale of 400 shares Golden Reef Mining Co., Ltd., @ 115½, as per contract of 26th April, 1903 ....£462 0 0 *Less* Brokerage and stamp 2 10 0	459	10	0				
22	June 24.	To cash received of Mr James for "The Elms," Hertford Road, St. Albans (Leasehold):— Purchase-money ....£620 0 0 *Less*: Deposit 62 0 0	558	0	0				
23	June 26.	To cash received of Messrs Jameson & Co (auctioneers) being the deposit in respect of "The Elms" .... £62 0 0 *Less* Auctioneer's charges 18 3 6	43	14	8				
24	June 27.	GENERAL INVESTMENTS (No 3) To amount of Queensland 4% Inscribed Stock purchased on this date	....			600	0	0	
25	Oct. 15.	APPORTIONMENTS (No 10). To cash being amount due to Capital in respect of unauthorized investments as per Suspense Apportionment Account, Appendix D., p 251	69	18	5				
		Carried forward	£2,494	17	6	£3,976	15	0	

(PERSONALTY)—*continued.* PAYMENTS AND TRANSFERS *Cr.*

No.	Date.	Name of Person to whom, and for what purpose paid or transferred.	Cash	Investments
	1903	Brought forward..............	£ s. d. 868 2 10	£ s. d. 1,250 0 0
		GENERAL INVESTMENTS (No. 3).		
21	April 26	By amount of $500 St. Louis Bridge Railroad Co. First Mortgage Gold Bond sold on this date	....	100 0 0
22	April 26	By ditto 400 shares Golden Reef Mining Co., Ltd., sold on this date	...	400 0 0
		LEGACIES (No. 9).		
	May 2	By cash paid the following pecuniary legacies —		
23		Mr. Alexander Richards .... £100 0 0 *Less:* Duty on real estate so far as it contributed to this legacy* .. 0 10 0	99 10 0	
24		Mr. Edward Ford .... £400 0 0 *Less·* Duty on real estate as above* 2 0 0	398 0 0	
25		Miss Ethel Roberts.................. £400 0 0 *Less* Duty on real estate as above* 2 0 0	398 0 0	
26		By cash transferred to Real Estate Account, being amount of duty deducted above, including Item 5....	5 0 0	
		INVESTMENTS PURCHASED (No. 12).		
27	June 29.	By cash paid Messrs Bishop & Co being price of £600 Queensland 4% Inscribed Stock @ 99¼ as per contract of 27th June, 1903.. ....£596 10 0 Brokerage and stamp 1 10 6	597 0 6	
		Carried forward	£2,365 13 4	£1,750 0 0

* See p 45.

Dr. RECEIPTS GENERAL CAPITAL

No.	Date.	Name of Person from whom, and on what Account received.	Cash	Investments.
	1903	Brought forward	£ s. d. 2,494 17 6	£ s. d. 3,976 15 0
26	Oct. 16.	GENERAL INVESTMENTS (No 3). To amount of Brighton Corporation 2½% Stock purchased on this date	...	85 2 5
27	Nov. 1	GENERAL ASSETS (No. 2). To cash from Income Account being income of that part of the testator's estate which was applied in payment of debts, legacies, &c., the particulars being as follows:—£1,405 : 6s. 4d. capital, which produced £6 : 13s. 9d. income. To raise £1,402. 16s. 5d. out of these sums rateably income pays £6 : 12s. 10d.; capital pays £1,396 : 3s. 7d.*	6 12 10	
			£2,501 10 4	£4,061 17 5

* For working of this item see p. 105.

(PERSONALTY)—*continued.*   PAYMENTS AND TRANSFERS   Cr.

No.	Date.	Name of Person to whom, and for what purpose paid or transferred.	Cash.			Investments		
			£	s.	d.	£	s.	d.
	1903	Brought forward	2,365	13	4	1,750	0	0
28	Oct. 18	INVESTMENTS PURCHASED (No 12). By ditto being price of £85 : 2s 5d. Brighton Corporation 2½ % Stock @ 82, as per contract of 16th October, 1903 .... £69 16 0 Brokerage and stamp 0 2 5	69	18	5			
29	Nov. 1.	EXECUTORSHIP EXPENSES (No. 6). By cash paid Mr. Gresham (Solicitor) being his costs of general administration to date	65	18	7			
		By aggregate amount of investments carried forward..	....			2,311	17	5
			£2,501	10	4	£4,061	17	5

Dr.   RECEIPTS   GENERAL CAPITAL

No.	Date.	Name of Person from whom, and on what Account received.	Cash.			Investments.		
			£	s.	d.	£	s.	d.
	1903 Nov 1	To aggregate amount of investments brought forward consisting of the following:—						
		1 Consols £600 0 0						
		2 Five Shares in Standard Bank of South Africa. 500 0 0						
		3. Mr. Wilson's mortgage 500 0 0						
		4 Advanced to pay Settlement Estate Duty on Mrs. Ford's settled share .. 26 15 0						
		5. Queensland 4% Inscribed Stock 600 0 0						
		6. Brighton Corporation 2½% Stock.. .. 85 2 5				2,311	17	5
28	1904 April 7	To cash received of Messrs. Roberts, Wallis & Co. being testator's share in partnership as per account stated by the surviving partners in accordance with the articles including interest on capital and share of profits to date of death	650	0	0			
		GENERAL INVESTMENTS (No. 4).						
29	April 20	To amount of India 3% Stock purchased on this date .	..			400	0	0
30	April 20	To ditto Lancs & Yorks 3% Debenture Stock	...			418	0	0
31	May 7	INVESTMENTS SOLD (No. 11). To cash received of Messrs. Bishop & Co. being proceeds of sale of five shares of £100 each in Standard Bank of South Africa, Limited, at 79½, as per contract of 2nd inst. .... £397 10 0 Less Brokerage and stamp 4 3 6	393	6	6			
32	June 6	GENERAL ASSETS (No. 2). To cash received of the Trustee in Mr. Henry Wood's bankruptcy, being second and final dividend of 5s. in the £ on £100 due to Testator	25	0	0			
33	Oct 7	To cash being amount due to capital in respect of unauthorised investments as per Suspense Apportionment Account, Appendix D, p. 247*	35	6	10			
		Carried forward................	£1,103	13	4	£3,129	17	5

* See p. 110.

PERSONALTY)—*continued*.   PAYMENTS AND TRANSFERS   Cr.

No.	Date.	Name of Person to whom, and for what purpose paid or transferred.	Cash.			Investments.		
			£	s.	d.	£	s.	d.
	1904	Brought forward.............						
		INVESTMENTS PURCHASED (No 12)						
30	April 24	By cash paid Messrs Bishop & Co., being price of £400 India 3% Stock @ 96¾ as per contract of 20th April, 1904 ....£387 0 0 Brokerage and stamp 1 7 8	388	7	8			
31	April 24	By ditto being price of £418 Lancs & Yorks 3% Debenture Stock @ 90 . ... £376 4 0 Brokerage and stamp 4 11 0	380	15	0			
		GENERAL INVESTMENTS (No 3)						
32	May 2	By amount of five shares of £100 each in Standard Bank of South Africa, Limited, sold on this date	...			500	0	0
		MISCELLANEOUS (No 13).						
33	Nov. 18	By cash transferred to income being amount applicable to income in respect of the testator's reversionary interest in the funds subject to his parents' marriage settlement *	54	13	0			
		Carried forward	£823	15	8	£500	0	0

* See pp 101—103

Dr.

No.	Date.
	1904
34	Nov. 18
35	1906 June 3
36	July 16
37	July 16

PERSONALTY)—*continued*.   PAYMENTS AND TRANSFERS   *Cr.*

No.	Date.	Name of Person to whom, and for what purpose paid or transferred.	Cash.			Investments.		
			£	s.	d.	£	s.	d
	1906	Brought forward................	823	15	8	500	0	0
34	June 3	By ditto Mr. Wilson's mortgage discharged by realisation of security*	....			500	0	0
		EXECUTORSHIP EXPENSES (No. 6).						
35	July 10	By cash paid Mr. Gresham (Solicitor) being his costs of general administration and winding-up of the estate	39	18	3			
		GENERAL INVESTMENTS (No. 3)						
36	July 10	By amount of Lancs & Yorks 3% Debenture Stock sold on this date†....................................	....			18	0	0
37	July 10	By amount of Brighton Corporation 2½% Stock sold on this date	....			85	2	5
		By balance of cash (personalty) carried forward for distribution	757	2	10			
		By the like aggregate amount of investments	....			3,004	0	1
			£1,620	16	9	£4,107	2	6

* See pp. 53, 54.
† See p 128.

C.   Q

Dr.   RECEIPTS   GENERAL CAPITAL

No.	Date.	Name of Person from whom, and on what Account received.	Cash.			Investments.		
			£	s.	d.	£	s.	d.
	1906 July 16	To balance of cash brought forward for distribution ..	757	2	10			
		To aggregate amount of investments brought forward for distribution consisting of the following:—*						
		1. Consols £1,577 5 1						
		2. Advanced to pay Settlement Estate Duty on Mrs. Ford's share 26 15 0						
		3. Queensland 4% Inscribed Stock 600 0 0						
		4. India 3% Stock 400 0 0						
		5. Lancs & Yorks 3% Debenture Stock.. 400 0 0	....			3,004	0	1
			£757	2	10	£3,004	0	1

* See Chap. V., p. 60 *et seq*, as to Balancing.

(Personalty) PAYMENTS AND TRANSFERS Cr.

o.	Date.	Name of Person to whom, and for what purpose paid or transferred.	Cash.	Investments.
			£ s. d.	£ s. d.
38	1906 July 16	GENERAL INVESTMENTS (No. 3). By amount of advance to pay Settlement Estate Duty on Mrs Ford's settled share of residue now charged against that share	....	26 15 0
39	July 16	GENERAL ASSETS (No. 2). By cash transferred to the account of Mr. James Roberts, being his share of residue (personalty)	391 18 11	
	July 16	GENERAL INVESTMENTS (No. 3). By amounts of the following investments transferred to the account of Mr. James Roberts being his share of residue.—		
40		Consols	....	788 12 6
41		Queensland 4% Inscribed Stock	....	300 0 0
42		India 3% Stock..	....	200 0 0
43		Lancs and Yorks 3% Debenture Stock	....	200 0 0
44	July 16	GENERAL ASSETS (No. 2). By cash retained in trust for Mrs A Ford and her children and carried to their account, being their share of residue (personalty) .... £391 18 11 Less Amount of advance as above. 26 15 0	365 3 11	
	July 16	GENERAL INVESTMENTS (No. 3). By amounts of the following investments retained in trust for Mrs. A. Ford and her children and carried to their account.—		
45		Consols	....	788 12 7
46		Queensland 4% Inscribed Stock	....	300 0 0
47		India 3% Stock..	....	200 0 0
48		Lancs and Yorks 3% Debenture Stock	....	200 0 0
			£757 2 10	£3,004 0 1

GENERAL CAPITAL

Dr. RECEIPTS

No	Date.	Name of Person from whom, and on what Account received.	Cash.			Investments.		
			£	s.	d.	£	s.	d.
1	1903 May 2	"WEST VIEW" (No 1). To cash being Estate Duty deducted from the following pecuniary legacies so far as they issued out of the Real Estate, viz.:—* Mrs. Roberts .... £0 10 0 Mr. A. Richards .... 0 10 0 Mr. E. Ford .... 2 0 0 Miss E Roberts 2 0 0	5	0	0			
2	1906 May 27	To cash received of Mr Forward for "West View," St. Albans (Freehold) — Purchase-money ...... £600 0 0 *Less* Deposit............. 60 0 0	540	0	0			
3	May 31	To cash received of Messrs. Jameson & Co. being deposit in respect of "West View" .... £60 0 0 *Less* Auctioneer's charges....... 15 12 0	44	8	0			
			£589	8	0	....		

* See p. 45.

(REALTY).*

Payments and Transfers Cr.

No.	Date.	Name of Person to whom, and for what purpose paid or transferred	Cash.			Investments.		
			£	s.	d.	£	s.	d.
	1903	"West View" (No. 1).						
1	April 10	By cash paid the Commissioners of Inland Revenue for estate duty on "West View," St. Albans............	15	0	0			
2	1906 July 16	By ditto Mr. Gresham (Solicitor) for expenses appertaining to Real Estate..........................	14	10	5			
3	July 16	By share of balance of cash (Realty) transferred to the account of Mr. James Roberts................	279	18	10			
4	July 16	By ditto retained in trust for Mrs. Ford and her children, and carried to their account	279	18	9			
			£589	8	0	£	....	

* As to this account, see pp. 43, 44.

THE ACCOUNT OF

Dr. RECEIPTS

No	Date.	Name of Person from whom, and on what Account received	Cash. £ s. d.	Investments. £ s. d.
	1906 July 16	To amounts of the following investments and cash transferred to this account —		
1		Consols	....	788 12 6
2		Queensland 4% Inscribed Stock	....	300 0 0
3		India 3% Stock..	....	200 0 0
4		Lancs & Yorks 3% Debenture Stock............	....	200 0 0
5		Cash transferred from Real Estate Account	279 18 10	
6		Ditto from Personal Estate Account	391 18 11	
7	July 20	To cash received of Messrs. Bishop & Co., being proceeds of sale of £300 Consols at 89, as per contract of the 16th inst. .... £267 0 0 *Less:* Power of Attorney, Brokerage and Stamp 1 0 0	266 0 0	
			£937 17 9	£1,488 12 6

Mr. JAMES ROBERTS' Share

Payments and Transfers   Cr.

No.	Date.	Name of Person to whom, and for what purpose paid or transferred.	Cash.			Investments.		
			£	s.	d.	£	s.	d.
1	1906 July 16	By amount of Consols sold on this date, as per contra..	....			300	0	0
2	July 22	By cash paid the British Reversionary Society in discharge of principal, interest, and costs due under Mr. James Roberts' mortgage of his share (amounts, &c. agreed by mortgagor*) :— Principal .... £700 0 0 Interest .... 26 17 0 Costs 4 4 0	731	1	0			
3	July 22	By cash paid Mr. Gresham, being his costs appertaining to the payment off of the British Reversionary Society's mortgage..	3	3	0			
	July 22	By amounts of the following investments transferred to Mr. James Roberts, being balance of his share of residue :—						
4		Consols	....			488	12	6
5		Queensland 4% Inscribed Stock	....			300	0	0
6		India 3% Stock	....			200	0	0
7		Lancs & Yorks 3% Debenture Stock.............	....			200	0	0
8	July 22	By cash paid Mr. James Roberts to balance	203	13	9			
			£937	17	9	£1,488	12	6

* See p. 187, *ante*

The Account of Mrs.

Dr.   Receipts

No.	Date.	Name of Person from whom, and on what Account received.	Cash.			Investments.		
	1906		£	s.	d.	£	s.	d.
	July 16	To amounts of the following investments and cash retained in trust for Mrs. Ford and her Children, being Share of Residue, less Settlement Estate Duty thereon —						
1		Consols	....			788	12	7
2		Queensland 4% Inscd. Stock	....			300	0	0
3		India 3% Stock	....			200	0	0
4		Lancs and Yorks 3% Deb. Stock	....			200	0	0
5		Cash transferred from Real Estate Account	279	18	9			
6		Ditto from Personal Estate Account	365	3	11			

LOAN

Dr.

Serial No.	Date.	Name of Person from whom, and on what Account received.	Cash.		
	1902		£	s.	d.
1	Nov. 9	To cash received from the Hertford Bank by way of loan, the deeds of "West View" being deposited as security................	200	0	0

ALICE FORD AND HER CHILDREN'S SHARE

PAYMENTS AND TRANSFERS . *Cr.*

No.	Date.	Name of Person to whom, and for what purpose paid or transferred.	Cash.	Investments.
			£ s. d	£ s. d.
		NOTE.—These assets, constituting as they now do a separate trust, will be transferred to and future records made in a separate book, a specimen of which is given on pp. 235—237, post.		

ACCOUNT.*

Cr.

Serial No.	Date.	Name of Person to whom, and for what purpose paid.	Cash.
	1902		£ s. d.
1	Dec. 11	By cash paid the Hertford Bank in discharge of loan	200 0 0

* See pp. 49, 50.

IN THE MATTER OF THE ESTATE

OF

Mr. WILLIAM ROBERTS deceased

SEPARATE ACCOUNT

OF THE SHARE SETTLED ON

Mrs. ALICE FORD and her Children

(*See Chap. V., p. 64, as to this Account.*)

NOTE.—The account overleaf may be preceded by a copy of so much of the Will as relates to the legacy and a Memoranda added

SEPARATE ACCOUNT OF MRS.

Dr. RECEIPTS PART I.—

No.	Date.	Name of Person from whom, and on what Account received.	Cash.			Investments.		
			£	s.	d.	£	s.	d.
	1906 July 16	To amounts of the following investments and cash retained in trust for Mrs Ford and her Children—						
1		Consols	....			788	12	7
2		Queensland 4% Insed Stock	....			300	0	0
3		India 3% Stock...........................	....			200	0	0
4		Lancs and Yorks 3% Deb. Stock	....			200	0	0
5		Cash transferred from Real Estate Account	279	18	9			
6		Ditto from Personal Estate Account	365	3	11			
7	July 30	To amount of Mortgage by Mr. Henry Ford, of "Fircroft," London Road, Reading.................	....			600	0	0
8	July 30	To amount of Consols purchased on this date	....			50	0	0

PART II.—

	1907 July	*Note.*—All Income is received by the Tenant for life direct until further order.	£	s.	d.

ICE FORD AND HER CHILDREN

'ITAL   PAYMENTS AND TRANSFERS   Cr.

Date.	Name of Person to whom, and for what purpose paid or transferred.	Cash			Investments.		
		£	s.	d.	£	s.	d.
1906							
July 30	By cash advanced to Mr. Henry Ford on Mortgage of "Fircroft," London Road, Reading	600	0	0			
July 30	By cash paid Messrs. Bishop & Co., being price of £50 : 0s. 0d. Consols @ 90 as per contract of this date .... £45 0 0 Brokerage and Stamp 0 2 8	45	2	8			

:OME

APPENDIX B

ACCOUNT OF APPORTIONMENTS UNDER THE STATUTE OF DIVIDENDS ACCRUING DUE AT THE DEATH OF THE TESTATOR

(*See Chap. VII.*, *p.* 85 et seq., *as to this Account.*)

current at the death (the 1st November, 1902) and apportioned as between Capital and Income

(Income Tax for the years 1902-3 and 1903-4 was at the rate of 1s. in the £)

Voucher No. and Serial.	Date when received.	Nominal or Face Value of Security.	Description of Security.	Rate of Interest.	Date from and to which the Income is calculated.	Amount apportion-able after deducting tax.	Proportion due to Capital.	Proportion due to Income.	Proportion carried to Suspense Apportion-ment Account.
1	2	3	4	5	6	7	8	9	10
	1903	£ s. d				£ s. d.	£ s d.	£ s. d.	£ s. d.
1	Jan. 5	600 0 0	Consols	2¾%	5th Oct. 1902, to 5th Jan. 1903.	3 11 3	1 1 1	2 10 2	
2	Feb. 19	500 0 0	London & North Western Railway Guaranteed Stock	4%	30th June to 31st Dec. 1902.	9 10 0	6 9 1	3 0 11	
3	Mar. 1	100 0 0	$500 St. Louis Bridge Railroad Company First Mortgage Gold Bond*	5%	1st Sept. 1902, to 1st Mar. 1903.	2 7 6	0 15 10	....	1 11 8
4	April 4	500 0 0	5 shares in the Standard Bank of South Africa, Ld:—* Final dividend for the year @ 3¾% free of tax ...... 19 0 0 *Less* Proportion of £38 (being dividend for the year) as from 1st Nov. to 31st Dec. 1902 (60 days), due to income .. 6 4 11 ────── £12 15 1	7⅝%	31st Dec 1901, to 31st Dec. 1902.	19 0 0	12 15 1	....	6 4 11

240

241

5	April 10	400	0	0	400 shares in Golden Reef Mining Company, Ltd.:—* Final dividend for the year @ 2% less 8s tax .... 7 12 0 *Less*: Proportion of £38 (being dividend for the year) as from 1st Nov. 1902, to 31st March, 1903 (150 days), due to income .... 15 12 4 (This deduction being impossible, no part of the final dividend is due to capital.)†	10%	31st Mar. 1902, to 31st Mar. 1903.	7 12 0	...	...	7 12 0
6		50	0	0	50 shares of £1 each in the English Investment Trust *	..	....	....	....	....	....
7	Jan 10	500	0	0	Mortgage by Mr. Wilson, of "Weston Cottage," Hatfield, Herts	4%	8th Oct. 1902, to 8th Jan. 1903.	4 15 0	1 5 0	3 10 0	....
8	April 7	650	0	0	Testator's share in the partnership of Messrs. Roberts, Wallis & Co.	10%	1st Nov. 1902, to 7th April, 1903.	26 11 3	....	....	26 11 3
								£73 7 0			
							Transferred to Capital	£22 6 1	....	....	
								Transferred to Income	£9 1 1	....	....

* See *ante*, p. 88.
† As to this, see p. 89, *ante*.

Note.—The Apportionments in this Account have been arrived at by calculating interest for the number of days expired at the death since the date to which the last payment was calculated on the capital sum and at the rate involved in each case, Income Tax (if necessary) then being deducted.

If an Apportionment Account has to be prepared upon the death of a tenant for life, the above form can be used, except that column 8 will be headed "Proportion due to the executors of the late tenant for life," and column 9 "Proportion due to the remaindermen," or "second tenant for life," as the case may be, and column 10 will be omitted.

C.

R

APPENDIX C

ACCOUNT OF APPORTIONMENTS UNDER THE STATUTE OF RENTS ACCRUING DUE AT DEATH OF THE TESTATOR

(*See Chap. VII., p.* 89 et seq., *as to this Account.*)

APPENDIX C

APPORTIONMENTS IN PURSUANCE OF THE STATUTE

Account or Rents of the property of the late Mr. WILLIAM ROBERTS, deceased, current at the death (the 1st November, 1902) and apportioned as between Capital and Income

PART I.—FREEHOLDS AND COPYHOLDS

(Property Tax for the year 1902-3 was at the rate of 1s. in the £)

No of Item.	Date when received	Names of persons from whom received, or to whom paid or allowed	On what account and in respect of what part of the estate received or paid, and when due.	Gross rent received.	Deductions.	Net amount apportionable.	Proportion due to Capital.	Proportion due to Income.
1	2	3	4	5	6	7	8	9
				£ s. d.		£ s. d.	£ s. d.	£ s. d.
1	1903 Jan 6	Mr James Roberts (Specific Devisee)	One quarter's rent of Stevenage Farm due Christmas, 1902, on an annual Michaelmas tenancy.	15 0 0	....	15 0 0	5 8 6	9 11 6
				Transferred to Capital............			5 8 6	....
				Transferred to Income			....	9 11 6

PART II.—LEASEHOLDS

No. of Item.	Date when received.	Names of persons from whom received, or to whom paid or allowed.	On what account and in respect of what part of the estate received or paid, and when due.	Gross rent received	Deductions.	Net amount apportion-able	Proportion due to Capital.	Proportion due to Income.	Proportion carried to Suspense Apportionment Account.
1	2	3	4	5	6	7	8	9	10
				£ s. d.	£ s. d	£ s. d.	£ s. d.	£ s. d.	£ s. d.
2	1903 Jan. 11	Mr. Strong (Tenant)	One quarter's rent of "The Elms" due Christmas, 1902	10 0 0					
			Deduct One quarter's ground rent from 29th Sept. 1902, at £6 per ann.		1 10 0	8 10 0			
						8 10 0	3 1 5		5 8 7
						Transferred to Capital.	3 1 5		
						Transferred to Income	..	..	..

APPENDIX D

SUSPENSE APPORTIONMENT ACCOUNT

(See Chap. VII., p. 110 et seq., as to this Account.)

APPEN

APPORTIONMENTS IN PURSUANCE

SUSPENSE APPORTION

No.	Date when received.	Description of Property and Particulars of Deductions.	Value of property at death, or amount produced by sale within the first year after or value at end of first year according to circumstances.			Notional amount of Consols produced by value at end of first year.		
1	2	3	4			5		
			£	s.	d.	£	s.	d.
1	1903 Jan 11	Proportion of one quarter's rent of "The Elms," less tax	620	0	0	....		
2	Mar. 1	Proportion of six months' dividend on $500 St. Louis Bridge Railroad Co. First Mortgage Gold Bond, less tax	139	5	0	....		
3	April 4	Proportion of one year's dividend on five shares in the Standard Bank of South Africa, Ltd., less tax	400	0	0	443	15	0
4	April 15	Proportion of one year's dividend on 400 shares in Golden Reef Mining Co., Ltd., less tax	459	10	0	....		
5	April 7	Proportion of *interest* on £650, being testator's share in the partnership of Messrs. Roberts, Walhs & Co., less tax	650	0	0	....		
6	Mar 28	One quarter's rent of "The Elms," less property tax £2 and ground rent £3	620	0	0	....		
7	Sept. 1	Dividend on $500 St. Louis Bridge Railroad First Mortgage Gold Bond	139	5	0	....		
8	Oct. 4	Interim dividend on five shares in Standard Bank of South Africa, Ltd.	400	0	0	443	15	0
9	Oct. 15	Dividend on 400 shares in Golden Reef Mining Co., Ltd.	459	10	0	....		

DIX D

OF THE RULES IN EQUITY

MENT ACCOUNT

Testator died.... 1st Nov. 1902

Date of Notional Conversion.... 1st Nov. 1903

Price of Consols on that date .. 90

Rate at which interest is payable to the Tenant for Life.	Period for which gross Income in Column 8 is paid.	Gross Income.	Deductions	Net Income	Proportion of net Income due to Tenant for Life.	Balance due to Capital.
6	7	8	9	10	11	12
		£ s. d.	£ s. d.	£ s. d.	£ s. d.	£ s. d.
3%	1st Nov. to 25th Dec. 1902.	5 8 7	....	5 8 7	2 12 3	2 16 4
3%	1st Nov. 1902, to 1st Mar. 1903.	1 11 8	....	1 11 8	1 6 1	0 5 7
2½%	1st Nov. to 31st Dec. 1902.	6 4 11	....	6 4 11	1 14 8	4 10 3
3%	1st Nov. 1902, to 31st Mar 1903.	7 12 0	....	7 12 0	5 7 8	2 4 4
3%	1st Nov. 1902, to 7th April, 1903.	26 11 3	....	26 11 3	7 19 4	18 11 11
3%	25th Dec. 1902, to 25th Mar 1903.	10 0 0	5 0 0	5 0 0	4 8 5	0 11 7
..	....	Sold 26th April, 1903.	....	....	....	..
2½%	Interim— say 6 months.	....	....	19 0 0	5 5 5	13 14 7
..	...	Sold 26th April, 1903.	..	....	....	....
		Carried forward....		£71 8 5	28 13 10	£42 14 7

See note (e) on p. 99, *ante*, as to interest at 3 %.

APPENDIX D

No.	Date when received.	Description of Property and Particulars of Deductions	Value of property at death, or amount produced by sale within the first year after or value at end of first year according to circumstances.	Notional amount of Consols produced by value at end of first year.
1	2	3	4	5
	1903		£ s. d.	£ s. d.
10	Oct 7	Six months' interest on £650, being testator's share in the partnership of Messrs. Roberts, Wallis & Co	650 0 0	..
11	June 28	One quarter's rent of "The Elms" ..	620 0 0	.
12	Oct.	Ditto	620 0 0	....
	1904			
13	April 4	Final dividend on five shares in Standard Bank of South Africa, Ltd.	400 0 0	443 15 0
14	April 7	Six months' interest on £650, being testator's share in the partnership of Messrs. Roberts, Wallis & Co.	650 0 0	..
15	Oct. 4	Dividend on five shares in Standard Bank of South Africa, Ltd.	400 0 0	443 15 0
16	Oct. 7	Six months' interest on £650, being testator's share in the partnership of Messrs. Roberts, Wallis & Co	650 0 0	...

The figure to be inserted in Column 4 will be the value of the property at the date of the of one year from the death. As to which of these principles should be adopted, see pp. 98—101, *ante*.

The figure to be inserted in Column 11 will either be a sum equal to 2½% per annum on the Column 4, and the appropriate rate of interest will be inserted in Column 6. If the figure in in Column 12.

As to whether "Consol interest" or 3% on value is payable, see pp. 98—101, *ante*.

—continued

Rate at which interest is payable to the Tenant for Life	Period for which gross Income in Column 8 is paid.	Gross Income	Deductions.	Net Income	Proportion of net Income due to Tenant for Life.	Balance due to Capital.
6	7	8	9	10	11	12
		£ s. d.	£ s. d.	£ s. d.	£ s. d.	£ s. d
		Brought	forward....	71 8 5	28 13 10	42 14 7
3%	7th April to 7th Oct. 1903	32 10 0	1 12 6	30 17 6	9 5 3	21 12 3
3%	25th Mar to 24th June, 1903	10 0 0	....	10 0 0	4 8 5	5 11 7
..	24th June to 29th Sept. 1903.	Sold 24th June, 1903.	....	....	....	.
				£112 6 1	....	..
			Transferred	to Income ..	42 7 6	....
			Transferred	to Capital ..		69 18 5
2½%	31st Dec 1902, to 31st Dec. 1903 (less No. 8, ante).	....	....	19 0 0	5 5 5	13 14 7
3%	7th Oct. 1903, to 7th April, 1904.	32 10 0	1 12 6	30 17 6	9 5 3	21 12 3
2½%	....	Sold 2nd May, 1904.	....	....	....	....
3%	7th April to 7th Oct. 1904	Paid off 7th April, 1904	....	....	....	....
				49 17 6	....	....
			Transferred	to Income ..	14 10 8	...
			Transferred	to Capital ..		35 6 10

estator's death, the amount actually produced by sale within the year, or the value at the end
otional amount of Consols in Column 5, or 3% per annum on the value of the property appearing in
Column 11 is then deducted from that in Column 10, the balance will be the amount to be inserted

See note (e) on p. 99 as to interest at 3 %.

APPENDIX E

INCOME ACCOUNT

(See Chap. VI. as to this Account.)

IN THE MATTER OF THE ESTATE OF

THE EXECUTORS' AND TRUSTEES' ACCOUNT OF

Dr.   RECEIPTS

No.	Date.	Name of Person from whom, and on what Account received.	Cash.
			£ s. d.
1	1903 Jan. 6	To cash being proportion of rent of freehold property current at the death as per Apportionment Account, Appendix C., Part I., p. 244.....	9 11 6
2	Jan. 10	To cash transferred from capital, being proportion of property tax in respect of "West View," from 5th April to 1st November, 1902 (210 days), @ £2 per annum*........	1 3 0
3	April 5	To cash being dividend for the quarter from 5th January to 5th April, 1903, on £600 Consols @ 2½ %, less tax	3 11 3
4	April 12	To cash being interest for the quarter from 8th January to 8th April, 1903, on £500 @ 4 % due from Mr. Wilson, less tax	4 15 0
5	April 15	To cash being proportion of dividends and interest current at the death as per Apportionment Account, Appendix B., p. 239	9 1 1
6	April 16	To cash received of the Hertford Bank, St. Albans Branch, being deposit interest on £400 at 2½ % from 12th January to 16th April, 1903 (94 days)	2 11 6
		Carried forward................	£30 13 4

* See Income Tax Act, 1842, Schedule A., No. IV., Rule 12.

THE LATE MR. WILLIAM ROBERTS Deceased

RECEIPTS AND PAYMENTS APPERTAINING TO INCOME

PAYMENTS   Cr.

No	Date.	Name of Person to whom, and for what purpose paid.	Cash £ s d
1	1902 Nov. 12	By cash paid the Commissioners of Inland Revenue for interest @ 3 % on £182 16s 8d Estate Duty from 1st to 12th November, 1902 (11 days)*	0 5 6
2	Dec. 11	By cash paid the Hertford Bank for interest on £200 @ 4 % from 9th November to 11th December, 1902 (32 days)	0 14 0
3	1903 Feb. 1	By cash paid Mrs. Ross being a quarter's annuity from 1st November, 1902, to 1st February, 1903, @ £26 per annum ....£6 10 0 Less : Tax 0 6 6	6 3 6
4	Feb. 21	By cash paid Mrs. Alice Ford being proportion of dividend for six months from 30th June to 31st December, 1902, on £500 London & North Western Railway Stock as per Apportionment Account, Appendix B. p 197	3 0 11
5	Feb 24	By cash paid Mr James Roberts being proportion of rent of 'Stevenage' current at the death, retained in hand until consent to devise granted (as per Item 1, contra)	9 11 6
6	April 8	By cash paid John Ross (Administrator of Mrs Ross) being proportion of annuity from 1st February to 21st March, 1903 (48 days), the day of the annuitant's death ....£3 8 5 Less Tax 0 3 5	3 5 0
7	April 10	By cash paid Commissioners of Inland Revenue for interest at 3 % on £n further Estate Duty from 1st November, 1902, to 10th April, 1903 (160 days)*	0 1 7
		Carried forward	£23 2 0

* This interest is payable out of Income See Earl Howe v. Kingscote, (1903) 2 Ch at 83, and Finance Act, 1896, s. 18 (1), repealing the words "interest . . shall form part of the Estate Duty" in section 6 (6) of the Finance Act, 1894

Dr. RECEIPTS INCOME

No	Date.	Name of Person from whom, and on what Account received.	Cash.		
	1903	Brought forward.........	£ 30	s. 13	d. 4
7	July 1	To cash being dividend for six months on £600 Queensland 4 % Inscribed Stock, less 12s. tax	11	8	0
8	July 5	To ditto being dividend for the quarter from 5th April to 5th July, 1903, on £600 Consols at 2½ %, less 3s. 9d. tax	3	11	3
9	July 10	To ditto being interest for the quarter from 8th April to 8th July, 1903, on £500 at 4 % due from Mr. Wilson, less 5s. tax	4	15	0
10	Oct. 5	To ditto being dividend for the quarter from 5th April to 5th October, 1903, on £600 Consols at 2½ %, less tax	3	11	3
11	Oct 8	To ditto being interest for the quarter from 8th July to 8th October, 1903, on £500 at 4 % due from Mr. Wilson, less 5s. tax	4	15	0
12	Oct 15	To cash being amount due to income in respect of unauthorised investments as per Suspense Apportionment Account, Appendix D., p. 251....	42	7	6
13	Nov. 1	To cash being dividend for the half-year from 1st May to 1st November, 1903, on £85 : 2s 5d Brighton Corporation Stock @ 2½ %, less 1s. tax....	1	0	3
			£102	1	7

I, Margaret Roberts, approve and agree this statement of account, and agree to accept the Income from the assets thereby disclosed for the periods therein stated.

Dated this 1st November, 1903

Account—*continued.*

Payments

Cr.

No.	Date.	Name of Person to whom, and for what purpose paid	Cash
	1903	Brought forward........	£ s. d. 23 2 0
8	Nov. 1	By cash to Capital Account (Item 27) being income of that part of the Testator's Estate which was applied in paying debts, legacies, &c.	6 12 10
9	Nov. 1	By cash paid Mr Gresham (Solicitor) being his costs appertaining to the collection and distribution of income....	3 7 5
10	Nov. 1	By cash paid Mrs. Roberts being balance of income	68 19 4
			£102 1 7

sum of £68 : 19s. 4d. thereby shewn to be due to me in discharge of all claims in respect of

(Signed)　M. ROBERTS.

C.

S

INCOME ACCOUNT FROM

Dr. RECEIPTS

No.	Date.	Name of Person from whom, and on what Account received.	Cash.		
			£	s.	d.
14	1906 April 5	To cash being dividend for the quarter from 5th January to 5th April, 1906, on £1,577 · 5s. 1d. Consols @ 2½%, less 9s. 10d tax	9	7	3
15	April 5	To ditto being dividend for the quarter from 5th January to 5th April, 1906, on £400 India 3% Stock, less 3s. 0d. tax	2	17	0
16	April 12	To ditto being interest for the quarter from 8th January to 8th April, 1906, on £500 @ 4% due from Mr Wilson, less 5s. tax	4	15	0
17	May 1	To ditto being dividend for the half-year from 1st November, 1905, to 1st May, 1906, on £85 : 2s 5d Brighton Corporation 2½ % Stock, less 1s. tax	1	0	3
18	July 1	To cash being dividend for six months from 1st January to 1st July, 1906, on £600 Queensland 4% Inscribed Stock, less 12s. tax	11	8	0
19	July 1	To ditto from 1st January to 1st July, 1906, on £418 Lancs & Yorks 3% Debenture Stock, less 6s 3d. tax	5	19	1
20	July 5	To ditto for the quarter from 5th April to 5th July, 1906, on £1,577: 5s. 1d. Consols, less 3s. 9d tax	9	7	3
21	July 5	To ditto from 5th April to 5th July, 1906, on £400 India 3% Stock, less 3s 0d. tax	2	17	0
			£47	10	10
	July 16	To balance brought down for distribution	44	4	7
			£44	4	

We, the undersigned, approve and agree this statement of account, and agree to accept the respect of Income from the assets thereby disclosed for the periods therein stated.

Dated this 22nd July, 1906.

16th OF JANUARY, 1906

PAYMENTS *Cr.*

No.	Date.	Name of Person to whom, and for what purpose paid.	Cash		
	1906		£	s	d.
		NOTE.—Mrs. Roberts, the tenant for life, died 16th January, 1906.			
10	July 1	By cash paid the Executors of the late Mrs Roberts being the proportion of income accrued prior to 16th January, 1906, as per Apportionment Account	3	6	3
		By balance carried down	44	4	7
			£47	10	10
11	July 16	By cash paid Mr Jas. Roberts being his share of balance	22	2	3
12	July 16	By ditto Mrs. Ford being her ditto	22	2	4
			£44	4	7

respective sums of cash thereby shewn to be due to us respectively in discharge of all claims in

(Signed) JAMES ROBERTS, } *Children of the Testator entitled*
             A. FORD,   } *to the above in equal moieties.*

(End of Estate Book)

APPENDIX F

IN THE MATTER OF THE ESTATE
OF
Mr. WILLIAM ROBERTS deceased

FINAL STATEMENT

FOR THE

BENEFICIARIES

(*See Chap. X as to this Account.*)

Note.—Here will be set forth a copy of the will *in extenso*, or an epitome thereof, if not previously supplied to the Residuary Legatee.

In the matter of the Estate of Mr. WILLIAM ROBERTS Deceased

THE SCHEDULE

Part I.

REAL ESTATE of which the Testator died possessed

No.	Particulars of Property	References.*
1	A Freehold House called "West View," situate at St. Albans, in the Parish of Belmont, in the County of Hertford, with 2 acres adjoining in the Testator's occupation and assessed under Sch. A at £35 per annum Valuation for Land Duties £700	SOLD 31st March, 1906 (Items 2 and 3, p 266)
2	A Freehold Farm known as "Stevenage," situate in the Parish of Hatfield, in the County of Herts, containing 12 acres, and let to Mr. Henry Green on an annual tenancy @ £60. Valuation for Land Duties £1,000. Mortgage thereon dated 7th October, 1890, created by the Testator in favour of Mr. Henry Bates to secure £500 and interest @ $4\frac{1}{2}\%$ which interest had been paid by the Testator down to the 7th October, 1902.	SPECIFICALLY DEVISED

* These references, except where otherwise appears, are to the Serial Numbers of the Real Estate Account in the Final Statement, which commences on page 266.

THE SCHEDULE—continued.

PART II.

PERSONAL ESTATE of which the Testator died possessed

No	Nominal or Face Value (if any).	Particulars of Property	References †
	£ s. d.		
3	....	A Leasehold Messuage and premises known as "The Elms," situate in Hertford Road, St Albans, held for a term of 99 years expiring September 29th, 1974, granted by John England, of 100, Pall Mall, London, at a ground rent of £6 per annum, and let to Mr Strong on a 21 years' lease at £40 per annum expiring 25th December, 1921 * Valuation for Land Duties £	SOLD. (Items 7 and 8, p 268)
4	600 0 0	Consols	DIVIDED IN SPECIE.
5	3 11 3	1 quarter's dividend due 5th October, 1902	RECEIVED. (Item 3, p 268.)
6	500 0 0	London & North Western Railway 4% Guaranteed Stock	SPECIFICALLY BEQUEATHED.
7	300 0 0	London & North Western Railway 4% Guaranteed Stock	SOLD. (Item 18, p. 272)
8	100 0 0	$500 St. Louis Bridge Railroad Company First Mortgage Gold Bond Nº 25 @ 4s. per dollar.*	SOLD. (Item 19, p. 272.)
9	500 0 0	5 shares of £100 each in the Standard Bank of South Africa, Limited *	SOLD. (Item 21, p. 272.)
10	400 0 0	400 shares of £1 each in Golden Reef Mining Company, Limited.*	SOLD. (Item 20, p 272.)
11	50 0 0	50 shares of £1 each in the English Investment Trust, Limited *	Valueless. (Item 1, p. 279.)
12	12 5 6	Cash in the house	RECEIVED (Item 1, p. 268.)
13	47 4 2	Cash at The Hertford Bank, St Albans, on drawing account	RECEIVED. (Item 2, p. 268.)
14	500 0 0	Mortgage by Mr Wilson to Testator of "Weston Cottage," Hatfield, Herts.	SECURITY REALISED (Item 12, p. 270.)

No	Nominal or Face Value (if any).	Particulars of Property	References.†
	£ s d		
15	200 0 0	Policy No. 10,864 in the Equitable Assurance Company on the life of the Testator	RECEIVED. (Item 4, p. 268.)
16	160 0 0	Bonuses thereon	
17	100 0 0	Debt due from Mr. Henry Wood (adjudicated bankrupt 29th September, 1901), for money lent by Testator—proof admitted for.	DIVIDENDS RECEIVED. (Items 5 and 6, p. 268.)
18	Produced:— £977 : 5s. 1d. Consols, £120 9s. 5d. Cash.	The Testator's one-third share in the investments subject to the trusts of his parents' marriage settlement, dated 21st January, 1850 (The rule in *Chesterfield's Case* applies in respect of this asset.)	RECEIVED. (Item 14, p 278, Item 11, p 270.)
19	....	Furniture	SPECIFICALLY BEQUEATHED.
20	650 0 0	Testator's share in partnership of Messrs. Roberts, Wallis & Co as per account to be stated by the surviving partners in accordance with the articles, including interest on capital and share of profits to date of death.*	RECEIVED (Item 10, p 268.)
21	5 8 6	Proportion of rent of Freehold property current at the death as per separate Apportionment Account.	RECEIVED (Item 13, p 270.)
22	3 1 5	Ditto in respect of Leasehold property	RECEIVED (Item 14, p 270.)
23	22 6 1	The like proportion of dividends and interest........	RECEIVED. (Item 15, p 270.)
		(The Testator died 1st November, 1902.)	

* The rule in *Howe* v. *Earl of Dartmouth* applies to the income derived from these assets

† These references, except where otherwise appears, are to the Personal Estate Account in the Final Statement, which commences on p 268

In the matter of the Estate of

THE EXECUTORS

in Account

the RESIDUARY LEGATEES

CAPITAL

Dr.   RECEIPTS

Serial No.	Account No	Date	Name of Person from whom, and on what Account received				Cash		
				£ s. d.	£ s d		£	s.	d.
1	1	1903 May 2	"WEST VIEW." To cash being Estate Duty deducted from the following pecuniary legacies, so far as they issued out of the Real Estate, viz. — Mrs. Roberts .... 0 10 0 Mr. A. Richards .... 0 10 0 Mr. E Ford .... 2 0 0 Miss E. Roberts 2 0 0		5 0 0				
2	2	1906 May 27	To cash received of Mr Forward for "West View," St. Albans (Freehold) — Purchase-money ....600 0 0 *Less* Deposit 60 0 0		540 0 0				
3	3	May 31	To ditto Messrs. Jameson & Co being deposit in respect of "West View" .... 60 0 0 *Less* Auctioneer's charges........ 15 12 0		44 8 0		589	8	0
							£589	8	0

Note —Where a voucher exists for any receipt or payment

Mr. WILLIAM ROBERTS Deceased

and TRUSTEES

with

of the above-named Testator

(REALTY)

PAYMENTS   Cr.

Serial No	Account No	Date.	Name of Person to whom, and for what purpose paid.	Cash
				£ s. d.
1	1	1903 April 10	"West View" By cash paid the Commissioners of Inland Revenue for estate duty on "West View," St. Albans £15 0 0	
2	2	1906 July 16	By ditto Mr. Gresham (Solr) for expenses appertaining to Real Estate 14 10 5	29 10 5
3	3	July 16	By share of balance of cash (Realty) transferred to the Account of Mr. James Roberts	279 18 10
4	4	July 16	By ditto retained in trust for Mrs Ford and her children, and carried to their Account	279 18 9
				£589 8 0

it bears the number as in the Capital Account

CAPITAL ACCOUNT

Dr.   RECEIPTS

Serial No	Account No.	Date.	Name of Person from whom, and on what Account received.		Cash.		
					£	s	d.
		1902	**GENERAL ASSETS.**				
1	1	Nov 8	To cash in the house at the date of testator's death.. £12 5 6				
2	2	Nov. 15	To cash received from the Hertford Bank being balance of testator's drawing account		47	4	2
3	10	Nov. 25	To ditto being 1 quarter's dividend on £600 Consols @ 2½ % due 5th October, 1902, less 3s. 9d. tax		3	11	3
4	12	Dec. 10	To ditto of the Equitable Assurance Co being the amount payable under Policy No. 10864 for. £200 0 0 Bonuses on ditto 160 0 0	360	0	0	
5	13	Dec. 10	To ditto of the Trustee in Mr. Henry Wood's bankruptcy, being first dividend of 2s. 6d. in the £ on £100 due to Testator		12	10	0
6	32	1903 June 6	To ditto being second and final dividend of 5s. in the £		25	0	0
7	22	June 24	To ditto Mr. James for "The Elms," Hertford Road, St. Albans (Leasehold):— Purchase-money .... £620 0 0 Less Deposit 62 0 0	558	0	0	
8	23	June 26	To ditto Messrs. Jameson & Co. (Auctioneers), being the deposit in respect of "The Elms" .... £62 0 0 Less Auctioneer's charges 18 3 6	43	14	8	
9	27	Nov. 1	To cash from Income Account being income of that part of the testator's estate which was applied in payment of debts, legacies, &c., the particulars being as follows:—£1,405:6s. 4d. capital which produced £6. 13s. 9d. income; to raise £1,402:16s. 5d. out of these sums rateably, income pays £6 : 12s. 10d., capital pays £1,396 · 3s 7d.		6	12	10
10	28	1904 April 7	To ditto Messrs. Roberts, Wallis & Co, being testator's share in partnership as per account stated by the surviving partners in accordance with the articles, including interest on capital and share of profits to date of death.. .... 650 0 0				
			Carried forward..... .£1,718 18 5				
			Carried forward.... ...		....		

(PERSONALTY)

PAYMENTS

Cr.

Serial No.	Account No.	Date.	Name of Person to whom, and for what purpose paid				Cash.		
		1902	FUNERAL EXPENSES				£	s.	d.
1	4	Nov. 17	By cash paid Messrs. Hinton & Co for testator's funeral				33	10	0
			ESTATE DUTY.						
2	1	Nov. 12	By cash paid Commissioners of Inland Revenue for estate duty	£182	16	8			
3	15	1903 April 16	By ditto for further estate duty on corrective affidavit in respect of personalty	6	0	0			
							188	16	8
		1902	EXECUTORSHIP EXPENSES.						
4	7	Dec. 10	By cash paid Mr. Gresham (Solr), for obtaining probate :—						
			Court fees £5 16 1						
			Costs 20 3 5						
		1903		25	18	6			
5	29	Nov. 1	By ditto being his costs of general administration to date..	65	18	7			
6	35	1906 July 10	By ditto being his costs of general administration and winding up of the estate	39	18	3			
							131	15	4
		1902	DEBTS DUE AT THE DEATH						
7	8	Dec 12	By cash paid the following debts due from testator.— Dr Thorpe (Medical Attendance)	17	10	6			
8	9		Mr. H. James (Wines, &c)	10	15	10			
9	10		Mr. J. Walters (Provisions)	7	3	4			
							35	9	8
			GENERAL EXPENSES						
10	3	Nov. 15	By cash paid Mis Roberts (testator's widow) for maintenance of " West View "				20	0	0
		1903 April 16	LEGACIES By cash paid the Commissioners of Inland Revenue for legacy duty on the following legacies :—						
11	16		£100 to Mr. Alexander Richards (Executor)..	£10	0	0			
12	17		£400 to Mr. Edward Ford (Nephew)	12	0	0			
13	18		£400 to Miss Ethel Roberts (Niece)	12	0	0			
14	19		Annuity of £26 to Mrs. Susan Ross	3	0	0			
			Carried forward........	£37	0	0			
			Carried forward......				£409	11	8

CAPITAL ACCOUNT

Dr. RECEIPTS

Serial No.	Account No.	Date.	Name of Person from whom, and on what Account received.	Cash.					
							£	s	d
			Brought forward.				....		
			Brought forward £1,718 18 5						
		1904	GENERAL ASSETS—*continued*.						
11	34	Nov 18	To cash received of the Trustees of Mr. and Mrs. Arthur Roberts' marriage settlement, being the Testator's share of cash subject thereto	120	9	5			
12	35	1906 June 3	To ditto Mr. Weeks being purchase-money of Weston Cottage	300	0	0	2,139	7	10
		1903	APPORTIONMENTS.						
13	14	Jan. 6	To cash being proportion of rent of Freehold property current at the death as per Apportionment Account, Appendix C., Part I., p. 244	5	8	6			
14	15	Jan. 11	To cash being proportion of rent of Leasehold property current at the death as per Apportionment Account, Appendix C., Part II , p 245	3	1	5			
15	18	April 15	To cash being proportion of dividends and interest current at the death as per Apportionment Account, Appendix B , p. 239	22	6	1			
16	25	Oct. 15	To cash being amount due to Capital in respect of unauthorised investments as per Suspense Apportionment Account, Appendix D., p 247	69	18	5			
17	33	1904 Oct. 7	To ditto	35	6	10	136	1	3
			Carried forward				£2,275	9	1

(PERSONALTY)—*continued.*

PAYMENTS   Cr.

Serial No.	Account No.	Date.	Name of Person to whom, and for what purpose paid.	Cash.
				£ s. d.
			Brought forward........	409 11 8
			Brought forward...... £37 0 0	
			LEGACIES—*continued.*	
			By cash paid the following pecuniary legacies:—	
15	5	1902 Nov. 17	Mrs Roberts (testator's widow) ....£100 0 0 *Less:* Duty on Real Estate so far as it contributed to this legacy at, say, ⅛th .. .. 0 10 0 ———— 99 10 0	
16	23	1903 May 2	Mr Alexander Richards.. 100 0 0 *Less:* Duty on Real Estate as above...... 0 10 0 ———— 99 10 0	
17	24		Mr. Edward Ford.. ... 400 0 0 *Less* Duty on Real Estate as above.. ... 2 0 0 ———— 398 0 0	
18	25		Miss Ethel Roberts .. .. 400 0 0 *Less* Duty on Real Estate as above...... 2 0 0 ———— 398 0 0 ———— 995 0 0	1,032 0 0
19	26		By cash transferred to Real Estate Account being amount of duty deducted as above	5 0 0
			Carried forward........	£1,446 11 8

CAPITAL ACCOUNT

Dr. RECEIPTS

Serial No	Account No.	Date	Name of Person from whom, and on what Account received		Cash		
		1902	Brought forward..		£ 2,275	s. 9	d. 1
18	11	Dec. 10	INVESTMENTS SOLD To cash received of Messrs Bishop & Co , being proceeds of sale of £300 London & North Western Railway 4 % Guaranteed Stock @ 120 cum dividend as per contract of the 30th November, 1902. ...... £360 0 0 Less Brokerage and stamp 1 17 6	358 2 6			
19	20	1903 May 1	To ditto $500 St. Louis Bridge Railroad Co. First Mortgage Gold Bond, at 140 as per contract of the 26th April, 1903 .... £140 0 0 Less Brokerage and stamp 0 15 0	139 5 0			
20	21	May 1	To ditto 400 shares Golden Reef Mining Co., Limited, @ 115½ as per contract of 26th April, 1903.. £462 0 0 Less Brokerage and stamp 2 10 0	459 10 0			
21	31	1904 May 7	To ditto five shares of £100 each in the Standard Bank of South Africa, Ltd , @ 79½ as per contract of the 2nd inst. .... £397 10 0 Less Brokerage and stamp 4 3 6	393 6 6			
22	36	1906 July 16	To ditto £18 Lancs & Yorks 3 % Debenture Stock sold for the purpose of distribution @ 147½ as per contract of the 10th inst.. .. .. £26 11 0 Less Brokerage and stamp 0 7 6	26 3 6			
23	37	July 16	To ditto £88 · 2s rd. Brighton Corporation 2½ % Stock @ 83 .... £70 13 0 Less Brokerage and stamp 0 2 6	70 10 6	1,446	18	0
			Carried forward........		£3,722	7	1

PERSONALTY)—*continued.*

PAYMENTS   Cr.

No.	Account No.	Date	Name of Person to whom, and for what purpose paid.	Cash		
		1903		£	s	d.
			Brought forward.....	1,446	11	8
			INVESTMENTS PURCHASED			
20	27	June 29	By cash paid Messrs. Bishop & Co being price of £600 Queensland 4% Inscribed Stock @ 99¼ as per contract of 27th June, 1903 .... £595 10 0 Brokerage and stamp .... 1 10 6 ———— £597 0 6			
21	28	Oct. 18	By ditto £85:2s 5d Brighton Corporation 2½% Stock @ 82 as per contract of 16th Oct , 1903.. £69 16 0 Brokerage and stamp....... .. .. 0 2 5 ———— 69 18 5			
		1904				
22	30	Nov. 24	By ditto £400 India 3% Stock @ 96¾ as per contract of 20th November, 1904 .... £387 0 0 Brokerage and stamp . ... 1 7 8 ———— 388 7 8			
23	31	Nov. 24	By ditto £418 Lancs and Yorks 3% Debenture Stock @ 90.. .. ..£376 4 0 Brokerage and stamp............. 4 11 0 ———— 380 15 0	1,436	1	7
			MISCELLANEOUS.			
24	11	Jan. 11	By cash transferred to income, being proportion of property tax in respect of "West View," from 5th April to 1st November, 1902 (210 days), @ £2 per annum..	1	3	0
25	30	Nov. 18	By cash transferred to income being amount applicable to income in respect of the Testator's reversionary interest in the funds subject to his parents' marriage settlement	54	13	0
		1903				
26	20	April 16	By cash paid Commissioners of Inland Revenue for Settlement Estate Duty on share of residue bequeathed in trust for Mrs. Ford and her children	26 15 0 ———— 82	11	0
			Carried forward	£2,965	4	3

C.   T

CAPITAL ACCOUNT

Dr. — RECEIPTS

Serial No.	Account No.	Date.	Name of Person from whom, and on what Account received.	Cash
				£ s. d
			Brought forward	3,722 7 1
				£3,722 7 1
		1906 July 16	To balance brought down	757 2 10
				£757 2 10

(PERSONALTY)—*continued.*

PAYMENTS   Cr.

Serial No.	Account No.	Date.	Name of Person to whom, and for what purpose paid	Cash.
				£ s. d.
		1906	Brought forward........	2,965 4 3
		July 16	By balance carried down for distribution	757 2 10
				£3,722 7 1
			GENERAL ASSETS	
27	39	July 16	By cash transferred to separate account of Mr. James Roberts, being balance of his share of residue £391 18 11	
28	45	July 16	By cash, retained in trust for Mrs Alice Ford and her children, and carried to their account £391 18 11 *Less:* Amount of advance for Settlement Estate Duty .... 26 15 0 ——————— 365 3 11	
				757 2 10
				£757 2 10

SUMMARY OF THE

Dr.

Receipts.	Cash.
	REAL
	£ s. d
"West View"	589 8 0
	PERSONAL
	£ s d.
General assets	2,139 7 10
Apportionments	136 1 3
Investments sold	1,446 18 0
	£3,722 7 1
Cash balance brought down for division	£757 2 10

A copy of the Income Account, appearing on
Alternative forms of Income Account will be

CAPITAL ACCOUNT

Testator died 1st November, 1902.

Cr.

	PAYMENTS.	Cash.
ESTATE		£ s. d.
	"WEST VIEW."	
	Duty and expenses £29 10 5	
	Mr. James Roberts' share of balance 279 18 10	
	Mrs Ford and her children's share 279 18 9	589 8 0
ESTATE		
		£ s d.
	Funeral expenses	33 10 0
	Estate Duty	188 16 8
	Executorship expenses	131 15 4
	Debts due at the death........................	35 9 8
	General expenses	20 0 0
	Legacies	1,032 0 0
	Estate Duty to Real Estate	5 0 0
	Investments purchased......	1,436 1 7
	Miscellaneous	82 11 0
	Balance for division	757 2 10
		£3,722 7 1
	Mr. James Roberts' share £391 18 11	
	Mrs. Alice Ford and her children's share.. £391 18 11	
	Less · Amount of advance for Settlement Estate Duty 26 15 0	
	——— 365 3 11	
		£757 2 10

pp. 258 and 259, will accompany this Capital Account.
found in Appendices G. and H., pp. 285—287.

Dr. GENERAL

Serial No.	Account No.	Date	Receipts.	Investments. £ s. d.
		1902	To amounts of the following investments belonging to the testator at the date of his death:—	
1	3	Nov 8	Consols	600 0 0
2	4		London & North Western Railway 4% Guaranteed Stock	800 0 0
3	5		$500 St. Louis Bridge Railroad Co. First Mortgage Gold Bond @ 4s. per $	100 0 0
4	6		5 shares of £100 each in the Standard Bank of South Africa, Limited	500 0 0
5	7		400 shares of £1 each in Golden Reef Mining Co., Limited ..	400 0 0
6	8		Mortgage by Mr. Wilson to testator of "Weston Cottage," at Hatfield, Herts, to secure	500 0 0
7	9		50 shares of £1 each in the English Investment Trust	50 0 0
8	16	1903 Jan. 11	To amount of cash on deposit with the Hertford Bank, St. Albans Branch	400 0 0
9	17	April 16	To amount advanced to pay Settlement Estate Duty on the share of Mrs. Ford and her children	26 15 0
10	24	June 27	To amount of Queensland 4% Inscribed Stock purchased on this date	600 0 0
11	26	Oct 16	To amount of Brighton Corporation 2½% Stock purchased on this date	85 2 5
12	29	1904 April 20	To ditto India 3% Stock ditto....................	400 0 0
13	30	April 20	To ditto Lancs & Yorks 3% Debenture Stock ditto	418 0 0
14	34	Nov. 18	To amount of Consols received of the trustees of Mr. and Mrs. Arthur Roberts' marriage settlement, being the testator's share in the investments subject thereto	977 5 1
				£5,857 2 6

INVESTMENTS*

Cr.

Serial No.	Account No.	Date	Transfers.	Investments.		
				£	s.	d.
		1902				
1	2	Nov. 12	By amount of 50 shares of £1 each in English Investment Trust, Limited (valueless, company liquidated in 1900)	50	0	0
2	6	Nov 30	By ditto London & North Western Railway 4% Guaranteed Stock sold on this date...........................	300	0	0
3	14	April 16	By amount of cash on deposit with the Hertford Bank, St. Albans Branch, withdrawn	400	0	0
		1903				
4	13	Feb 1	By amount of London & North Western Railway 4% Guaranteed Stock transferred to Mrs. Alice Ford, being her specific legacy .	500	0	0
5	21	April 26	By ditto $500 St. Louis Bridge Railroad Co. First Mortgage Gold Bond sold on this date	100	0	0
6	22	April 26	By ditto 400 shares Golden Reef Mining Co., Limited	400	0	0
		1904				
7	32	May 2	By ditto 5 shares of £100 each in Standard Bank of South Africa, Limited....................... ..., ...	500	0	0
		1906				
8	34	June 3	By ditto Mr Wilson's mortgage discharged by realization of security	500	0	0
9	36	July 10	By ditto Lancs & Yorks 3% Debenture Stock sold on this date ..	18	0	0
10	37	July 10	By ditto Brighton Corporation 2½% Stock	85	2	5
			By balance carried forward	3,004	0	1
				£5,857	2	6

* See p 208

Dr.   GENERAL

Serial No.	Account No.	Date	Receipts.	Investments.
		1906 July 16	To balance brought forward for distribution, consisting of the following investments :— 1. Consols .... £1,577 5 1 2. Advanced to pay Settlement Estate Duty on Mrs. Ford's share........................ 26 15 0 3. Queensland 4% Inscribed Stock .... 600 0 0 4. India 3% Stock ... . 400 0 0 5. Lancs & Yorks 3% Debenture Stock 400 0 0	£ s. d. 3,004 0 1
				£3,004 0 1

INVESTMENTS—*continued.*   *Cr.*

Serial No	Account No.	Date.	Transfers				Investments.		
							£	s	d.
11	38	1906 July 16	By amount of advance to pay Settlement Estate Duty on Mrs. Ford's settled share of residue charged against that share in Cash Account, Item 28				26	15	0
		July 16	By amounts of the following investments transferred to the account of Mr. James Roberts:—						
12	40		Consols	£788	12	6			
13	41		Queensland 4% Inscribed Stock	300	0	0			
14	42		India 3% Stock	200	0	0			
15	43		Lancs & Yorks 3% Debenture Stock	200	0	0	1,488	12	6
		July 16	By ditto retained in trust for Mrs. Alice Ford and her children and carried to their account:—						
16	45		Consols	£788	12	7			
17	46		Queensland 4% Inscribed Stock	300	0	0			
18	47		India 3% Stock	200	0	0			
19	48		Lancs & Yorks 3% Debenture Stock	200	0	0	1,488	12	
							£3,004	0	1

THE ACCOUNT OF

Dr. RECEIPTS

No.	Date.	Name of Person from whom, and on what Account received	Cash.			Investments.		
			£	s.	d.	£	s.	d.
	1906 July 16	To amounts of the following investments and cash transferred to this account :—						
1		Consols	....			788	12	6
2		Queensland 4% Inscribed Stock	....			300	0	0
3		India 3% Stock......	...			200	0	0
4		Lancs and Yorks 3% Debenture Stock..........	....			200	0	0
5		Cash transferred from Real Estate Account	279	18	10			
6		Ditto from Personal Estate Account	391	18	11			
7	July 20	To cash received of Messrs. Bishop & Co., being proceeds of sale of £300 Consols at 89, as per contract of the 16th inst .... £267 0 0 *Less* · Power of Attorney, Brokerage and Stamp.... ..:... 1 0 0	266	0	0			
			£937	17	9	£1,488	12	6

I, James Roberts, the undersigned, approve and agree this statement of account, and me in discharge of all claims upon the assets thereby disclosed.

Note.—The Schedule and statement for the beneficiaries are common to the class. The carried to a separate account, which will be rendered to the beneficiary in question only. and is merely a copy of that special account in the Estate Book.

Mr. JAMES ROBERTS' Share

Payments and Transfers   Cr.

No.	Date	Name of Person to whom, and for what purpose paid or transferred.	Cash.			Investments.		
			£	s	d	£	s	d
1	1906 July 16	By amount of Consols sold on this date, as per contra..	....			300	0	0
2	July 22	By cash paid the British Reversionary Society in discharge of principal, interest, and costs, due under Mr James Roberts' mortgage of his share (amounts, &c agreed).— Principal .. .. £700 0 0 Interest........ .... 26 17 0 Costs 4 4 0	731	1	0			
3	July 22	By cash paid Mr. Gresham, being his costs appertaining to the payment off of the British Reversionary Society's mortgage	3	3	0			
	July 22	By amounts of the following investments transferred to Mr. James Roberts, being balance of his share of residue.—						
4		Consols	....			488	12	6
5		Queensland 4% Inscribed Stock	....			300	0	0
6		India 3% Stock.........	..			200	0	0
7		Lancs & Yorks 3% Debenture Stock	..			200	0	0
8	July 22	By cash paid Mr. James Roberts to balance..........	203	13	9			
			£937	17	9	£1,488	12	6

gree to accept the sum of £203 : 13s 9d and the investments thereby shewn to be due to
Dated this 22nd of July, 1906.
(Signed)   JAMES ROBERTS
(one of the Residuary Legatees under the Testator's Will).

ssets belonging to each beneficiary, if there have been any dealings with those assets, are
ne specimen of such separate account has been given above in the case of the son's share,

RENT ACCOUNT

Receipts

No. of Item.	Date when received.	Tenants' Names	Description of Premises.	Annual Rent	Arrears due at 25th Mar. 1907.	Amount due at 25th Mar. 1907.	Amount received.	Arrears remaining due.	Observations.
				£ s. d.	£ s. d.	£ s. d.	£ s. d.	£ s. d.	
1	1907 Mar. 29	Mr Jno Scott	100 Piccadilly. House, &c	100 0 0	Nil.	25 0 0	25 0 0	Nil.	*Held on repairing lease for 7 years from Xmas, 1901

* In the first Account the nature of each tenancy should be stated in this column, and any alteration noticed in the subsequent accounts In this column should also be entered any remarks the collector may think proper to make as to the arrears of rent, the state of repairs or otherwise.

Payments and Allowances

No. of Item	Date of Payment or Allowance.	Names of Persons to whom paid or allowed.	For what purpose paid or allowed.	Amount.
				£ s. d.
	1907		100 Piccadilly	
1	March 29	Sun Insurance Office	One year's insurance against fire in respect of Policy No. 10,876, due 25th inst	1 10 0
2	March 29	Thomas Carpenter	Repairs	2 7 0
3	March 29	James Francis	Income tax	5 0 0

APPENDIX H

This is merely a specimen of an Annual Income Account to be rendered to a beneficiary.

Account of Rents of the property forming part of the Residuary Estate of Mr. WILLIAM ROBERTS, Deceased, for the Half-Year ending 24th June, 1903

No	Description of Property.	Name of Tenant.	Annual Rent.	Arrears.	Amount due.	Nature of Deductions.	Amount deducted.	Amount received.	Arrears remaining due.	Observations.
			£ s. d.	£ s. d.	£ s. d.	£ s. d.	£ s. d.	£ s. d.	£ s. d.	
					Part I—Freehold					
1	"Stevenage Farm," St. Albans	Henry Green	60 0 0	....	....	..	..	..	..	Specifically devised.
					Part II—Leasehold					
2	"The Elms," Hertford Road, St. Albans.	W. Strong	40 0 0	....	8 16 10	..	..	8 16 10		Leased for 21 years expiring 25th December, 1921. Amount dues as per Suspense Apportionment Account Sold 24th June, 1903.

Account of the Income of the Investments forming part of the Residuary Estate of the late Mr. WILLIAM ROBERTS, deceased, for the half-year ending 8th July, 1905.

(Income Tax for the year 1906 was at the rate of 1s. in the £)

Amount.	Description.	Gross Income accruing during the period.	Deductions.	Amount actually received during the period.
£ s. d.		£ s. d.	£ s. d.	£ s. d.
1,577 5 1	Consols 2½% .... (5th Jan. to 5th July)	*		
400 0 0	India 3% Stock .... (5th Jan. to 5th July).	6 0 0		
	Less Income tax	....	0 6 0	5 14 0
600 0 0	Queensland 4% Inscribed Stock ...... (1st Jan to 1st July)	12 0 0		
	Less Income tax.............	....	0 12 0	11 8 0
418 0 0	Lancs and Yorks 3% Deb. Stock...... (1st Jan. to 1st July)	6 5 4		
	Less Income tax....	...	0 6 3	5 19 1
		£24 5 4	£1 4 3	£23 1 1

Item —* The dividends on this Investment are paid by the bank to the tenant for life direct

Note —Particulars will be given on the face of this Account of any income in arrear.

See Chap. VI. as to this Account.

APPENDIX I

IN THE MATTER OF THE TRUSTS
OF
Mr. & Mrs. THOMAS' MARRIAGE SETTLEMENT

ESTATE BOOK

(*See Chap. XI. as to this Estate Book.*)

The following are specimen Epitome, Memoranda, Schedule, and Register of a marriage settlement trust, dealing with cash and securities only.

The dividends on the investments are paid to the tenant for life direct, so do not appear.

The Bank Pass-book with the counterfoils of the cheque and payment-in books are alone relied upon for transactions with the Bank.

In the matter of the Trusts of Mr. and Mrs. Thomas' Marriage Settlement

EPITOME OF THE SETTLEMENT

Date.

March 12, 1880.

Parties.

1. Mr. Frederick John Thomas, of 102, Piccadilly, W.
2. Miss Mary Rees, of Brighton.
3. Mr. Frederick Rees, of 79, Cheapside, E.C.,
   Mr. Alfred Thomas, of 102, Piccadilly, W., } Trustees.
   Mr. Charles Guppey, of 25, Regent Street, W.,

Property Settled.

(See Schedule.)

Trusts after Marriage.

To convert and invest as below, with usual power to hold any investment received as part of any settled share, and to postpone sale of reversionary interests.

Investments.

To be made, with the consent of the tenant for life, in the public stocks or funds or Government or parliamentary securities of the United Kingdom, or of India, or of any British colony or dependency or possession the interest or income whereof is payable in England; any securities the interest on which is guaranteed by Parliament; the stock of the Bank of England, or any mortgage of freeholds, copyholds, or leaseholds in England, such leaseholds having at the date of investment at least sixty years to run; the debentures or debenture stock, preference stock, or preference shares or bonds of any railway company in Great Britain or the United States of America or guaranteed railway company in India which shall have paid dividends of not less than £2 per cent. per annum on its ordinary capital for at least three years prior to investment.

Power.

To purchase residence out of one or both funds.

Covenant.
> By the wife to settle after-acquired property exceeding £200 in value.

Trusts of Husband's Fund.
> Income to be paid to husband for life or until he attempts to charge, sell, or incumber the same, then to the wife for life.
>
> Capital and income to be divided between the issue of the marriage after determination of prior life interests, as the parents or survivor shall appoint, but in default of appointment amongst the children equally.
>> If no issue, then subject to the life interests, the husband, his executors, administrators, and assigns will be entitled to the whole fund.

Trusts of Wife's Fund.
> Income to be paid to wife for life for her separate use without power of anticipation, then to the husband for life or until he attempts to charge, &c the same.
>
> Capital and income to be divided between the issue of the marriage after determination of prior life interests, as the parents or survivor shall appoint, but in default of appointment amongst the children equally.
>> If no issue, and subject to the life interests, the settled funds are to be held in trust for such person or persons as the wife shall by will appoint, and in default of appointment, in trust for such persons as would have been her next of kin if she had died intestate without having been married.

Advancement.
> Power for the trustees, at the request of the husband and wife, or the survivor, to raise one-half of the expectant share of any child or grandchild for advancement in life.

Hotchpot.
> Hotchpot clause.

New Trustees.
> Appointed by husband and wife during their joint lives and by the survivor during his or her life.

MEMORANDA

1.—13*th March*, 1880. The marriage was duly solemnised at St. Margaret's, Westminster.

2.—30*th June*, 1881. William Brown Thomas, the first child of the marriage, was born at 100, St James'.Square, London.

3 —10*th December*, 1882. Frances Mary Thomas, the second child of the marriage, was born at 100, St. James' Square, London

4 —10*th January*, 1895. Mr. Frederick Rees retired from the Trusts and Mr. Walter Atkins was appointed in his stead, jointly with the two continuing trustees, and the securities set forth in the "Balance of Stocks, &c.," in the register under this date were transferred to the new trustees

5.—10*th January*, 1895. The accounts were examined on this day by Mr. Walter Atkins, one of the Trustees, assisted by Mr. Parke, the Solicitor, and balances found to be correct. All the scrips for the various investments and the Trust documents (which are now deposited in the names of the Trustees at the Metropolitan Bank, St. James' Branch) were inspected and found to be in order.

(Signed)   W. ATKINS (Trustee),
(Signed)   J. PARKE (Solicitor).

6.—10*th January*, 1895. The expenses appertaining to the appointment of new trustees were raised and paid out of the Husband's Trust Funds, one-half of which must be charged against the Wife's Trust Funds when cash is available.

7.—*17th June*, 1896. Mr. Frederick John Thomas (the settlor) died at 100, St. James' Square, London.

8.—*8th August*, 1896. Mr Henry Rees (the father of Mrs. Thomas) died at Brighton.

9.—*12th February*, 1897. The stocks and cash under this date in the register were received in respect of the wife's share in her parents' Marriage Settlement Trust Fund, and all duties were paid, the Inland Revenue reference being "*Re* Rees, deceased," R. 30466—1897.

10.—*12th February*, 1897. The share of the expenses payable out of the Wife's Trust Funds was repaid to the Husband's Trust Funds.

11.—*1st March*, 1897. The stocks and cash under this date in the register were received in respect of the wife's share in Lady Brown's Settlement Trust Fund, and all duties were paid, the Inland Revenue reference being "*Re* Lady Brown, deceased," B. 78646—1897.

12.—*12th July*, 1904. Notice was received on this date of a settlement, dated the 7th July, 1904, executed by Miss Frances Mary Thomas in anticipation of her marriage with Mr. Charles Walter Nelson whereby she assigned to her trustees, Messrs. William Brown Thomas and Arthur James Nelson, her share in the Trust Estate.

13.—*6th April*, 1905. John Thomas (the settlor's father) died at Basingstoke.

14 —*10th May*, 1906. The stocks and cash under this date in the register were received in respect of the husband's share in his parents' Marriage Settlement Trust Fund, and all duties were paid, the Inland Revenue reference being "*Re* Thomas, deceased," T. 19742—1906.

15.—21st *May*, 1906. Mrs. Mary Thomas (the settlor) died at 100, St. James' Square, London. Inland Revenue reference T. 19621—1906.

16.—John Thomas (the settlor's father) by his will dated 17th June, 1890, and proved in the Principal Registry on the 28th May, 1905, by James Watkins, the executor therein named, declared (*inter alia*) " as to the share of my son Frederick John Thomas in my residuary estate I direct the same to be transferred to the trustees of his marriage settlement and be held by them upon the trusts thereof."

17.—10th *June*, 1906. The sum of £2,250 Consols, under this date in the register, was received in respect of the husband's share in his father's Residuary Estate, and all duties were paid, the Inland Revenue reference being T. 13482—1905.

THE SCHEDULE

Part I. Real Estate Settled

Nil

Part II. Personal Estate Settled

No.		Particulars.	References.
1	£1,000 0 0	**HUSBAND'S TRUST FUNDS** Policy No 1,001 in the Equitable Assurance Society on the husband's life.	Transferred. See Item No. 1, p. 300.
2	....	Bonuses in respect of husband's policy....	Carried down.
3	£5,000 0 0	India 3% Stock	Transferred. See Item No. 2, p. 300.
4	£800 0 0	40 Pennsylvania Railroad Bonds $100 each and No^d 1 to 40 *at 4s. per dollar*.	Transferred. See Item No. 3, p. 300.
5	....	The husband's one-third share in the investments subject to the trusts of his parents' marriage settlement, dated June 23, 1841, expectant upon the death of his father.	Carried down.
6	....	**WIFE'S TRUST FUNDS.** The wife's one-tenth share in the investments subject to the trusts of her parents' marriage settlement, dated Dec. 26, 1854, expectant upon the death of her father, Henry Rees.	Carried down.
7	....	The wife's one-tenth share in the investments settled by the late Lady Brown upon the wife and her brothers and sisters subject to their father's life interest.	Carried down.
8	Produced — £562: 3s. 10d. cash.	Covenant by the wife to settle after-acquired property.	Received. See Item No 8, p 308. Carried down.

BALANCE OF ASSETS REMAINING IN SCHEDULE ON 10TH JANUARY 1895 WHEN MR. WALTER ATKINS WAS APPOINTED TRUSTEE IN THE PLACE OF MR. FREDK. REES (RETIRED) JOINTLY WITH MESSRS. ALFRED THOMAS AND CHARLES GUPPEY THE CONTINUING TRUSTEES.

PART II. PERSONAL ESTATE

Original No in Schedule		Particulars	References
2	£472 0 0	**HUSBAND'S TRUST FUNDS.** Bonuses in respect of husband's policy.	Received. See Item No 5, p 302.
5	Produced :— £440 London County 3 % Stock £320 North Eastern Railway 3 % Debenture Stock. £178 . 9s. 2d. cash	The husband's interest in his parents' marriage settlement trust estate.	Proceeds received. See Items Nos 10, 11 & 12, p. 304
9	Produced : £2,250 Consols.	The husband's share in the residuary estate of his father, John Thomas, Esq., deceased, bequeathed by the testator to the trustees of this settlement to be held upon the trusts therein declared concerning the husband's trust funds. (See Mem. Item No. 17.)	Received. See Item No 14, p 304
6	Produced — £100 Midland Railway 4 % Stock £80 G. W. Railway Guaranteed ditto. £200 Consols. £682 · 9s. 1d cash	**WIFE'S TRUST FUNDS.** The wife's interest in her parents' marriage settlement trust estate.	Proceeds received. See Items Nos 1, 2, 3 & 4, p. 308.
7	Produced — £11 E. I. R. Annuity, " Class B " £200 G I. P Guaranteed Stock. £197 · 3s 10d. cash.	The wife's interest in Lady Brown's trust estate	Proceeds received. See Items Nos 5, 6 & 7, p. 308.
8	....	Covenant to settle after-acquired property	Nil.

BALANCE OF ASSETS remaining in Schedule on 14th June, 1906.

PARTS I. and II.—*Nil.*

I.B.—Part III , INCUMBRANCES, has been omitted in this case, having regard to the nature of the property settled.

1

IN THE MATTER OF THE TRUSTS
OF
Mr. & Mrs. THOMAS' MARRIAGE SETTLEMENT

Trustees { Mr. FRED^{K.} REES
Mr. ALFRED THOMAS
Mr. CHARLES GUPPEY }

Inl. Rev Ref. T. 20473—1896

GENERAL CAPITAL
(CASH AND INVESTMENTS)

IN THE MATTER OF THE TRUSTS OF MR.

THE ACCOUNT OF THE TRUSTEES OF

Dr. GENERAL

No.	Date.	Name of Person from whom, and on what Account received.	Cash. £ s. d.	Investments. £ s. d
				HUSBAND'S TRUST
1	1880 Mar. 12	To amount of policy in the Equitable Assurance Society	....	1,000 0 0
2	Mar. 12	To ditto India 3% Stock	....	5,000 0 0
3	Mar. 12	To ditto 40 Pennsylvania Railroad Bonds $100 No^d 1 to 40 at 4s. *per dollar*............................	....	800 0 0
				£6,800 0 0
	1895 Jan. 10	To aggregate amount of investments brought down, consisting of the following :— 1. Policy ....£1,000 0 0 2. India Stock .... 5,000 0 0 3. 40 Pennsylvania Railroad Bonds 800 0 0	....	6,800 0 0
		Carried forward	....	£6,800 0 0

Note —Where a voucher exists for any receipt or payment

AND MRS. THOMAS' MARRIAGE SETTLEMENT

THE ABOVE-MENTIONED SETTLEMENT

TRUSTEES : { MR. FREDK. REES,
MR. ALFRED THOMAS,
MR. CHARLES GUPPEY.

CAPITAL *Cr.*

No.	Date.	Name of Person to whom, and for what purpose paid or transferred	Cash.			Investments.		
			£	s	d.	£	s.	d.
FUNDS.	1895 Jan 10	By aggregate amount of investments carried down	....			6,800	0	0
						£6,800	0	0
		Trustees on Jan 10, 1895, { Mr. Alfred Thomas, Mr Charles Guppey, Mr. Walter Atkins.						

it bears the serial number, as in the Register.

Mr. Frederick John Thomas (the Settlor) died on the 17th June, 1896.

Dr. The Account of the Trustees of the

No.	Date	Name of Person from whom, and on what Account received.	Cash.	Investments
			£ s. d.	£ s. d.
				HUSBAND'S TRUST
	1895	Brought forward............ ...	....	6,800 0 0
4	Jan 13	To cash received of Messrs. Flint & Co. being proceeds of sale of £24 17s. 6d. India 3% Stock @ 110 as per contract of 11th January, 1895...... £27 7 3 *Less:* Power of Attorney, Brokerage and Stamp............... 0 14 1	26 13 2	
5	1896 July 10	To cash received of the Equitable Assurance Society being the amount payable under Policy No. 1001— £1,000 0 0 Bonuses thereon 472 0 0	1,472 0 0	
6	July 18	To amount of Consols purchased on this date as per *contra*	....	1,046 9 4
7	1897 Feb. 12	To cash transferred from the Wife's Trust Fund, being the wife's trustees' share of expenses of appointment of new trustees	13 6 7	
8	1899 Mar. 6	To cash received of Messrs. Flint & Co. being proceeds of sale of £360:10s. 9d. India 3% Stock @ 102 as per contract of 2nd March, 1899 . ... £367 15 0 *Less:* Power of Attorney, Brokerage and Stamp 1 1 7	366 13 5	
9	Mar. 6	To amount of advancement for William Brown Thomas charged against his share...............	...	380 0 0
		Carried forward	£1,878 13 2	£8,226 9 4

3fore-mentioned Settlement—*continued.* Cr.

o.	Date.	Name of Person to whom, and for what purpose paid or transferred	Cash.			Investments.		
			£	s.	d	£	s.	d
FUNDS.								
	1895	Brought forward		..			..	
1	Jan 11	By amount of India 3% Stock sold on this date as per *contra*		...		24	17	6
2	Jan. 13	By cash paid Mr Parke being his costs of and appertaining to appointment of new trustees	26	13	2			
3	1896 July 10	By amount of Policy No. 1001 in the Equitable Assurance Co. received as per *contra*		....		1,000	0	0
4	July 17	By cash paid Commissioners of Inland Revenue for Estate Duty payable on the death of Mr Frederick John Thomas	354	14	4			
5	July 17	By cash paid Mr. Parke, Solicitor, being his costs of obtaining payment of the policy moneys and preparing and passing Estate Duty Account	6	10	8			
6	July 18	By cash paid Messrs. Flint & Co being price of £1,046 9s 4d. Consols @ 106 as per contract of this date .. £1,109 5 1 Power of Attorney, Brokerage and Stamp .. 1 9 11	1,110	15	0			
7	1899 Mar. 2	By amount of India 3% Stock sold on this date as per *contra*		....		360	10	9
8	Mar. 6	By cash paid Mr Parke being his premium and stamp on Articles of Clerkship of William Brown Thomas*	380	0	0			
		Carried forward	£1,878	13	2	£1,385	8	3

Interest at 4% per annum will have to be paid on this advance from the time when it has to be brought into hotchpot. *Re Davy,* (1908) 1 Ch 61. See also p. 114, *ante.*

Mrs. Mary Thomas (the Settlor) died on the 21st May, 1906

Dr.   The Account of the Trustees of the

No.	Date.	Name of Person from whom, and on what Account received.	Cash.			Investments.		
			£	s.	d.	£	s.	d.
			HUSBAND'S TRUST					
	1906	Brought forward	1,878	13	2	8,226	9	4
	May 10	To the following investments and cash received of the trustees of Mr and Mrs. John Thomas' Settlement being the husband's one-third share in the funds subject thereto:—						
10		London County Council 3% Stock	...			440	0	0
11		North Eastern Rly. 3% Debenture Stock	....			320	0	0
12		Cash	178	9	2			
13	June 3	To cash received of Messrs. Flint & Co. being proceeds of sale of £440 London County Council 3% Stock @ 90 as per contract of May 24th, 1906 .... £396 0 0 *Less.* Power of Attorney, Brokerage and Stamp 1 3 9	394	16	3			
14	June 10.	To amount of Consols received of the Trustees of the Will of John Thomas, Esq., deceased, being the husband's share in the Residuary Estate of his father, John Thomas, Esq., deceased	...			2,250	0	0
			£2,451	18	7	£11,236	9	

before-mentioned Settlement—*continued*.　　　　　　　　　　　　Cr.

No.	Date.	Name of Person to whom, and for what purpose paid or transferred.	Cash. £ s. d.	Investments. £ s. d.
		FUNDS.		
	1906	Brought forward	1,878 13 2	1,385 8 3
9	May 24	By amount of London County Council 3% Stock sold on this date	....	440 0 0
10	June 14	By cash paid Mr. Parke being his costs appertaining to the winding-up and distribution of the Trust Estate..	24 13 3	
		By cash balance carried forward.................	548 12 2	
		By aggregate amount of investments carried forward	....	9,411 1 1
			£2,451 18 7	£11,236 9 4

C.　　　　　　　　　　　　　　　　　　　　　　　　　　　　　　　X

The Account of the Trustees of the

Dr.

No.	Date.	Name of Person from whom, and on what Account received.	Cash.			Investments.		
			£	s.	d.	£	s.	d.
			HUSBAND'S TRUST					
	1906 June 14	To aggregate amount of cash and investments brought forward for division consisting of the following:—						
		Cash	548	12	2			
		1. India 3% Stock.................. £4,614 11 9	....					
		2. 40 Pennsylvania Railroad Bonds ... 800 0 0	....					
		3. Consols........................... 3,296 9 4	....					
		4. Advanced for Mr. W. B. Thomas' Articles of Clerkship 380 0 0	....					
		5. North Eastern Railway 3% Debenture Stock 320 0 0	....			9,411	1	1
			£548	12	2	£9,411		1

)efore-mentioned Settlement—*continued*.

Cr.

No.	Date	Name of Person to whom, and for what purpose paid or transferred.	Cash £ s. d.	Investments. £ s. d.
	FUNDS			
	1906			
	June 14	By amounts of the following investments transferred to Mr. W. B. Thomas being his share of the Trust Estate :—		
11		India 3% Stock....	....	2,307 5 11
12		20 Pennsylvania Railroad Bonds....	....	400 0 0
13		Consols................	....	1,648 4 8
14		North Eastern Railway 3% Debenture Stock....	....	160 0 0
15		By amount of advancement made for Mr. W. B. Thomas' Articles of Clerkship and now charged against his share....	....	380 0 0

16		By cash paid Mr W B Thomas being his share of balance made up as follows :—
		Cash balance on the Estate £548 12 2
		Add for purposes of computation advance as per Item No. 15*...... 380 0 0
		                                            2)928 12 2
		                                              464 6 1
		       Deduct advance 380 0 0
		Net cash balance due to Mr Thomas.............
			84 6 1	

		By amounts of the following investments transferred to Messrs. W. B Thomas and A J Nelson, trustees of Mrs. Nelson's settlement, being her share of the Trust Estate:—		
17		India 3% Stock................	....	2,307 5 10
18		20 Pennsylvania Railroad Bonds	....	400 0 0
19		Consols	....	1,648 4 8
20		North Eastern Railway 3% Debenture Stock....	....	160 0 0
21		By cash paid Messrs W. B Thomas and A. J Nelson being Mrs Nelson's share of balance as per Item No. 16.	464 6 1	
			£548 12 2	£9,411 1 1

* In the Income Account Mr. W. B. Thomas' share will be charged with interest at 4% on £380 as from the date of the death of the last tenant for life. *Re Davy*, (1908) 1 Ch. 61. See also p. 114, *ante*

Mr. Frederick John Thomas (the Settlor) died on the 17th June, 1896.

Dr.   The Account of the Trustees of the

No.	Date	Name of Person from whom, and on what Account received.	Cash.			Investments.		
			£	s	d.	£	s	d.
						WIFE'S TRUST		
	1897							
	Feb. 12	To the following investments and cash received of the trustees of Mr. and Mrs Henry Rees' marriage settlement being the wife's one-tenth share in the funds subject thereto —						
1		Midland Railway Consolidated 4% Perpetual Preference Stock	....			100	0	0
2		G. W Railway 5% Guaranteed Preference Stock....	....			80	0	0
3		Consols	....			200	0	0
4		Cash	682	9	1			
	Mar. 1	To the following investments and cash received of the trustees of Lady Brown's settlement being the wife's one-tenth share in the funds subject thereto —						
5		East Indian Railway annuity, "Class B."	....			11	0	0
6		Great Indian Peninsula Railway 5% Guaranteed Stock	....			200	0	0
7		Cash	197	3	10			
8	Mar 3	To cash received of the trustees of Henry James, Esq., deceased, being the wife's share in the Residuary Estate of the above-named testator	562	3	10			
9	Mar 5	To amount of Victorian Government Inscribed Stock purchased on this date.				1,209	14	5
10	Mar. 5	To ditto Great Indian Peninsula Railway 5 % Guaranteed Stock				110	0	0
		Carried forward	£1,441	16	9	£1,910	14	5

before-mentioned Settlement—*continued.*   *Cr.*

No	Date	Name of Person to whom, and for what purpose paid or transferred.	Cash. £ s. d.	Investments. £ s. d.
	FUNDS 1897			
1	Feb 12	By cash transferred to the Husband's Trust Fund being the wife's trustees' share of the expenses of appointment of new trustees	13 6 7	
2	Mar 5	By cash paid Messrs. Flint & Co for the purchase of £1,209 : 14s. 5d. Victorian Government 3½% Inscribed Stock, 1921–1926, at par .... £1,209 14 5 Brokerage and stamp 1 13 6	1,211 7 11	
3	Mar. 5	By ditto £110 Great Indian Peninsula Railway 5% Guaranteed Stock at 178¼................ £196 1 6 Brokerage and stamp... ... .. 1 8 6	197 10 0	
4	Mar. 5	By ditto Mr. Parke (Solicitor) for professional charges..	19 12 3	
		Carried forward	£1,441 16 9	....

Dr.   The Account of the Trustees of the

No.	Date	Name of Person from whom, and on what Account received.	Cash.			Investments.		
			£	s.	d	£	s.	d.
						WIFE'S TRUST		
	1898	Brought forward..	1,441	16	9	1,910	14	5
11	April 1	To amount of Midland Railway Consolidated 2½ % Perpetual Preference Stock received in exchange as per contra				160	0	0
12	May 6	To ditto Great Indian Peninsula Railway annuity, "Class B.," ditto				20	14	0
			£1,441	16	9	£2,091	8	5
	1900							
	Jan. 10	To balance brought down, consisting of the following investments —						
		1. Midland Railway 2½ % Preference Stock £160 0 0						
		2. G W. Railway 5% Guaranteed Stock 80 0 0						
		3. Consols............. ... ... 200 0 0						
		4. East Indian Railway annuity, "Class B." . 11 0 0						
		5. Great Indian Peninsula Railway Annuity, "Class B" 20 14 0						
		6. Victorian Government Inscribed Stock, 1921—1926 .... 1,209 14 5						
						1,681	8	5
		Carried forward....	....			£1,681	8	5

before-mentioned Settlement—*continued.*   *Cr.*

No.	Date.	Name of Person to whom, and for what purpose paid or transferred	Cash	Investments.
			£ s. d.	£ s. d.
	FUNDS.			
	1898	Brought forward........	1,441 16 9	....
5	April 1	By amount of Midland Railway Consolidated 4 % Perpetual Preference Stock surrendered in exchange for Consolidated 2½ % Perpetual Preference Stock as per *contra*		100 0 0
6	May 6	By ditto Great Indian Peninsula 5 % Guaranteed Stock surrendered in exchange for annuities as per *contra*		310 0 0
	1900 Jan. 10	By balance carried down		1,681 8 5
			£1,441 16 9	£2,091 8 5

Mrs. Mary Thomas (the Settlor) died on the 21st May, 1906.

Dr.   The Account of the Trustees of the

No	Date.	Name of Person from whom, and on what Account received.	Cash.	Investments.
			£ s. d.	£ s. d.
				WIFE'S TRUST
	1906	Brought forward........	....	1,681 8 5
13	June 8	To cash received of Messrs Flint & Co., being proceeds of sale of £160 Midland Railway 2½ % Preference Stock @ 74 as per contract of 29th May, 1906..118 8 0 *Less:* Brokerage and stamp 0 16 0	117 12 0	
14	June 8	To ditto of 14s. Great Indian Peninsula Railway, "B." Annuity, as per contract of 29th May, 1906, @ 21 for purpose of distribution............ 14 14 0 *Less* · Brokerage and stamp 0 2 7	14 11 5	
15	June 8	To ditto £1 East Indian Railway Annuity, Class "B.," as per contract of 29th May, 1906, sold @ 26 for purpose of distribution .... 26 0 0 *Less* · Brokerage and stamp 0 2 7	25 17 5	
			£158 0 10	£1,681 8 5

before-mentioned Settlement—*continued.*   *Cr.*

No	Date	Name of Person to whom, and for what purpose paid or transferred.	Cash. £ s d	Investments. £ s. d
	FUNDS. 1906	Brought forward........	....	....
7	May 29	By amount of Midland Railway 2½ % Preference Stock sold on this date		160 0 0
8	May 29	By cash paid Commissioners of Inland Revenue for Estate Duty payable on the death of Mrs Thomas ...	63 12 8	
9	May 29	By amount of Great Indian Peninsula Railway, "B" Annuity, sold on this date		0 14 0
10	May 29	By ditto East Indian Railway Annuity, Class "B.," ditto............................		1 0 0
11	May 29	By cash paid Mr. Parke being his costs appertaining to the winding-up and distribution of the Trust Estate	33 18 4	
		By cash balance carried forward	60 9 10	
		By aggregate amount of investments carried forward..		1,619 14 5
			£158 0 10	£1,681 8 5

Dr. The Account of the Trustees of the

No.	Date.	Name of Person from whom, and on what Account received.	Cash	Investments.
			£ s. d.	£ s. d.
				WIFE'S TRUST
	1906 June 14	To aggregate amount of cash and investments brought forward for division consisting of the following —		
		Cash	60 9 10	
		1 G. W. Railway 5% Guaranteed Stock.. £80 0 0		
		2. Consols 200 0 0		
		3. East Indian Railway Annuity, Class "B." . 10 0 0		
		4. Great Indian Peninsula Railway Annuity, Class "B." . 20 0 0		
		5. Victorian Government Inscribed Stock . 1,209 14 5	....	1,519 14 5
			£60 9 10	£1,519 14 5

We, the undersigned, approve and agree this statement of account, and agree to accept the discharge of all claims upon the assets thereby disclosed.

Dated this 14th day of June, 1906.
(Signed)   WILLIAM B THOMAS

before-mentioned Settlement—*continued*.   Cr.

No	Date.	Name of Person to whom, and for what purpose paid or transferred	Cash £ s d.	Investments. £ s. d
	FUNDS. 1906 June 14	By amounts of the following investments transferred to Mr. W. B Thomas being his share of the Trust Estate :—		
12		G W. Railway 5% Guaranteed Stock	....	40 0 0
13		Consols	.. .	100 0 0
14		East Indian Railway Annuity, Class " B ".........	....	5 0 0
15		Great Indian Peninsula Railway Annuity, Class " B."	....	10 0 0
16		Victorian Government Inscribed Stock	....	604 17 3
	June 14	By the like transferred to Messrs. W. B. Thomas and A. J. Nelson, Trustees of Mrs. Nelson's Settlement, being her share of the Trust Estate —		
17		G W. Railway 5% Guaranteed Stock	.. .	40 0 0
18		Consols	....	100 0 0
19		East Indian Railway Annuity, Class " B "	....	5 0 0
20		Great Indian Peninsula Railway Annuity, Class "B."	....	10 0 0
21		Victorian Government Inscribed Stock	...	604 17 2
22	June 14	By cash paid Mr. W. B Thomas being his share of balance	30 4 11	
23	June 14	By cash paid Messrs. W. B. Thomas and A. J. Nelson being Mrs. Nelson's share of balance	30 4 11	
			£60 9 10	£1,519 14 5

respective sums of cash and the investments thereby shewn to be due to us respectively in

(Signed) WILLIAM B THOMAS, } *Trustees of Mrs Nelson's*
(Signed) A. J NELSON,   } *Settlement.*

INDEX

"ACCOUNT CHARGE AND DISCHARGE," 2

"ACCOUNT RENDERED," 179

ACCOUNTS,
- apportionment of dividends, 85.
-                     rents, 92.
- Chancery, 15.
- Charitable Trusts Act, under, 19
- Charity Acts, 19.
- constantly ready, 9.
- copies of, 10.
- costs of keeping, 10
- Custodian trustee, of, 22.
- Inland Revenue, for, 18
- Judicial Trustee Act, under, 22.
- Lunacy, in, 20
- Probate Division, in, 13
- to be rendered without demand, 9.
- Trustee in Bankruptcy, of, 20, 21.

ACCOUNTS FOR APPORTIONMENT OF DIVIDENDS AND INTEREST PURSUANT TO STATUTE, 81.

ACCUMULATION
- of income, 179.

ACCURATE ACCOUNTS
- to be kept, 8.

ADEMPTION, 179

ADMINISTRATION,
- costs of, 181.

ADMINISTRATION ORDER
- in Chancery, 14, 15.

ADVANCEMENT,
- entry of, 34.
- what it is, 54.

INDEX.

ADVANCES, 179.

ADVERTISEMENTS
for claims, 179.

AFTER-ACQUIRED PROPERTY, 179.

AGENT
collecting rents, 69.
employed to keep trust account, 10.

AGENT'S
ledger, 32.
rent book, 70.
vouchers of payments made ex trust money, 65.

AGENT'S ACCOUNT
not a trust account, 32.

ALLHUSEN *v.* WHITTELL, 103—7.

ANNUITANT
as to estate duty, 179.

ANNUITIES,
generally charged on capital in aid, 179.

ANNUITY,
belonging to deceased, sale of, 180
commences at death and payable annually, 180
covenant to pay, how apportioned between capital and income, 109, 110.
funds set aside to meet, proving insufficient, 180.
payable by deceased, 180.

ANNUITY ARREARS,
no interest on, until judgment, 179—80.

APPENDIX A,
estate book, 195—235.

APPENDIX B.,
apportionments of dividends and interest, form and contents, 239.
explained, 82, 83, 84, 85, 89.

APPENDIX C.,
apportionments of rents, form and contents, 243
explained, 90—94.

APPENDIX D.,
suspense apportionment account, form and contents, 247.
explained, 82, 83, 110—112.

APPENDIX E.,
income account, form and contents, 253.

INDEX.

APPENDIX F.,
  final statement for beneficiaries, form and contents, 261—282.

APPENDIX G ,
  rent account, 285.

APPENDIX H ,
  income account, 286.

APPENDIX I.,
  estate book for a marriage settlement trust, 289—308.

APPLICATION
  for an audit, 148.

APPORTIONMENT ACCOUNT,
  rent, form of, 244

APPORTIONMENT ACT, 1870   74.
  sects. 1, 2, 3. .75.
       4, 5...76.
       6, 7 .77.

APPORTIONMENT
  at death of tenant for life, 81
  at death of testator, 74
              dividends, 74
              interest, 74
              rents, 74
  calculation of interest, 84, 85
              interim dividend, 88.
              dividends on Government securities, 86.
                  stocks and shares, 86.
          rents, 89—94.
  income tax, 85.
  mining rents, 80.
  purchase-money of lands less than freeholds, 80.
  sale or purchase of investments, none, 80.
  sub Settled Land Act, 1882, s. 11, mining rents, 79.
                    s. 34, purchase-money, 80.
                    s. 35, timber, 80.

APPORTIONMENTS,
  Chap. VII., 74—112.
  according to Rules of Equity, 74, 96—108.
      Allhusen v. *Whittell*, 103—107
      Earl of Chesterfield's Case, 101—103.
      Howe v. *Lord Dartmouth*, 98—101.
      insufficient mortgage security, 107—8.
      narrative in, 82.
      sub statute, form of account, 239
      when tenant for life and remainderman involved, 97.

INDEX.

APPROPRIATION,
>none, ex unauthorised securities, 181.
>to meet a legacy, 180

ASSETS
>brought into account, 46.
>remaining in schedule, 62.
>value of, immaterial, 17.

ASSIGNMENTS,
>absolute, 127

AUDIT
>*sub* Act and Master's certificate on the account, difference, 137.
>and investigation, Chap. XII, 137—171
>application form, 148.
>application for, 148.
>>for, contents of, 141.
>
>conduct of, 155—168.
>>advances, 166.
>>analysis of trust, 156.
>>appointments, 166.
>>apportionments, 160.
>>balancing, 162.
>>capital cash payments, 161
>>>receipts, 159.
>>>>payments and transfers to beneficiaries, 166.
>>
>>conversion of stocks and shares, 164.
>>different kinds of accounts, 156.
>>income account, 167
>>original assets, 157.
>>outstanding assets, 166.
>>production of deeds, scrips, &c., 165.
>>sales, purchases, mortgages and transfers of investments, 163.
>>verification of inscribed stock, 164.
>
>expenses of, primarily ex estate, 145.
>limitation of, 138
>notice of application, 149.
>notices served through the post, 147.
>penalty for not producing documents at, 146
>>false statement at, 147.
>>power in Court, 147.
>
>Public Trustee's fee, 146.
>the, 151.
>who can apply for, 140.

INDEX.

AUDITOR,
    appointment of, 140, 141.
    removed by Court alone, 144.
    who may be appointed, 138.
    when appointed, parties cannot limit his powers or duties, 141.

AUDITOR'S
    account, 170.
    certificate, 141, 170
    certificate, form of, 151
    duties, 151—5.
        to forward to (1) applicant; (2) every trustee; (3) public trustee—
            copy of accounts, 142.
                report, 142
            certificate that accounts are true and securities produced, 142.
    powers—
        access to books, accounts and vouchers, 142.
            securities and documents, 142.
        to require information, 142.
    remuneration, 142.
            parties entitled to be heard, 145
            Public Trustee fixes, and who to pay, 144, 146.
    reminders for, 179—191.
    report, form of, 150
    report, 150, 170.
    statutory duties, 141.

BALANCING THE ACCOUNTS, 60
    assets remaining in schedule, 62.
    cash balance, 62.
    investment balance, 62

BANK
    account, Chap IX , 122—126.
        advantages of a separate, 122—3.
        balance of, 124
    of England, authority to answer, 11.

BANKRUPTCY,
    accounts in, 20.

BENEFICIARY,
    who is a, 8.
    every, entitled to inspect accounts, report and certificate of auditor, 143.

INDEX.

BENEFICIARY—*continued.*
    entitled personally or by agent to—
        inspect accounts, &c., 8, 10.
        take copies of accounts, &c., 10.
        examine deeds, scrips, &c., 10, 12.

BOND
    to deliver inventory, 6.

BONUS
    in cash or shares by company, 87.
    is usually capital, 181.
    on shares sometimes apportionable, 78.

BROKERS'
    notes as vouchers, 65

BUSINESS,
    account of a, 28.
    carrying on, 181.

"BY CASH," 44.

CALCULATION
    of dividend and interest, 85—89.
    of rent apportionments, 89—94.

CAPITAL
    account, Chap. V., 43—68.
        form and contents, 211.
        object of, 44.
        payments to beneficiaries, 166.
        when to be rendered, 9.
    money ex mining rents, 80.
    payments, 47.
    receipts, 46.

CASH
    and investment account, 26.
    bonus declared by company, 87.
    entries, 45
    entries in capital account, 45.

"CASH AND INVESTMENT ACCOUNT," 26.
    objects of, 43.
    as by Paymaster-General, 43.
    form and contents, 211.

CHANCERY DIVISION, 14.
    accounts in, form of, 24.
    administration order in, 14.

INDEX.

"CHARGE AND DISCHARGE"
  account, 2.
CHARITABLE TRUSTS ACTS,
  accounts under, 19.
CHARITY,
  gift to, 181.
CHARITY COMMISSIONERS,
  form of account prescribed by, 19.
CHESTERFIELD'S CASE,
  rule in, 39, 101—103.
CHRONOLOGICAL
  order, importance of, 59, 60
CLASSIFICATION
  of entries, 47.
  of investment entries, 52.
COMMISSIONERS OF INLAND REVENUE,
  account to, 7.
COMPANY
  dissolved, entry of, 51.
COMPANY'S
  power to fix period for dividend, 86—7.
COMPENSATION
  on extinction of license is capital, 181.
CONDEMNATION
  by judges of practice of mixing trust moneys, 126
CONTINGENT
  legacies, interest on, when, 185
CONVERSION
  of original investment, 63.
  of real estate, 181.
  trust for, 181.
COPIES
  of accounts, 10.
COSTS
  of administration, 181.
  of ascertaining legatees, 182.
COUNTERFOILS
  of cheques, 124.
COVENANT
  by deceased to pay an annuity, 109, 110

INDEX.

COVENANTS
    to settle after-acquired property, 39, 135

"CR.," 45—6.

CUSTODIAN
    trustee, 22.

DEATH
    duties, 182
    of tenant for life, apportionment on, 81

DEBTS,
    priority of, 182.

DEBTS AND LEGACIES
    charged on mixed fund, 182.

DEEDS,
    custody of, 182.

DEPOSIT
    for audit, 139
    on contract for sale, forfeited is capital, 189

DEPOSITS
    by trustees, 53.

DEVASTAVIT, 182.

DILAPIDATION
    money, who it belongs to, 182.

DISCHARGE
    to executors and trustees, 175

DISSOLUTION
    of company, entry of, 51.

DIVIDENDS
    declared after death for period prior to, apportionable, 78
    in arrear not apportionable, 74.
    on consols, apportionment, how calculated, 86
    on stocks and shares, apportionment, how calculated, 86.
    paid to account of tenant for life, 72.
    paid to trustee's account, 72

DIVISION
    in specie, 128.

DOMICILE, 182.

DONATIO MORTIS CAUSA, 183

"DR ," 45, 46.

INDEX.

DUTIES,
> direction to pay, 182.
> on beneficiary's share, 48.
> on death, 182.

EMBLEMENTS, 183.

ENTRIES,
> narrative of, 48.

ESTATE
> at the death, particulars of, 15.

ESTATE BOOK, 31, 32
> form of, 195.

ESTATE DUTY, 183.
> affidavit, 47, 48.
> on an annuity, 179

EXAMINATION
> of accounts, periodical, 63.
> of trust deeds by beneficiary, 12.

EXECUTORS,
> and trustees should not allow money to remain in hands of either, 124.
> compromise of debts by, 183.
> entitled to undisposed-of residue if no next of kin, 187.

EXECUTORSHIP,
> end of, close the account, 64.

EXPENSE
> of keeping trust accounts, 10.

EXPENSES
> of ascertaining legatee, 184
> of audit, by whom paid, 139, 140.

FINAL STATEMENT
> for beneficiaries, Chap. X., 127—132.
>> form and contents, 261.
> arrangement of account in, 128, 129.
> classification for, 129.
> contents of, 128.

FIRE INSURANCE, 183.

FIRST FRUITS AND TENTHS,
> apportionable, 78.

FIXTURES, 183.

FOREIGN
> money, 28.

INDEX.

FORM
of income account, 70.

FRIENDLY SOCIETY, 183.

FUNERAL
expenses, 183.

FURNITURE,
insurance of, 184.

HISTORY
of the subject, Chap. 1., 5—23.

HOTCHPOT, CHAP. VIII., 113—121.
advance which is subject to estate duty, deduct the duty when fixing value, 120.
advance to be brought into account pursuant to direction, 13
           Statute of Distribution, 13.
amounts which formed part of the estate, 115.
       did not form part of the estate, difference between, 115.
    may be either a sum of money or a proportion of the whole estate, 115.
effect is given to direction, how, 113 *et seq.*
if the amount exceeds the share, excess is not recoverable, 114.
interest on advance, from when, 114.
period of distribution is date from which interest accrues, 114.
proportion of fund, no interest, but reduced share in income, 116.
    the fund and a sum of cash, difference, 115.
rate of interest, usually 4 per cent. per annum, 114
statement of the law by Cozens-Hardy, M. R., 121
two funds involved, application of clause when—
    tests are (1) Is there really a separate settlement? 120.
        (2) Is there an amalgamation? 120.
        (3) Could separate trustees be appointed? 121
valuation of advance, as of what date, 118, 119.

HOUSEKEEPING
expenses after death, 184.

HOWE *v* LORD DARTMOUTH, 36, 79, 83, 90, 98.
rule does not apply in marriage settlements, 136.

IMPORTANCE
of trust accounts, 1.

INDEX.

INCOME,
> apportionable *sub* the statute, 77, 78.
> not apportionable, *sub* statute, 79.
>> profits in partnership, 79.
>> rent payable in advance, 79.
>> poor and local rates, 79.
>> jointure *sine* any covenant, 79
>
> proportion to death, 38.

INCOME ACCOUNT, 26, 29.
> annual, arrangement of items in, 71.
> Chap. VI., 69—73.
> explained, 70.
> form and contents, 253—259, 287.

INCOME TAX,
> return of, 184

INCUMBRANCES
> affecting real estate, 15.
> created by *c.q t.*, no duty of trustee to state, 11.
> created by testator, 42.
>> trustee, 42.
>
> arising by operation of law, 42.
> particulars of, 26.
>> to be entered, 41.

INFANT'S LEGACY,
> interest on, 169
> 4 per cent from one year from testator's death, 184

INFORMATION
> as to the trust, 11.
> by Public Trustee, 12.
> to be furnished by trustee, 9.
> what a beneficiary entitled to, from trustee, 11.

INLAND REVENUE,
> accounts for, 18
> residuary account, 47, 48.

INSPECTION
> of accounts, 9
> of vouchers, 9.

INSUFFICIENT
> mortgage security, 107

INSURANCE
> by trustees, 185.

INDEX.

INTEREST
    accrues due from day to day, 78.
    apportionable, how calculated, 85, 86
    in arrear not apportionable, 74.
    on legacies, 185, 186.
    on contingent legacies, 185.
    on legacy to testator's child from testator's death, 186.

INTERIM DIVIDENDS, 88.

INVENTORY, 3, 6.
    of personal estate, 3, 6, 7, 15.

INVESTIGATION
    and audit, Chap. XII., 137—171.
    of condition of trust, 168.
    of the conditions of a trust, 1

INVESTMENT
    entries, 51.

INVESTMENTS,
    balance, 62.
    entries, 51—55
    order of, in income account, 71.
    verification of, 11.
    in hand, 58.
        slip for, 59.
    new, 16.

JUDGMENT
    against executors, priority of, 186.

JUDICIAL
    factor, 2.

JUDICIAL TRUSTEE ACT,
    accounts under, 22.

LAND TAX
    redeemed, 36

LAPSE
    of share in residue, next of kin takes, 186.

LAPSED
    legacy, 186

LEASEHOLDS,
    rents of, liability of executor for, 186

LEGACIES,
    payment of, twelve months after testator's death, 188.

INDEX.

LEGACY,
> fund to meet it, 186.
> duty account, cost of, 186
> to testator's child, interest on, from testator's death, 186

LEGATEE
> abroad, costs occasioned by, 186.

LEGATEE'S DEBT,
> set-off, 186.

LIABILITIES
> apportionable, 77

LIABILITY
> as to accounts, 8. (n.)

LIMITATION
> of audit, 139, 140, 141.

LOAN
> by widow to husband, 187.

LOANS TO TRUSTEES, 49.

LOCKE KING'S ACTS, 187.

LUNACY,
> accounts in, 20.

LUNATIC'S
> real estate, 36.

MAINTENANCE, 187

MARRIAGE SETTLEMENT
> estate book, form and contents, 289.
> trust, Chap XI., 133—136

MARSHALLING, 187.

MASTER'S CERTIFICATE
> on taking account, 137.

MEETINGS
> of trustees, 34.

MEMORANDA,
> Chap. III , 33
> form and contents, 205.

MINES,
> leases of, rents, how apportionable, 80.

MIX TRUST MONEYS,
> wrong to, 126.

INDEX.

MIXED FUNDS
  charged with debts and legacies, 187

MORTGAGE,
  trustee, by, 49.

MORTGAGE SECURITY,
  insufficient, 107, 108, 155.
      on sale, distribution of purchase-money when there is tenant for life, 187.

MORTGAGEE,
  payment to, of debt, &c. only, 128.
  security falling into possession, sum to cover principal, interest and costs alone paid, 187.

MORTGAGES
  by beneficiaries, 128.
  by legatee, costs occasioned by, 186.
  by trustees, 49.

MORTMAIN ACT OF 1891...187.

MOURNING,
  cost of, 187.

NARRATIVE
  of entries, 48
  of investment entries, 52.

NEW RIVER
  shares, 36.

NEW TRUSTEES,
  duty of, 2.

NOTICE
  of application for audit, 149.
  of application for audit, to whom sent, 141.
  of intention to hold audit, on whom served, 139
  to trustees, 187.

NOTICES
  of incumbrances, &c., 127.

OBJECTS
  attained by system prescribed—
      to shew original assets, schedule, 25.
          dealings with assets, cash and investment account, 25.
          what estate consists of on any given day, schedule and account, 25.
          income, account, 26.

INDEX.

ORDER IV. R. 10A...25.
    judges' use of, 25.

ORDER XXIX. OF 1852 ..27.

ORDER LV R 75...14, 15.

ORIGINAL
    assets, 40
        schedule of, 26.
    investment received, 57.

OUTSTANDING
    personal estate, 15, 16.
    real estate, 16.

PARTICULARS
    of money received and paid, 16.
    which accounts must contain, 8

PASS BOOKS, 124

PAYMASTER-GENERAL'S
    cash and investment account, 16.

PAYMENT
    to mortgagees, balance to beneficiary, 128.

PENALTY
    for making use of trust money, 125.
    on trustee in bankruptcy for not paying money to separate account, 125.
    on judicial factor, 126.

PERIODICAL
    examination of accounts, 63.

PERPETUITIES,
    rule against, 188.

PERSONAL ESTATE,
    inventory of, 3, 6, 7.
    particulars of, 26.
    schedule of, 37.

POWER
    in Public Trustee and Court to limit audit, 139, 140.

PREMIUM
    on fire insurance, 183

PROBATE
    of wills, 3.

PROBATE DIVISION
    will order—
        inventory of real and personal estate, 13.
        cash account of receipts and payments, 13.

INDEX.

Property
without pecuniary denomination, 57.

Property Tax, 91.

Proportion
of income due at death, 38.
of rents due at death, 38.

Public Trustee
may refer solicitor's costs for taxation, when, 142.
must pay moneys to the bankers of the trust, 126.

Public Trustee Act, 1, 137.
provisions of, considered, 138.

Public Trustee's
audit fee, 146.
duty as to information, 12.

Purchase
of investment, no apportionment of accruing dividend, 80.

Purchases,
entry of, 163.

Real and Personal Funds
to be separated, 44, 45.

Real Estate,
incumbrances affecting, 15.
particulars of, 15, 26.
schedule of, 37.
upon trust for sale, 36.

Reconstruction
of a company, 181.

Release
at present day, 175.
beneficiary who has assigned, position of, 176.
breaches of trust must be stated in, 178.
by purchaser, 176.
by trustees of sub-settlements, 176
conditions precedent to, 172.
executors' right to, 173.
general words, effect of, 178.
preparation of, 177.
prior to Judicature Act, 176.
recitals in, importance of, 177, 178.
trustees' duty before taking a, 172.

INDEX.

RELEASES, 9.
    Chap. XIII, 172—178.
    executors and trustees, former difference between, 173.
                           present right, 175.
    trustees' power to grant, 176.

RELIEF
    of trustees, 169.

REMUNERATION
    of auditor, fixed by Public Trustee and by whom to be paid, 144, 146.

RENT,
    interest and dividends in arrear not apportionable, 74.

RENT ACCOUNT,
    form and contents, 285, 286.

RENTS,
    apportionment explained, 93, 94.
    due prior to death, 39.
    of mines, how apportionable, 80.
    proportion to death, 38.

REPAIRS, 188.

REPORT
    on audit, 150.

RESIDUARY ACCOUNT
    to Inland Revenue, 47.

RESTRAINT
    on anticipation, removal of, 188

RETAINER
    by creditor administrator, none, 189.
    executor's right of, 188.

REVERSIONARY
    interest, 39
          and rule in *Chesterfield's Case*, 189.
    interests in marriage settlement trust, 135.

REVIEW
    of the account, 66.

SALE
    of investment, no apportionment of accruing dividend, 80.

SALES,
    entry of, 163.

SATISFACTION
    of debts by legacies, 189.

INDEX.

SCHEDULE, 26.
    Chap. IV., 35—42.
    form and contents, 207.
    Part I. (real estate), 37.
    Part II. (personal estate), 37.
    Part III. (incumbrances), 41.
        Division A.—created by deceased or settlor, 42
                      trustee *sine* covenant, 42.
              charges arising by operation of law, 42.
        Division B.—mortgages by trustees with covenant, 42.
    contents of—
        particulars of real estate, 26.
                personal estate, 26.
                incumbrances, 26.
    of original assets, 26.
    references, 55.

SCOTLAND,
    form of trust accounts, 2.

SECURED DEBT
    not paid in full, 53.

SEPARATE
    account, form and contents, 235.
    trusts, 64.

SET-OFF
    by beneficiary, 189.

SETTLED LAND ACT,
    trust account, 64.

SETTLEMENT
    estate duty, 189

SHARE,
    bonus on, declared by company, 87.

SIMPLE
    contract and specialty creditors, 189.

SOLICITOR (AGENT)
    employed to keep trust account, 10.

SOLICITOR'S
    account not a trustees' account, 32.
    charges in insolvent estate disallowed, 184, 188.
    costs, taxation of, in an audit, 142.

SPECIE,
    division in, 128.

INDEX.

SPECIFIC
    bequests, income of, apportionable, 78.
    bequest, dividends on, 189.
        expenses concerning, 189.
    devise, 57.
        rents of, apportionable, 78.
    legatee of shares, pays for transfer, 190.

STATUTE-BARRED
    debts, payment of, 190.

STOCKS AND SHARES,
    executors when qualified to vote in respect of, 190.

STOCKS, SHARES, ETC.,
    when to be entered in account, 51.

STREET
    paving charges, 190.

SUB-TRUSTEE,
    duty of, when receiving payment, 177.

SUCCESSION DUTY, 190.

SUMS
    accruing due alone apportionable, 77

SURVIVORSHIP, 190.

SUSPENSE APPORTIONMENT ACCOUNT, 85, 101
    explained, 110—112.
    form and contents, 247.

SYSTEM
    explained, Chap. II., 24—32.

TABULAR
    forms, advantages of, 95.

TAXATION
    of solicitor's costs in audit, 142.

TENANT
    for life, equitable, repairs by, 190.

TESTAMENTARY
    expenses, 190.

TITHE
    rent charge, apportionable, 78.

TITLE DEEDS,
    possession of, 191.

"TO CASH," 44.

INDEX.

TOMBSTONES,
 expense of, 191.

TRACING
 an item in the account, 57, 58.

TRANSFER
 of investments, 51.

TRUST,
 deeds, when beneficiary may examine, 12.
 estate, 5.
 for sale of real and personal property, effect of, 191

TRUST ACCOUNTS, 7.
 what they should contain, 8.
 to be kept separate, 8.
 must be constantly ready, 9.
 vouchers must be produced, 8.
 duty to keep, 7.
    common form for, 2, 3.
 expense of keeping, 10

TRUSTEE,
 duty to answer, as to incumbrances, none, 11

TRUSTEE'S
 duty to inform his beneficiary, 9.
 liability to account in Chancery, 3.
 right to a discharge, 174.

UNAUTHORISED
 investments, 110—12.

UNDERTAKING
 to deliver inventory, 6.
 to pay trustee's costs, 12.

VALUE
 of trust estate, not necessary to ascertain for account purposes, 17.

VALUELESS SECURITIES, 54.

VOLUNTARY SETTLEMENTS, 191.

VOUCHERS, 64.
 of payments made by trustee's agent, 65.
 to be produced, 8.

WIDOW'S
 interest on husband's intestacy *sine* issue, 182

WITNESS,
 gift to, is void, also to his or her wife or husband, 191

LONDON: PRINTED BY C. F. ROWORTH, 88, FETTER LANE, E.C.

CPSIA information can be obtained
at www.ICGtesting.com
Printed in the USA
LVHW081340270621
691274LV00002B/50